# LOOKING AHEAD

Life, Family, Wealth and Business
After 55

Palisades Hudson Financial Group LLC

Ali Elkin
Editor

Edited by Ali Elkin

ISBN-13: 978-1503003002
ISBN-10: 1503003000

Library of Congress Control Number: 2014919240
CreateSpace Independent Publishing Platform
North Charleston, South Carolina


Book design by Ashley A. Dandridge

# LOOKING AHEAD

Life, Family, Wealth and Business
After 55

Also by Palisades Hudson Financial Group LLC founder
Larry M. Elkin

*Financial Self-Defense for Unmarried Couples:*
*How to Gain Financial Protection Denied by Law*

For our families, friends and clients.

# Acknowledgments

$\mathbf{M}$any businesses publish their own books, but it is rarely the case that an entire company actually takes part in creating one. This book is one of those rare cases.

Every client service professional who was working at Palisades Hudson when we started this project two years ago contributed to writing *Looking Ahead*, though after completing her chapter on long-term care, Anna Pfaehler left our firm when she moved to Ohio with her family for personal reasons. She chose to remain part of this effort, however, and we are pleased that she will always be one of us in print.

It is not easy to give a single voice to a book that has so many authors. Ali Elkin, our editor, gave this book its voice with her judicious and considerate suggestions. A professional journalist, Ali has never been employed at Palisades Hudson, but she literally grew up here, along with her older sister Jessica (who actually did work at the firm while in high school). Ali was 2 years old when her father founded the firm; Jessica was 6. They make an appearance in Chapter 4, which discusses family businesses.

A book gets its personality from its design, its unique look and feel. Ashley Dandridge gave this book its personality. The typeface selections, layout, cover design and graphics are all Ashley's. Not many financial advisory firms the size of Palisades Hudson are lucky enough to have a graphic artist on staff. Ashley joined us in a part-time capacity while attending graduate school, and she has since stayed because her talents fit so well with our emphasis on clearly communicating what we know.

This is also why we are the professional home of Amy Laburda, our editorial manager and resident wordsmith. Amy helped draft many of the chapters in this book. Though she has never prepared a client's tax return, developed an estate plan or rebalanced a portfolio, Amy knows a great deal about all those things — and many more — after having spent years working with our staff to write articles, and now a book, about them. Eliza Snelling, who preceded Amy in this role before leaving to attend graduate school, also helped with some of the drafting.

Our client service team could not have written *Looking Ahead* without the constant support of the administrative staff that keeps a firm like ours running smoothly. Jeffrey Howard, our technology specialist, maintains our technical platforms with the assistance of administrative associate Cristina DeLuca and applied science consultant Jonathan Zornow. Pascale Bocchino manages the financial and administrative side of the business. Nicole Merigliano handles travel and other necessities. Stephen Grady III, Kirstie Ward, Carmelo Bueti and Timothy Meyer, who round out our client service group, joined our staff while this book was being prepared. Marketing manager Melissa DiNapoli and our outside contractors Henry Stimpson and Helen DiNetta helped *Looking Ahead* find its audience, and vice versa, under the guidance of marketing director Linda Elkin.

Linda also happens to be the wife of our firm's founder and mother of this book's editor. Without her support and encouragement, in every possible way, neither our firm nor this book would exist.

A thank-you is owed to the spouses, children, parents, domestic partners and other loved ones who support all of us in our work and give it meaning when we come home.

The final word belongs to our clients, who offer us so much more than their patronage. They open their homes, families and lives to us, and remind us every day that personal finance is much more personal than finance. If there is any wisdom in this book, it comes from many years of working closely with some of the most thoughtful and accomplished families to be found anywhere. We are privileged, and grateful.

# Contents

# 1

# LOOKING AHEAD WHEN YOUTH IS BEHIND US
## Larry M. Elkin, CPA, CFP®

---

Nobody plans for the past.

Like all planning, financial planning is about the future. We plan our financial affairs because we want to enjoy more secure, more productive, more comfortable and more harmonious lives if things work out as we hope. We plan because we want to be prepared for whatever happens otherwise. Most of us want to be free to change our plans, and that sort of flexibility requires good planning.

Not many people pay attention to financial planning when they first enter adulthood. This is not to say that most young people don't need financial planning; they do, from the moment they become independent of their parents, and sometimes sooner. But most pay little heed to personal finances, beyond day-to-day bill-paying and the financing of education and cars, as young adults. It is the things that come with time and maturity, such as building a career, starting a family, buying a home and devoting ourselves to important endeavors or causes, that gradually direct our attention toward the future rather than the present.

I have been a financial planner for 28 years. In my experience, the people who are most diligent, but also the most anxious, about planning tend to be about 55 years old or older. I believe I am only slightly biased by the fact that I turned 56 at the end of 2013.

This later-in-life focus on financial planning is counterintuitive. At 55 or older, the future is like the flexibility in your joints and (for men, at least) the hair on your head: You find less of it every time you check, but what remains is all the more precious. This may be why so many people focus more intently on planning as they get older.

I am not talking just about estate planning, which is one area where older people understandably are highly engaged. And I am not talking just about planning for incapacity and the potential need for long-term care, which is also a preoccupation of older people.

People near and in retirement tend to pay very close attention to saving and investing. This attention is deserved, although young people – who have longer time horizons over which to accumulate assets – have even more reason to focus on thrift and wealth building.

If you are older, there is a good chance you are more careful about how you use credit, how you budget and spend money, and about how you keep records, than you were when you were younger. Together with thrift, these are the basic tools of financial management. Use them well and you will most likely be happy with the results. Use them poorly, or not at all, and your chances of a good outcome are much less. You can borrow and spend recklessly and still end up with a small fortune, but you will need to start with a large fortune.

Don't overlook taxes. From the moment we engage in economic activity, whether by spending money or earning it or saving it, taxes are a big part of our financial lives. Yet there may be nobody, not even someone like me who is a CPA and an experienced financial planner, who really knows how much we pay in total taxes.

For people of modest or average means, income taxes are typically quite low and might even be zero. But various other payroll taxes, mainly for Social Security and Medicare in the United States, can take a significant chunk from earned income. Then there are general sales taxes, often structured as value-added taxes in countries outside the U.S., which can tack on 5 percent to 20 percent of every dollar you spend on taxable goods and services. Property taxes are a significant expense for homeowners and other holders of real estate. In some jurisdictions there are personal property taxes on items such as cars and boats, too.

On top of these well-known items, there is a raft of hidden taxes that affect most of us but are designed to escape our notice. If you stay in a hotel or rent a car, you will discover that the easiest people to tax are the ones who live and vote somewhere else. Special taxes get added in many locations to utility bills, because few consumers read or understand them. Taxes are slapped on every airline ticket and every gallon of gasoline you buy. Many of the imported products you purchase were subject to import duties. One purpose of such duties is to protect domestic producers, but another is to raise money for the Treasury in a way that consumers do not see.

These are just the taxes that affect our daily activities of acquiring money and spending it. What happens to the wealth we manage to accumulate through our savings and investments? As you might expect, there are taxes on that, too, in the form of gift, estate and inheritance taxes. But there are special breaks for assets that we bequeath to charities, or wealth held in certain forms, such as family farms or closely held businesses.

This is not a diatribe against taxes. We need government, and government costs money. The appropriate type and level of taxes, and the proper reach and cost of government, are political questions that lie beyond the scope of a book on financial planning. Yet no book on this topic would be complete without addressing the way taxes affect how much we keep of the money we earn, how much things cost us when we spend it, how much we can pass to our heirs or other beneficiaries, and how we might be affected by future changes in the law. So we will consider these topics, among many others, in later chapters.

Since this is a book about financial planning, and the primary audience is a reader who is around 55 years old or older, we probably should begin by defining the term "financial planning." My colleagues and I consider ourselves financial planners, but we view our field in a way that is different from many members of the public, and even from many other financial planners.

Many people use the terms "financial planning" and "investment management" interchangeably. We do not. Investment management, albeit important, is just one element among many that must be part of any thoughtful and effective financial plan for an individual or family. In fact, "investment management" by itself is almost meaningless in the context of an individual's portfolio.

If you run a mutual fund whose mission is to invest aggressively in stocks, your goal is pretty simple: Generate the highest return you can possibly achieve, because you want people to invest in your fund, and people are more likely to invest if you have a stellar performance record. Chances are, you will take considerable risk in pursuit of this goal, because high returns invariably are accompanied by high risk. But the risk is someone else's problem. Your prospective investors have to decide how much of your risky fund they really want to buy; you hope your performance record will be good enough to attract and keep investors despite the risk. You just want maximum results, meaning maximum returns for your investors, maximum assets in your fund and maximum compensation for you.

Individuals and families don't usually operate this way. I have yet to meet anyone whose most important financial goal in life is to die with the maximum possible net worth. If this were your goal you would never give anything to charity and never give anything to relatives. You would send your children to the cheapest possible colleges, or tell them to pay for college themselves. You would never take a vacation, at least not one that required you to spend money on travel or other leisure pursuits. Come to think of it, you probably wouldn't have leisure pursuits. You would just work as long as you are physically able, and then you would stay home and watch whatever happens to be available on basic cable TV.

We have a variety of personal goals, often interrelated, sometimes conflicting, and frequently not very clearly defined. We hold jobs or pursue careers not only because they pay adequately (or better) but because we find the work interesting, fun or personally rewarding. We want to be financially comfortable in old age, but we want to have active and engaging leisure pursuits while we are young and healthy enough to enjoy them. We want to raise our children to be healthy, well-rounded adults. We want to see them get good educations. We want to support charities and other causes that are important to us. We want to travel. And many of us want to be able to retire, at least from our primary careers, while we are still vigorous enough to pursue other activities that seem appealing.

So, for individuals, investment planning does not exist in a performance-driven, risk-taking vacuum. We invest to achieve specific short- and long-term goals. We must balance our desire to achieve good investment returns with our preparedness to tolerate risk, and with our potential need (if there is any) to convert the investments to cash sooner than planned. Managing an investment portfolio without first deciding on financial goals is like driving a car without first deciding on a destination.

To my colleagues and me, investment management is part of an interrelated set of planning activities that focus on setting goals and deciding how to achieve them. If a client asks us to help manage investments that will be used in retirement, we offer to help determine how much he or she will want to have in the portfolio when retirement commences. Then we look at how much is in the portfolio today and we try to estimate how much the client will be able to add to the portfolio, through savings, during the rest of his or her pre-retirement career. We estimate how rapidly the portfolio might grow, based on how aggressive the client is prepared to be with the investments. We determine whether the target amount is realistic. If not, we'll talk to the client about changing the parameters, such as planning to retire later, spend less in retirement, save more before retirement, or invest more aggressively.

We have a lot of tools at our disposal: computer-based cash flow and investment projections, the client's earning history, and decades of statistical information about how investments perform under various market and economic conditions. One tool we do not have is a crystal ball. The future never plays out exactly as we expect. So we typically produce more than one projection, using a range of scenarios and assumptions, to try to offer a realistic range of possible outcomes. That is the best we can do without being clairvoyant.

This is why I often tell people that financial planning is a process, not an event. You have to revisit it regularly so you can adjust your plans or your behavior when, inevitably, things fail to go precisely according to plan. I would not simply write a five-year budget for my business and then go away on a round-the-world trip and expect to return home, five years later, to find that everything has happened the way I expected. I can't do that for my personal financial plans, either.

But financial planning is much broader than just setting goals and devising the budgets and investment plans to reach them. Everybody's life includes one great certainty, which is taxes, and one great uncertainty, which is life and health. You can't draw up a well-rounded financial plan without considering these elements.

**Quick Tip:**
Always consider life's certainties as well as its uncertainties when planning your finances.

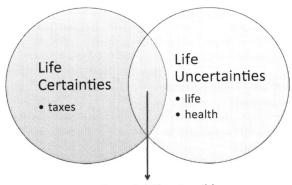

Best Financial Plan Possible

Taxes affect how we accumulate wealth, how we deploy it and how we ultimately dispose of it. Every advanced economy has a tax system that is complicated, because modern life is complicated. An income tax must define "income" so it does not become a tax on gross revenue or receipts, and it usually must contain some mechanism so the same income is not taxed more than once. This is why the U.S. government allows Americans who work abroad to exclude some foreign-earned wages from tax, and it allows U.S. taxpayers to claim a credit for some foreign taxes that are applied to income from sources outside the country. But income earned by large American corporations is, in fact, taxed twice – deliberately – through the corporate income tax, and then through the personal income tax that applies to dividends the corporation pays to its shareholders. This is a policy choice. It also is a planning opportunity, since most privately held businesses can be structured to avoid this double taxation.

Similarly, at the state level, a taxpayer's state of residence may allow a credit for taxes paid to another state, to avoid taxing the same income twice. But the credit is limited to the amount of tax that would be owed to the individual's home state. If you live in a low-tax state like Georgia but derive income from a high-tax state like California, you will pay tax at California's higher rate on income you obtain from that state. There may be opportunities to shift income away from California's aggressive taxes back to Georgia – or even to avoid Georgia's tax if the taxpayer's domicile can be shifted to an even less taxing jurisdiction, such as Georgia's neighboring states of Florida and Tennessee.

Over the course of many years, diligent tax planning can add up to a significant difference in the wealth a family accumulates. Such planning can also have a major impact in just a single year, especially if the year includes a major transaction such as the sale of a business. It is critical to plan carefully before a transaction is structured or consummated. The best approach is to build tax planning into a regular review of an individual or family's financial plan, and to update tax strategies periodically, especially if there is a significant change in the law or if a major financial event is on the horizon.

As we noted earlier, income taxes are just one of many taxes we pay as we go about our financial lives. For wealthier Americans, another major consideration is the potential impact of gift and estate taxes on the assets we hope to eventually transfer to children and other heirs. There is even a special tax, the generation skipping transfer tax, which applies to some transfers that we make to grandchildren, great-grandchildren and other beneficiaries who are much younger than ourselves. The sole purpose of the generation-skipping tax is to prevent us from planning around the estate tax by giving money directly to grandchildren, thus skipping potential taxes at our children's generation.

There are many ways to plan to minimize these taxes, too. We just need to plan properly.

We cannot plan around the fact that we are all human and mortal, but we can plan for the risks that this entails. Sickness, disability and premature death can happen to any of us. So can property loss due to theft or disaster, or liability because of an accident, or financial harm due to a failed relationship. We cannot make these risks disappear, but we can manage them by taking preventive steps – such as installing sprinkler system and burglar alarms, or getting a prenuptial agreement – and by buying suitable and adequate insurance.

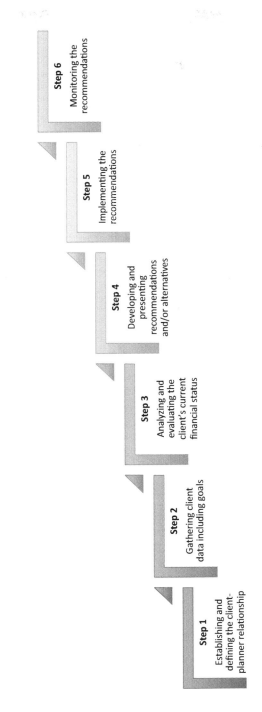

**The Financial Planning Process**

**Step 1**
Establishing and defining the client-planner relationship

**Step 2**
Gathering client data including goals

**Step 3**
Analyzing and evaluating the client's current financial status

**Step 4**
Developing and presenting recommendations and/or alternatives

**Step 5**
Implementing the recommendations

**Step 6**
Monitoring the recommendations

Figure 1

Source: CFP Board (www.cfp.net) -- used by permission.

We cannot insure against everything, however. Life insurance does not protect us financially against death, because everyone dies eventually. There is no place for the insurance company to spread the risk of death. Not everyone dies prematurely, however. In fact, highly premature death is so rare that the cost of insuring against a death of a healthy 20- or 30-something is quite low. On the other hand, life insurance for a 90-year-old who is in marvelous condition would be extremely expensive, if you could buy it at all.

We also cannot insure against old age. If we don't die prematurely, we all get old, and most of us don't die prematurely. So, once again, there is no place for an insurance company to spread risk. How, then, does long-term care insurance work? Such insurance is marketed as being something we all need when we get old, because most of us are going to need care at some point in our lives. The answer to my question, how does it work, is simple: not very well. My colleagues and I do not sell long-term care insurance (or any other insurance product), and we don't recommend it, either. This is going to upset a lot of people, as it has when we have written on this topic in our company newsletter and on our website. Most of the people it upsets, however, are in the business of selling long-term care insurance.

How should you deal with the costs of maintaining yourself in old age? Save for it and plan for it.

For some of us, building a closely-held business has been a big part of our life's work. Anyone who has successfully nurtured a startup enterprise knows that this can be one of the most rewarding experiences there is, emotionally as well as financially. I know this personally because I have spent more than 20 years building a business. I hope to be able to give my business another 20 years.

But, as I mentioned, we are all human. Eventually we all must leave the scene, voluntarily or otherwise. Planning a successful business transition is one of the most difficult of all financial planning tasks. It is also one of the most important.

Starting a business can also be a rewarding "second act," something constructive to do after retiring from a primary career. Often, financial gain is not the main motivator for someone who starts a business late in life. If your financial position is secure, starting a new enterprise can be a way to do important or enjoyable work and to remain engaged with the world. This can be a fine capstone to a professional life. There are, of course, some issues to consider when starting a business after concluding an earlier career. Even when future financial gain is not the major motivation, planning is important.

No business operates as an island. Even before you take your first order or deposit your first receipts, you are likely find yourself working with people who want very much for you to succeed. Yes, your landlord has a financial stake in your business, since a successful enterprise is more likely to pay its rent and renew its lease. But I found that the people with whom I did business – landlords, bankers and other vendors – really did root for my success, almost as though my venture was a sports team and they were our fans.

Our clients, too, have been major supporters, not to mention by far the best source of new business, via referrals. I have hired most of our staff straight out of college, in effect "raising" them professionally at our firm. Clients take a strong interest in our staff's development and success. When someone is quoted in a prominent publication or receives some sort of professional recognition, clients often take the trouble to send their congratulations.

The most satisfying part of building the business for me has been the opportunity to watch intelligent, caring young people grow into intelligent, thoughtful, caring professionals. You will get to know many of them through the chapters that follow.

I am not the author of this book. This book does not have a single author in the traditional sense. My colleagues at Palisades Hudson Financial Group collaborated with me to put this volume together. Each chapter was written by one or two of our experienced financial planners, with research and drafting help from members of our staff. Their efforts and those of others who made this book possible are acknowledged elsewhere.

We wrote the book this way for several reasons. The most important is described in the old adage, "Many hands make light work." We wanted to put together a book that captures the art and science of financial planning the way we see it, as a complex tapestry through which many strands are woven to create a picture that is rich, descriptive, useful and as unique as the person or family for which it was intended. This would have been far too much work for any one of us individually to accomplish without taking about a year off from other assignments. But divided among us, and with the help of our staff, it was manageable.

Another reason for collaborating was to allow our readers to get to know us as individuals. This is why we asked our writers to sign each chapter personally, rather than simply identify our firm as the book's author. It is also why I am writing this chapter in the first person. You will see "I" and "we" throughout this book.

A really good relationship between a financial adviser and a client is, inevitably, deeply personal – but in a professional way. In my opinion, a client is not well served by an adviser who tries too hard to be a friend or to become "part of the family." So, although all of us are comfortable discussing any of the topics in this book, we chose specific subject areas where we each feel we have something personal to say to the reader. That is why I chose to write Chapter 4 on business succession planning. It is a topic on which I, as a business owner, have a particular interest.

One of the nicest comments I ever heard from a client came a few years ago from a man who retired as the chief executive of an international corporation. "Elkin," he said to me, "your people are all different, but they're all good." Of course I agree, but it was good to hear him say it.

We do not have a homogenized style or personality at Palisades Hudson, even though my colleagues and I share a common approach to financial planning. Confronted with the same set of facts, we would offer similar alternatives and suggestions. But we each have our own way of communicating and our own experiences and war stories to offer.

You might think personal finance is a dry, often boring, topic. We don't see it that way. Our field is personal financial planning, but for us the dominant word is "personal," not "financial." In business, the bottom line is the bottom line. It doesn't work that way in personal life.

As professionals, we are always trying to prepare our clients for all the things that might possibly go wrong. Our contingency plans have contingency plans. Yet that does not stop us from being basically optimistic, hopeful and confident. Financial planning is about trying to create the future that we want to create.

The past is past. We need to understand it, but we don't need to plan for it.

# 2

## RELATIONSHIPS WITH ADULT CHILDREN
### Shomari D. Hearn, CFP®, EA
### Rebecca Pavese, CPA

---

Leo Tolstoy famously wrote, "All happy families are alike; each unhappy family is unhappy in its own way." Outside of fiction, though, most families don't fall neatly into the happy or unhappy category. For financial planners, each family is unique no matter how harmonious (or not), but all families are alike in the need for solid and well-communicated financial plans.

When navigating your relationship with your adult child or children, many factors come into play. Even if your child is financially responsible and easy to communicate with, you still face a variety of challenges and decisions. It's important not to let trust in your children lull you into the false sense that you don't need to initiate discussions with them about your financial plans or intentions. Even the children who are closest to their parents can't read minds.

Nor does every family, or even every part of every family, exist in such harmony. Interpersonal tensions between you and your children, between siblings and between in-laws can all contribute to the feeling that sitting down to discuss your financial plans is the last thing anyone in your family wants. While your particular situation may dictate how you proceed, intrafamily strife makes it all the more important to structure your plans to take into account any existing or potential relationship issues. It's also important to make the effort to open communication wherever you can. Surprises in a legacy, an estate or a business transfer are likely to aggravate existing tensions, not ease them.

No matter what the state of your personal relationship with your adult children, setting expectations – yours and theirs – is critical. Sitting down as a family, perhaps in a neutral space with a trusted financial adviser, attorney or other impartial third party, is the best way to ensure everyone is on the same page.

## Taking Stock

When approaching the financial aspects of your relationship with your adult children, it may sound obvious to suggest you first thoroughly examine your own financial situation. However, it is important not to neglect this step. Many parents want to be generous with their children and grandchildren in every way they can. While such generosity is admirable, it's imperative to consider other factors too.

For example, who is financially dependent on you and to what extent? Include your spouse or partner's needs and, of course, your own, but also those of any other dependents, possibly including siblings, children or grandchildren with special needs, your own parents or parents-in-law, and any adult children who continue to need your support. It is important to be realistic about what you and your dependents need, both now and in the future.

There are also future expenses and debts to be considered. You may wish to help your children now by helping to fund down payments on their first homes or educational expenses for your grandchildren. Yet you should also consider that the increase in longevity for most seniors means that you will need to allow for not only more years of life post-retirement, but also for medical care or assisted living costs for yourself and your partner. Such costs can be substantial. Avoiding passing them on to your children can be a different, but no less valuable, sort of generosity.

As in any stage of life, it is also important to allow for the unexpected. Financial and estate plans need flexibility for many reasons, but one is to allow you room to maneuver if circumstances change. These changes can be personal, such as marriage or divorce, births, illness, deaths, or major changes in economic circumstances. Circumstances can also change because of issues that have nothing to do with family members. Changes in tax law, for example, can have a profound impact on estate planning, and even seasoned professionals find them difficult to predict.

Few of us relish considering our own mortality, but it's something we all need to face. An uncertain tax environment, a volatile family situation, or uncertainty about a family member's health can all seem convincing reasons to justify delay. The reality is even a plan that needs revision is worlds better than no plan at all. If you die without a will or suitable trusts, state law will handle your final affairs for you – it's called dying "intestate," but the state's plan may be very different than what you had mind. If you die intestate, you have also either given up the opportunity to talk with your children about your plans or left your children without the legal standing to honor wishes you did express in the absence of a will. (For more information about planning your estate, see Chapter 5.) Being honest with yourself about the state of your finances and the need for planning is essential before you begin a conversation with your children about these topics.

**Quick Tip:**
Parents, remember to consider all of your financial commitments when planning financial help for adult children. You may have more obligations than you realize.

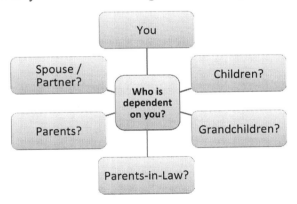

### Give With a Goal in Mind

Most parents want to help their children, but sometimes it is hard to know the best way to be helpful. It can be tempting to step in and save the day when your adult children run into money trouble of one kind or another, but it's wise to consider what sort of help you want to give.

Instead of just handing your adult child a lump sum, consider giving specifically to promote his or her independent success. Depending on your child, such a gift could take many forms. You could subsidize educational expenses through tuition or books; you could help underwrite a wardrobe for a young professional just starting up his or her career ladder; or you could help with the purchase of a first home by providing the down payment. Adult children will have many steps on the way to a successful, self-supported adulthood, and by helping them take those steps, you offer a sign of your affection and support while being sure your gift won't become a casualty in your child's next financial fender-bender.

For a child who is currently in financial trouble, you can also help in directed ways, such as paying their electric bill or buying them groceries. If your child makes a good faith effort to manage his or her finances, helping with particular needs is a good way to make them secure without enabling them to continue a pattern of poor decisions. You can also pay for your child to meet with your financial adviser to establish a manageable budget and a financial plan to help them address their current cash flow issues.

Giving your children money directly is not a bad idea in every case. Quite the opposite; giving your child money to manage can help him or her avoid larger financial mistakes down the road by offering hands-on experience under controlled circumstances. By letting your child direct your gift, you can help teach money management skills and responsibility that will be valuable to your child in dealing with money he or she earns, as well as any greater inheritance you may plan to leave.

While you may worry that handing a large sum of money to your children may spoil them, the choice to never give your children any money directly may inadvertently hinder their financial growth. Larger distributions will not only allow you to help them with their needs, but will demonstrate your confidence in them as well. A natural way to develop their skills is through trusts. Most trust documents are written to allow flexibility in the amounts distributed. Often a certain amount must be distributed annually, but the trustee has discretion to make additional distributions. These additional, discretionary distributions can be a valuable tool.

For example, if your children are the beneficiaries of a $20 million trust that will be paid to them outright at the death of the surviving parent, but the trust is currently making annual distributions of only $200,000, that amount may not adequately prepare them for the large inheritance they will eventually receive. It may also lead to unnecessary financial struggles in the meantime. After a family meeting, you may decide to increase the annual distribution to $500,000. Additional distributions during your lifetime will let you see how the children handle the money. Do they seek appropriate advisers, or do they spend the excess money in a fashion that makes you worry the $20 million inheritance will be dissipated within a few years of your death? The answers to these questions will allow the parent to help the child grow financially, as well as leaving time for such growth when the parent can still provide a safety net.

## Quick Tip:
Parents, don't let your adult child's needs unbalance your own finances.

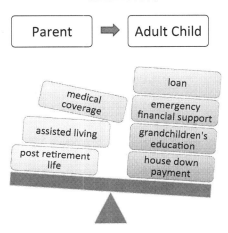

Many of these concerns also apply to adult grandchildren. Grandchildren bring an immense amount of joy to their grandparents and, as a result, grandchildren are often easier to spoil. Yet if you want your child to be a productive, responsible adult, you probably want the same for your grandchild. Many of the same concerns about helping without enabling bad behavior apply. Another complication is that, as a grandparent, you may also be in a position to make larger financial contributions than your child can, especially if a large portion of the middle generation's money is still held in trust.

You and your child may be able to meet your goals for your grandchild with a simple agreement. To ensure the grandchild remains productive, you may choose to make your gift or any distributions from a trust contingent on certain behavior. For example, you may tell your grandchildren that you will supplement their income with a monthly distribution of $5,000 as long as they are gainfully employed (or productive in some other defined fashion, such as participating in charitable endeavors or parenting a young child full-time). With grandchildren, as with children, tailoring a gift to the situation can make it a useful tool without preventing the recipient from growing as an independent adult.

If your children need help, sometimes it may make more sense to give them a loan than a gift. This is another good way to foster independence and responsibility in a child hoping to take a large personal step, such as the purchase of a car or a home. It also is a wise choice if your own finances won't allow for a large outright gift but can allow you the flexibility of a loan.

A loan can also be a useful solution for a child trying to escape the burden of credit card debt or the fallout of other poor financial choices. Don't hesitate to make the loan conditional – for example, requiring your child to enroll in a budgeting course or to make another good-faith effort to learn from his or her mistake before you finalize the loan. A loan can also help you to avoid enabling future poor behavior by suggesting that you will always bail your child out – or, worse, giving beyond your means simply because you find it hard to tell your child "no."

When you consider providing a loan, no matter what the circumstances, it is important to set up rules at the beginning. Set a rate of interest, and be aware that, if you want to avoid having the loan or the foregone interest treated as a gift for tax purposes, you can't set the interest rate below the Applicable Federal Rate, a rate the IRS sets each month and which varies based on the length of the loan. You should also set up a repayment schedule and decide in advance the penalty for your child failing to make payments on time. If your child "defaults" on a loan, there should be stated, concrete consequences, such as withholding future gifts or reducing their inheritance – if nothing else, you should be reluctant to lend again unless he or she demonstrates substantial improvement in responsibility.

Such intrafamily loans have distinct advantages: Children pay less than they likely would if they borrowed from a bank, and you can earn a decent return while helping your children help themselves. But be aware that such loans can also cause tension in relationships if your child can't or won't repay the borrowed amount. To avoid later headaches, it's essential that all terms be clear and set down in writing before you lend the money. Specifically, the terms of the loan should be documented in a promissory note that is signed by you and your child. Further, if the loan is intended to be a mortgage on your child's primary home, you may want to hire an attorney to draft the note, because the loan must be secured by the home and recorded under state or local law in order for your child to deduct the mortgage interest on his or her tax return.

### Quick Notes:
### On Intrafamily Loans

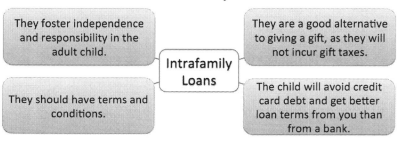

## Communication and Preparation

No matter what assets, if any, you plan to pass on to your children, it is crucial that you discuss your plans with them. Of course, as previously mentioned, in order to do this, you must first have plans to discuss. In addition to the information on estate planning in Chapter 5, you might also consider alerting your financial adviser that you intend to discuss your plans with your children. Your adviser may be able to help you make sure you have all the pertinent points in mind before you begin.

---

## Rebecca's Advice

---

### How much is *too much* financial support?

When deciding how much support to give your children, consider whether you are helping or hindering them in the long term. If you provide too much financial support you could dampen their own drive to become financially independent. You want to provide enough to let them grow to their true potential but not so much that they become lazy. It is reasonable to provide support to allow them to pursue goals and dreams, but not so much that they lose sight of the fact that their goals and dreams should provide them with a livelihood or purpose.

-RP

---

There are many reasons to discuss your plans with your children fully and frankly, once those plans are in place. First, it is important that at least one child know where to physically find your will, trust documents, financial and medical powers of attorney, and other important documents. Whether this is the child you've named as your executor, the child who lives closest to you, or simply all your children is up to you. What matters is avoiding a scramble to locate your documents if you are incapacitated – or an even worse scenario, in which no one knows that such documents exist at all. A will is important for many reasons, including serving as a road map for the orderly distribution of your assets. It does no good if no one can find it.

It's also important to have a conversation with your children about your living will, if you have prepared one, and your health care power of attorney. Sometimes these documents are combined into one. A living will, also sometimes called an advance directive, is a legal document that is used to express your wishes about life-prolonging medical treatment. It differs from a health care power of attorney because it relates only to life-prolonging decisions. If your medical situation is not terminal but you cannot act on your own behalf, a health care power of attorney will enable someone to make all medical decisions on your behalf. (See Chapter 3 for more information about planning for incapacity.) By documenting your wishes regarding medical circumstances that may make it impossible for you to act on your own behalf, you will both increase the chances that your wishes will be honored and relieve your children of the burden of making such difficult choices themselves. This can also help to avoid potential conflict among siblings or other family members by making your wishes about such situations clear and indisputable.

Wills and living wills become doubly important if you are a member of a same-sex marriage or long-term domestic partnership. Because of the varying laws in different states, and the varying levels of federal recognition you face as a result, a solid estate plan serves as the best method to ensure your partner and your children are provided for. Make sure your children know what you have set in place and how it is designed to work.

Other important information to communicate to your children includes the location of any safe deposit boxes you own, an inventory of any trust assets, and any passwords for important online accounts. You don't have to give these to your children outright if you are uncomfortable doing so, but you should make sure that at least one person knows where to find such information in the event anything happens to you unexpectedly.

All your children, but especially any who serve as your executors or who are the beneficiaries of trusts, should know who your family advisers are. At a minimum, you should provide them with the names, email addresses and phone numbers of your lawyers, financial advisers, accountants, and any other professionals you employ. To whatever extent possible, you should ideally introduce your adult children to your advisers in person. Arranging a family meeting can provide an excellent neutral ground for beginning what might otherwise be a delicate conversation about your estate plans, while also allowing your children and your advisers to meet one another.

Even in stable families, inheritance fights can break out unexpectedly. One of the primary factors in such fights is a lack of planning prior to the benefactor's death. You may help your children to avoid disagreements if you take time to make sure they all understand what you are doing and, almost as importantly, why you are doing so.

Not all children will intuitively understand that fair treatment is not always the same as equal treatment. Adult children are likely to have had different opportunities or career paths that vary significantly in terms of compensation. They will almost certainly have different needs, including different numbers of children of their own. For example, if your son receives a modest salary working for a nonprofit organization and your daughter is an investment banker making six or seven figures annually, you may decide that it is fair for your son to receive a larger inheritance than his sister, rather than dividing your wealth equally between the two of them. Ultimately, fairness is a subjective measure that is up to you, but if your children know the logic behind your decisions, they may find those decisions easier to accept.

If siblings do not get along, though, even the calmest and most logical discussions of your planning decisions may not placate them. In some situations, setting up a separate trust or bequest for each child may be a more logical option. This will keep management and decision-making separated and offer each child a measure of privacy; perhaps more importantly, setting up separate trusts will mean you won't require your children to come to a consensus for the trustee to take action. It is also important to consider your children-in-law – both their relationships with you and with your children – as you make and discuss inheritance plans. In many cases, adult children count on a certain inheritance that you may or may not intend to give, regardless of whether or not they have siblings. Children who help take care of aging parents often feel entitled to a greater share of the estate than other heirs. The treatment of stepchildren or children from prior marriages can also raise hackles. You may feel that you should leave more to children who needed less help during your lifetime, but what seems fair to you may be baffling and hurtful if it comes as a surprise.

You should also consider the disposition of illiquid assets. Will it be a burden to liquidate holdings such as real estate or a family business? Illiquid assets may also trigger a fight over memories as well as financial value, as in the case of a vacation home where your children spent their summers growing up. Once again, discussing your decisions with your children lets them avoid nasty surprises and can allow for modification before your plans are set in stone. You may find that one child would like to inherit your vacation home, while the other might see it as a burden. One child may show a keen interest in taking over your family business, while the other finds running an enterprise overwhelming or simply less interesting than pursuing other options. Based on your discussions with your children, you may ultimately decide it would be better to sell the property, either prior to or upon your death, in order to avoid making it a point of contention among your children.

## Shomari's Advice

### Where should you discuss finances with an adult child?

For such an important discussion, we recommend that you hold the family meeting in a location that provides privacy and is free of any distractions. The information discussed is often sensitive, so you want to conduct the meeting in a place where all participants will be comfortable speaking openly. Another factor to consider is the number of family members attending the meeting. The office of your financial adviser or a meeting room at a hotel typically make for good places to hold a family meeting.

-SH

A clear succession plan is essential for a business, whether the plan is to keep it in the family or to sell it, but the latter may ultimately be better for both the business and your children. A discussion between you and your children may help guide your decision about the business so that all of your children are treated fairly. For example, you can leave the children not interested in working for the family business an income stream from the business without forcing them to become involved in its operations; alternately, you can simply leave them other assets of equal value. (For more information about transferring a family business, refer to Chapter 4.)

Your attorney or financial adviser may help resolve disputes between children, should the need arise. It may also be a good idea to make meetings regarding your financial plans a regular occurrence, perhaps annual or bi-annual, in order to update your family on any changes to your plan.

As uncomfortable as some of these conversations will be, all of them boil down to one major idea: What do you want your legacy to be? Communicating your vision clearly to your children is the best way to ensure they can honor that legacy. Don't hesitate to make your final wishes known. Discuss your children's inheritance with them, especially in the context of any bequests you plan to leave to charity or other institutions outside the family. At its core, estate planning is about what is truly important to you. The better your children understand what you hope to leave behind, the better the chance that they will respect and accept your wishes.

How much specific information you share with your children about your finances and estate plan is ultimately up to you. If are concerned that providing too much information will result in your children trying to interfere in how you live your daily life, such as trying to curb your spending in order to preserve their inheritance, provide only a broad overview of your intentions instead of sharing every detail. If you establish and fund a trust of which your adult children are beneficiaries, you may be required to provide them with an annual financial accounting for the trust. These accountings must typically include the value of the assets held in the trust and any income, gain or loss activity that occurred within the trust during the year. Such requirements depend on your state law, so if you are concerned about the amount of financial information you share with your children, ask your estate planning attorney how much detail your trustee will be required to provide when initially considering the trust.

## Boomerang Kids

Of course, you need to talk to your children when they are young adults, not only once they are involved in their careers and raising children of their own. It is becoming increasingly common for multiple generations of adults to live together, often for economic reasons, which can trigger a whole new set of conversations.

"Boomerang kid" is a term for an adult child who returns home to live with his or her parents. Frequently, it describes young adults who have just finished their undergraduate education, but it can be adult children of any age who need to return home for a variety of reasons, including job loss, divorce or the end of a significant cohabitation, or economic difficulties of any kind. Your adult child may also move back in with you in cases where you might need extra care.

Depending on your relationship with your child, how long they've been away, and the reason for the move, your child's return to your home may be a more or less bumpy process. You and your child have both gotten used to some level of independence and, as with monetary gifts, you may be torn between feeling supportive and worrying about enabling bad behavior.

It helps to discuss some ground rules with a child who returns to your home when he or she first arrives – or, ideally, during the planning stages of the move back. Discuss your conditions for their living at home. These might include maintaining or actively seeking employment, paying rent, or helping out with a certain amount of house or yard work. Also discuss the timeline over which your child expects to stay. Strongly consider charging your child rent, even if the income is not crucial to you, to help them responsibly manage their money. In the event you don't need it yourself, you can place this money in an account for your child's future needs.

You should also set ground rules, especially with a younger adult child, about alcohol use, smoking, and overnight guests. You will need to respect their independence and their choices, but they also need to respect your home. It will be easier for you both to have a conversation up front, calmly and in the abstract, rather than a heated confrontation later, when competing expectations collide. Your child has changed since he or she moved out and so have you. It is a relationship you will both need to actively navigate.

While your children are living with you, you have a unique opportunity to enforce good financial habits. Encourage them to save, especially if you are not charging them rent; this will give them an emergency fund, a nest egg for when they eventually do move out, or a resource for paying down debt. If your child is employed and his or her employer offers a 401(k) plan, talk to your child about why it's a good idea to participate. If his or her employer doesn't offer such a plan, mention and perhaps help your child to set up a traditional or Roth IRA. Even if your children can only save a little, you can help them to establish good saving habits that will serve them well later in life.

Whatever rules you and your child agree on, be sure to treat him or her as an adult. Your adult children's choices are largely their own, and while the home is yours, avoid trying to actively parent the way you did when they were children or teenagers. Don't demand to know where they are at all times or try to make them ask your permission to come and go. Ground rules that are reasonable will be much less likely to cause strife.

Remember to re-evaluate your own finances when an adult child moves back in. How will having an additional person eating groceries, consuming utilities, and driving your vehicle impact your cash flow? Don't let yourself get into trouble because you failed to reassess your own budget while helping your child. This holds for all sorts of gifts, but it can be harder to say no when you share a living space and witness your child's struggles firsthand.

Financial discussions can be uncomfortable, even with those we care about most. Yet communication is the best tool for staying close. Talking to your adult children will give you a good sense of their capabilities and needs, and it will give them a good sense of your wishes and resources. Money is a source of tension in many families, and it may seem deceptively easy to just leave your kids in the dark. But no parent wants a bitter, messy inheritance fight for the children left behind, or ever-building resentment over how much or little help you provide during your life. However and whenever you decide to help your children with money, the best thing you can do for them is tell them what's on your mind.

# 3

## PLANNING FOR INCAPACITY
### Rebecca Pavese, CPA

T hough we all hope for a long life in which we remain active and independent, the reality is that many of us may one day face health problems or complications of aging that could lead to incapacity in one form or another. Just as you hope you will never face a catastrophic house fire but you insure your home just in case, it is important that you put time and effort into making sure one or more trusted people know and have the resources to carry out your wishes.

Discussions about future incapacity are seldom comfortable. Like estate planning, the subject is one that many people would prefer never to think about. By taking the time to consider your options, however, you can take steps toward securing your ideal outcome. Additionally, taking the time to have conversations early, awkward as they may be, can save your loved ones from the pressure of trying to guess what you want in the event you cannot tell them. By the time questions arise about your medical or financial affairs, it may be past the point where you can offer direct input. Many mechanisms allow you to avoid this eventuality, and you can give those you trust the tools they need to make sure your preferences are honored.

## Making Your Wishes Explicit

Perhaps the most important principle to keep in mind when planning for incapacity is the importance of making your wishes explicit as soon as possible. Procrastination is an easy trap to fall into. Likewise, it can be easy to convince yourself that your spouse, adult children or other loved ones naturally know your preferences. Until you state your preferences directly, however, there is no way to be sure that this is the case.

Discussion alone does not go far enough, however. If you are in a position in which you are no longer capable of making your own wishes known, it is important to keep the potential for guessing or arguments among your loved ones to a minimum. One way to achieve this end is through a living will, sometimes called an "advance health care directive."

### Living Will

A living will is a document that describes your preferences regarding treatment for a serious illness or injury in the case that you are not able to speak for yourself – for example, if you are in a coma or if you face a degenerative mental disorder. These documents are important for adults of any age. A living will allows you to spell out which medical procedures and life sustaining procedures you do or do not want, sparing your doctors and loved ones doubt or disagreement. You should also be explicit about your wishes for palliative care.

Though a do not resuscitate (DNR) order does not require an advance directive, it is a good idea to include it in your living will as well as in your medical chart, to be clear about your intentions. If you have wishes about organ donation, you can outline those in your advance directive as well.

Beyond the scope of a living will, you can designate someone as your health care agent by granting them medical power of attorney. The person you appoint is called your health care agent or proxy. This person should be someone you trust implicitly – don't pick a proxy out of feelings of obligation (for example, picking a spouse over a child, or a sibling over a friend). You should select the individual you believe will best be able to follow your wishes, regardless of their own emotions or outside pressure. Your proxy does not need to be a family member, though it can be helpful if the person lives in your area in case of unforeseen medical emergencies.

No living will can cover every possible situation. A designated proxy can help head off long and heated arguments among your loved ones, and can prevent a drawn-out process of determining what you would want if you could express your wishes. The high-profile, prolonged struggle between Terri Schiavo's husband and her parents provides a clear historical example of the emotionally devastating potential for legal and family battles when a patient cannot express his or her own wishes. Such battles can be largely avoided by a clear advance directive backed by a trustworthy health care proxy.

---

## Rebecca's Advice

---

**If my health wishes have been verbally expressed and accepted by loved ones do I still need an advance directive?**

A verbal advance directive it not sufficient. It is easy for your loved ones to be understanding, rational, and prepared to honor your wishes when your life is not on the line; it is harder during a crisis. Putting your wishes in writing gives family members the clear guidance they will need to make the decision you chose and not the one that their hearts want them to make.

-RP

---

### Medical and Legal Powers of Attorney

A medical power of attorney is not the same as a legal power of attorney, but the latter is equally important in making sure your wishes are clear in case you are incapacitated. In the case of a legal power of attorney, your agent may also be called an attorney-in-fact (as opposed to a lawyer, who is an attorney-at-law). Designating an agent to deal with your legal and financial affairs allows that person to make decisions about your assets, bank accounts and real property should you be unable to do so. A power of attorney can be broad or specific, according to your wishes.

Without a designated agent, your incapacity could mean that your financial and legal affairs are frozen until the court completes a long, often expensive process to designate a guardian for you. And, of course, there is no guarantee the guardian the court selects will be the person you would prefer. By selecting your agent yourself and discussing your wishes with him or her in advance, you can have greater peace of mind regarding that person's judgment and knowledge of your interests.

When selecting your agents, you may be tempted to name more than one person to avoid hurting someone's feelings or seeming to belittle someone's opinion. These are reasonable concerns, but having more than one agent often makes managing your affairs more difficult.

For your medical power of attorney, choosing one person is the best option. Once a decision requires two people to agree, there is the potential for deadlock and fighting. Telling your family why you chose a certain person to be your medical power of attorney can help prevent hurt feelings. Your children all have different personalities; one is likely better-suited to make such decisions because he or she can emotionally handle the consequences and, most importantly, can maintain a clear head during what will likely be a stressful time. Your children are more likely to gracefully accept your decision when they understand your logic.

It is less critical for you to name only one person as your agent for your legal and financial affairs. That said, if you name more than one person, each of them should have the power to act independently. You do not want to require two or more people to agree before they can take action. Having two agents may be appropriate if you have a child who lives nearby, who can manage the day-to-day affairs, but another child who is better suited to handle matters such as your portfolio's investment management.

Powers of attorney (POA) intended for general use (rather than related to a specific event), whether medical or financial, can be either durable or springing in nature. A durable power of attorney takes effect immediately once the documents are finalized. A springing power of attorney, on the other hand, is triggered by the occurrence of a specific event, such as your incapacity. While a springing power of attorney prevents your agent from acting before you need him or her to do so, it can cause delays and extra expense. For example, if the event that triggers the POA is your incapacity, determining whether you are incapacitated may not be legally straightforward. Doctors may be reluctant to take a firm stand, for example. This legal tangle can defeat the entire purpose of setting up a POA in the first place.

While you should only give POA to someone whom you trust completely, some people feel more secure knowing that their agent cannot speak on their behalf while they still have capacity. However, a springing POA is not the only way to accomplish this goal. You can execute a durable POA but, instead of giving your agent the document immediately, you can simply inform him or her where to find the document in your home in case it is needed. (Note: Never store a power of attorney in a safe deposit box. Banks will not allow anyone but you to access the box unless they already have a power of attorney in hand.)

For a power of attorney to stand up to a legal challenge, it is important that there be no doubt about your mental capacity at the time it is drafted. That is one reason why it is better to execute the document sooner than later, even if you do not immediately hand over the document to your agent. Depending on your state and locality, the power of attorney may need to be witnessed or notarized, and even in places where these measures are not required, a notarized document is more likely to stand up in court. Standardized forms are available for various sorts of powers of attorney, though it is important to review such forms carefully before using them.

## Making Your Assets and Personal Information Accessible

Once you have made your wishes for medical care clear and appointed one or more people to act on your behalf if necessary, consider how your loved ones will access your personal assets and information should you be unable to do so yourself. There are many options depending on your priorities, so it is important to consider them thoroughly.

### Revocable Living Trust

One option for assets is a revocable living trust, sometimes just called a revocable trust. When you set up a revocable trust, you typically serve as the maker, initial trustee or co-trustee and initial beneficiary. If set up properly, this sort of trust allows you to retain control of the trust's assets until you choose to cede control to someone else. A revocable trust can also include provisions for distribution of assets upon the grantor's death, making it a useful way to minimize probate concerns. While a revocable trust can be a useful tool, setting it up correctly is essential. You should rely on the help of your attorney or financial planner. See Chapter 5 for more information on trusts.

### Joint Tenancy With Rights of Survivorship

Another way to allow access to an asset when you are incapacitated is for one or more people to own an asset with you. There are many forms of ownership that allow for more than one owner. A common one is joint tenancy with rights of survivorship (sometimes abbreviated JTWROS). Though married couples often use this form of property ownership, joint tenants do not have to be spouses. Joint tenancy is a long-term financial commitment, however, and should not be undertaken lightly.

By jointly owning the asset, you ensure that your fellow tenant can access the asset immediately, even if you are incapacitated for any reason. However, if one joint tenant is incapacitated, legal steps may be necessary before the remaining tenant or tenants can sell or mortgage the asset. When one joint tenant dies, the asset passes directly to the other joint tenant or tenants. This bypasses the need for probate as long as at least one tenant is living. Though it can be tempting to add more tenants to make sure probate is avoided for as long as possible, remember that you are granting anyone who shares the asset with you joint control, use and enjoyment of the asset. The asset will also be exposed to any of the tenants' liabilities, such as creditors or divorces. Adding a joint tenant who is not your spouse may also trigger unintended gift tax consequences.

*Alternative Ownership Sharing Options*

The variety of ways you can legally share ownership of assets or property is beyond the scope of this chapter. However, depending on where you live and what sort of asset you're sharing, you may also have the option of tenancy in common, tenancy by the entirety, or community property. Certain states allow for community property with right of survivorship. Additional statutory non-probate methods of transferring property or assets exist, but many of these are more useful for estate planning than planning for incapacity. It is important to research your options thoroughly while considering the question of access during incapacity, as well as eventual outright transfer. You should make sure the type of ownership you select is appropriate for you in health, incapacity, and with regard to your larger estate plans.

## Preparation of Personal Information

Do not surprise those closest to you should they need to step in and help manage your affairs when you cannot. Prepare copies of important documents, such as your will, and keep them in an accessible but secure location that you disclose to a few trusted individuals. Again, a safe deposit box is not appropriate in most instances, since the only person who can access it besides you is someone with a power of attorney giving them that right; if you plan to keep documents there, make sure your agent has a durable POA in hand, as well as a copy of the box's key. A secure location in your home may make more sense, but use your best judgment for your particular situation. In addition to copies of important documents, you should prepare a list of passwords for important websites, such as your bank or your primary email account. It can be very challenging for your agent or loved one to reset such passwords from scratch if you are not able to help.

## Discussion of Inheritance and Estate Plans

A more niche concept regarding incapacity relates to inheritance fights. Though this concern will not apply to everyone, it is not uncommon. If you have any indication that any of your estate planning documents will be contested by an heir or a family member, you should take steps in advance to ensure your wishes are carried out. The main argument usually presented by those who contest a will or trust is that the maker was not of sound mind when the documents were drafted or that the maker was coerced by an outside party. To defend against such arguments, you may consider recording a video with a doctor at the time you sign your will and other estate plan documents. This can demonstrate that you were of sound mind and under no duress.

Some individuals and couples prepare operating manuals describing exactly how their estate plans are intended to work. Often, when the time is right, they share these documents with their families so their adult children, siblings or other loved ones can understand the intent behind the plan. Explaining who has been selected to serve as a proxy or executor and why can defuse tensions that threaten to appear later in the process. Those leaving the legacy should have forthright conversations, to the extent possible, with their beneficiaries ahead of time, both about their plans for incapacity and their estate. (For more information on estate planning, refer to Chapter 5.)

*Further Preparation*

There are additional steps you can take to make it easier on those who may need to help manage your affairs one day. If recurring income sources, such as Social Security benefits or pension checks, are not already set up for direct deposit, consider arranging this. Not only will it save you time, but it will ensure payments continue uninterrupted even if your mail falls by the wayside for any reason. Likewise, you can set up automatic payments for many regular bills to keep them paid on time.

You can also consider involving a trusted friend, adult child or professional planner in your financial affairs prior to incapacity. Most banks and financial institutions make it relatively easy to send duplicate copies of your statements to someone that you authorize to receive them. In addition, you can give someone you trust the authority to sign checks for you, in case they need to step in unexpectedly to pay bills. As with the considerations above, these steps give the other person some power over your personal affairs, so you should only involve those whom you completely trust. The other side of this consideration, however, is that it is infinitely easier to arrange for someone to step in and help if you can involve them while you still have the capacity to handle matters yourself and explain things to them as needed.

## Maintaining Your Independence

While the previous section suggests reasons why allowing a trusted person to have a bit more involvement in your affairs can be useful, it is also important to realize that capacity and incapacity are not black and white states, but rather the ends of a broad spectrum of potential situations. Many of us, as we age, need some help from those around us, but how much help depends on individual situations.

There are many reasons that maintaining as much independence as possible is important. The primary reason is maintaining the highest quality of life your health and resources will allow. Staying independent can keep you healthier and more mentally stimulated, permit you to enjoy the home you have built for yourself over your working life, and secure a higher level of privacy than other options would allow. Conversely, if managing your financial affairs, especially day-to-day bookkeeping and bill-paying, is a bothersome and stressful task for you, consider delegating this responsibility to the person you have named as agent in your power of attorney, if they are interested in taking on these tasks, or hiring a professional firm to take care of them for you.

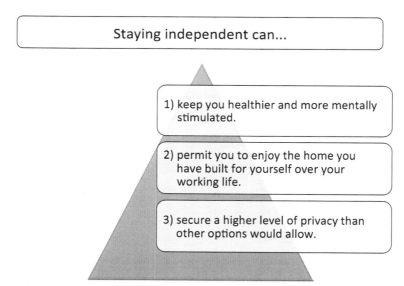

Staying independent can...

1) keep you healthier and more mentally stimulated.

2) permit you to enjoy the home you have built for yourself over your working life.

3) secure a higher level of privacy than other options would allow.

## Home Support

If you stay in your home, you can still build a support system that will give you greater peace of mind and take off the pressure of having to keep up with all your obligations yourself. Meals on Wheels, senior centers, and visiting nurses can all offer services in your home if mobility becomes a problem for you. Domestic employees can also offer a range of services, including home cleaning, shopping, reading mail and providing transport. With proper support from a network of people and services and with available means, you can often remain in the comfort of home even if you require help with some tasks. As people age, many of them are not technically incompetent but do lack the mental and physical strength to perform all their daily tasks unassisted.

An adult child may be able to take over your financial affairs and hire full- or part-time caregivers to help you with meal preparation, perform household chores, and provide daily companionship. If you are childless or you do not desire your children to take on these responsibilities, you can hire a professional to handle your financial affairs and arrange for your physical care at home.

Financial and medical needs may make living alone, even with help, an impractical choice in certain cases. Another option for some older adults is to move in with adult children. The viability of this option will depend on many factors, including your relationship with your child, your child's financial and living situations, and whether the move is meant to be temporary or permanent. With clear communication and a commitment to maintaining your independent lives, living with your children can offer a wonderful opportunity to reconnect with them and their families. It is essential, however, not to fall back into the role of trying to parent independent adult children; likewise, you need to set boundaries about your own independence and life outside the home. Moving in with adult children is not a step to be taken lightly, and you should discuss it calmly, fully and over time before you take any action at all.

## Alternative Living Options

In some cases, support systems in-home or living with adult children will be impractical, or even unsafe. Several levels of residential choices are available to older adults seeking community and social interaction, on-site medical care, or freedom from home maintenance and upkeep.

### Retirement Communities

Retirement communities cater to individuals who are mainly independent and can conduct most of their daily living activities without help. Besides living space, the community typically provides services such as meals, housekeeping, transportation and social activities. Retirement communities can offer individually owned homes or condominiums, or they can be based around rental apartments. The structured nature of the community and the opportunity for social interaction among others of the same age group may be attractive to some, though others might find such structured interaction intrusive.

*Assisted Living Facility*

The next step in level of care is an assisted living facility. These can also be called "board-and-care," "residential care," or "adult family care" facilities, and the level of care they offer varies widely. Broadly speaking, such facilities offer greater assistance with daily living activities than do retirement communities, but do not offer the level of care you would find in a skilled nursing home. Nursing homes offer the highest level of care, including comprehensive medical attention. While a nursing home would be few people's first choice, it can be the best option for individuals with acute, around-the-clock medical needs. Good nursing homes provide social interaction and physical activities as well as medical and personal care.

With any sort of residential facility, you and your loved ones should research the facility fully before making any sort of commitment. If you have long-term care insurance, make sure your plan covers the facilities and services you are considering. For more information on financing long-term care, see Chapter 9. It is important to speak with your adult children or loved ones about your preferences, just as you should discuss your advance health care directive with them. While you cannot anticipate every eventuality, giving those who care about you some idea of your preferences while you have the ability will also guide them in case they need to eventually make choices on your behalf.

## Conclusion

Making informed decisions about your lifestyle and support systems can allow you to remain independent as long as possible. But however much assistance you may one day need, you can gain greater peace of mind from the knowledge that you have made your affairs as simple and accessible as possible for the person or people you trust to oversee them. By discussing your wishes, setting up systems by which trusted people can speak on your behalf, and ensuring that your important information is accessible to those individuals, you establish a safety net for both yourself and your loved ones in the event of a difficult time ahead.

# 4

## THE FAMILY BUSINESS
### Larry M. Elkin, CPA, CFP®

———————————

I was 35 when I left my last salaried job just before Christmas in 1992. I was a senior tax manager in the Manhattan office of Arthur Andersen, and I had given notice that I was starting my own financial planning firm. But first my wife and I planned to drive to Florida for a family vacation.

So I walked to the Port Authority bus terminal that dreary December day, clutching a teddy bear that a co-worker had given me to bring to our 6- and 2-year-old daughters as a going-away present. I took the bus to a stop just off the New Jersey Turnpike. My wife, Linda, pulled up in our tiny Toyota Corolla station wagon. I handed the girls their bear, slid behind the wheel as Linda moved to the passenger seat, and pulled the car back onto the highway

I was now the self-employed founder of a family business.

I did not know whether any other member of my family would ever work at my business. I did not know if I truly had a viable business. There were no employees. There were no customers. I had already rented an office, but my first task after my vacation would be to assemble a desk so I would have a place to work.

My most pressing personal financial goals on the day I left Arthur Andersen were, first, to buy a minivan so we could travel more comfortably in the future and, second, to buy a home in a good suburban school district. My business eventually brought us those things and more – opportunities to travel as a family, to give the kids experiences that enriched their lives, and to provide them with good educations.

But the satisfaction that comes with having a business is not just a matter of money. Linda and I both have M.B.A. degrees. We could have had successful careers in corporate America. For us, the most important aspects of having our own business were the ability to mesh our work time with our family time, and the satisfaction that came with forging relationships that have now spanned two decades and are still going strong.

My background is in journalism, finance and accounting. My wife's is in psychology and marketing. Before we had children, Linda worked for several large publishers. When our first child was born, Linda asked for six months off, but her company allowed only three. She left that job and did not take another for eight years.

By that time I had started my own firm. I was a one-man show, doing everything from drafting financial plans and preparing tax returns to taking out the trash at the end of the day. But I had attracted a core group of excellent clients, who provided a reliable stream of revenue. I had written a book. I was ready to start hiring full-time employees. The business was tiny, but it was on solid footing.

My little office provided the perfect vehicle for Linda to re-enter the work force as a part-time executive. I put her in charge of marketing and human resources, which meant recruiting our first full-time employee. I let her set the days and hours she wanted to work.

Linda's computer skills were almost nonexistent. When she left her prior job to stay home with our children, marketing executives still had secretaries who used personal computers or workstations to type letters and enter data into spreadsheets. When she returned, PCs had mice and ran Windows. Business people were just learning about something called the Internet. Working at our business gave Linda an opportunity to bring her technology skills up to date.

Linda is still with the firm. She has recruited most of the employees who work at Palisades Hudson today, including all of the people who collaborated with me to write this book. She trained our marketing and human resource groups. She now has perfectly good computer skills.

In many ways, the colleagues who have joined our business have become part of our extended family. We hire most of our employees straight out of college and hope, if they prove to be a good fit with Palisades Hudson, to keep them as long as possible – ideally for their entire careers. We try to identify each employee's individual talents and interests, and we direct their career paths to take advantage of their strengths.

## Larry's Advice

### How do you give your small business the best chance to succeed?

You may be starting your own business to make more money, to create a legacy, to control your work environment or just to do something you love. To accomplish any of these things, you need your business to succeed, even though many startups do not. Improve your chances by:

1. Controlling expenses, especially fixed costs. Don't let overhead get ahead of revenue.

2. Focusing on products or services you can deliver efficiently and well.

3. Ensuring you have enough working capital. It takes time and money to generate sales, produce product and collect payment -- at which point you have to spend money again to generate more sales and more product.

4. Trying to have credit available, but use it sparingly and thoughtfully.

Be the sort of boss people want to work for, and the sort of vendor people want to buy from. The goodwill your business builds can be your most valuable asset.

-LME

We never forget that employees want their personal lives to mesh with their work lives just as well as ours did. We keep working hours flexible. We provide ample vacation time and, unlike some workplaces, we do not subtly discourage people from using it. When someone has a personal emergency, we accommodate it. And when someone has young children at home or some other personal need that requires flexible work arrangements, I let the employee tell me what he or she wants to do, just as I once let Linda tell me how much time she was prepared to spend at the office when she first came back to work.

None of these practices are unique to our firm or to family businesses in general. Large corporations can provide very good workplaces. Smaller firms that are not family-controlled can too. But a family-controlled business tends to take on the culture and priorities of the owners in ways that other businesses find hard to replicate.

The ultimate purpose of any business is to make a profit, yet I am free to do things that might cost me some profits – maybe only in the short term, or maybe forever. As sole owner of the business, it is my prerogative to sacrifice profits if I choose. As ownership of any business, public or private, becomes more diverse, it becomes more difficult to unify the owners behind any objective beyond the bottom line.

## Exactly What Is a Family Business?

Everyone understands the difference between a public corporation, whose shares are traded on a stock exchange, and other forms of business ownership, yet a lot of people toss around terms like "family business," "closely held business," and "owner-managed business" as though they are interchangeable. They are not. Before we discuss family businesses in detail, we need to define some terms.

When I started my business, I was a sole proprietor. I was the only owner of the business, and the business was not held in some form of legally organized entity, such as a corporation, a partnership or a limited liability company. In legal terms, I was the business and the business was me.

This did not change when Linda came to work in my office part-time, although some might say that this is when it first became a "family" business. I was still the sole owner, and I was the boss (but only at work). Nor did the business' status change when we began to hire full-time employees.

A big problem with sole proprietorships is that if the owner dies, legally the business dies too. As my firm took on more employees and became more complex (we added an investment management unit in 1997), I established new business entities whose legal existence is separate from me. The primary vehicle is a limited liability company, Palisades Hudson Financial Group LLC. The investment practice is conducted through a limited partnership (Palisades Hudson Asset Management L.P.), which has a corporate general partner (Palisades Hudson Asset Management Inc.). I continue to be the sole owner, but my estate plan is arranged so that these businesses will continue to operate even if I die unexpectedly.

This type of continuity planning was vital if I wanted my firm to grow and prosper, and especially if I wanted to attract and retain talented non-family employees. Now that I am in my mid-50s, I cannot expect young professionals to cast their lot with my firm unless they know the business is organized to go on without me. As I have gotten older, this type of planning has also become increasingly important to our clients. They want to know that the people who take care of them will still be around even if I am gone.

Often, a business' founder will admit co-owners as the company grows. The new partners (who are technically shareholders if the business is a corporation or members if it is an LLC) may be other experienced professionals who join forces with the founder. They may be employees who have grown up with the business and who are given, or are permitted to buy, a piece of the equity. Sometimes the new owners are outside investors who buy into the business. This can provide capital for expansion, or it can allow the founder to reduce her investment in the business and diversify her assets.

This type of business is still a private company, in the sense that its shares are not bought and sold by the general public on a stock exchange. But it is no longer a "family" business, at least in my eyes, because more than one family has a significant ownership stake. Even when the founder's family retains majority control, the controlling owner owes fiduciary duties to the other owners. It may no longer be appropriate to sacrifice profits for other purposes without the consent of the non-controlling owners. A well-run business will have an operating agreement, which is a contract among the various owners, to set out exactly how much power the party in charge retains to make decisions on the other owners' behalf.

Professional firms, such as those in which lawyers and accountants practice, are typically organized as partnerships. Some of them become quite large and profitable. As I said, even though these are no longer truly family businesses, they are still private (also called closely-held) businesses, not public companies. They can also be described as owner-managed businesses, because the owners – the partners – occupy the key management positions.

Most family businesses are owner-managed, but this is not always the case. For more than a decade prior to its acquisition by Colgate-Palmolive in 1992, The Mennen Company (a venerable maker of personal care products) had been run mostly by non-family senior executives. Family members still owned the company and controlled the board of directors, but after three generations of family leadership, they promoted a seasoned executive from outside the family, L. Donald Horne, to become chief executive in 1981. Horne and several other non-family executives took the company to more than $500 million in annual revenue before the $670 million sale to Colgate.

Another organizational variant is fairly common in the media industry, used by companies including The New York Times Co. The company has two classes of stock. Class A shares, representing about 90 percent of the company's equity value, are publicly traded. Class B shares, which are not publicly traded, hold a majority of the company's voting rights and are owned by descendants of Adolph Ochs, who bought The New York Times newspaper in 1896. The Times adopted this structure in 1967 because it wanted to list its shares on the stock exchange but did not want to risk an outside buyer acquiring enough shares to wrest control from the Ochs-Sulzberger family. So, to this day, the company remains publicly traded but family-controlled.

## Managing Family and Non-Family Employees

Non-family employees are often justifiably concerned when a member of the owner's family works in the business. These situations can lead to real or perceived unfairness that can hurt morale, create higher turnover, interfere with recruiting and generally damage the company. But these problems can be avoided if the owner is sensitive and responsive to employees' concerns.

In business, everyone wants to understand the terms of any deal. Employees want to know what sort of work is expected of them, how much time and effort it will take, how much they will be paid, how their performance will be judged, and what sort of advancement is possible in the future. It is in everyone's interest to be as clear and forthright about such matters as possible. The process starts at the job interview.

Once employees come aboard, they will watch carefully to see that the terms of their deal are being honored. This is where the presence of a family member can be disruptive.

The founder and CEO may have been eminently reasonable and quite impressive during the job interview. Yet once on the staff, the new employee could find himself working for or alongside the boss's offspring or siblings, who may not measure up. I cannot think of anything worse for company morale than a manager who is incompetent, inconsiderate or abusive, and who feels immune to criticism because of his relationship to the business owner – or because he is an owner himself.

The strongest businesses are meritocracies, where everyone advances based on performance. It is difficult to maintain a meritocracy if non-family employees know, or believe, that advancement beyond a certain level is only possible for people who share the founder's last name. Meritocracy can also easily dissolve into cynicism when high-level jobs go to people who are unqualified, merely because those people share the founder's DNA. Faced with these situations, the best non-family employees are the ones most apt to find work elsewhere. Not only is their own advancement blocked because they lack the requisite genetics, but they know that they either are currently, or eventually will be, working for someone not fit to lead.

From the viewpoint of the non-family employee, especially when the employee is important to the business' success, a major drawback of working for a family-owned firm is that the family may not be willing to grant an ownership stake. Public corporations often issue stock or options that allow valued employees to build substantial wealth. Executives frequently obtain this equity as part of performance incentive packages intended to align the executives' interests with those of shareholders, who want to increase the value of the enterprise over the long term. Can a family-owned enterprise compete?

Absolutely. There is no difference in the compensation tools available to a private company and those available to one that is publicly traded. The public company's only indisputable advantage is that, because its shares are freely traded, it always has a liquid market in which an equity holder can dispose of, or add to, her investment in the business.

A nonpublic corporation can issue shares or options, just as a public corporation can. In fact, being nonpublic, it can do so with less of a regulatory compliance burden than a publicly traded business. In many cases, it can offer different classes of shares with different entitlements for voting power, dividends and liquidation rights. It can also offer options, though this is uncommon because the lack of a readily ascertainable share price makes options difficult to exercise and almost impossible to trade unless the company is sold.

Often, however, the family in control of a closely-held business does not want to part with much of the equity, or maybe not with any of it. These enterprises can satisfy employees' aspirations through contractual arrangements that create "phantom equity." Such arrangements might entitle the employee to receive payments that are equivalent to the dividends paid on real stock. In the event the company is sold, the employee might have a vested right to a bonus that is equal to the value of the phantom shares based on the sale price. The phantom shares might vest only over a certain period of time, creating an incentive for employees to stay with the firm – a provision typical in corporate grants of stock or options. Such vesting usually becomes immediate if the company is sold.

These phantom equity arrangements do not receive the same favorable tax treatment that is typically available for genuine equity. An owner who sells shares held for more than one year is entitled under U.S. tax law to a favorable capital gains tax rate. Many public-corporation dividends are also eligible for lower tax rates. But payments under phantom equity plans are taxed as ordinary wages. In some cases, as part of the phantom equity deal, the business agrees to reimburse (or "gross up," to use legal and accounting jargon) the employee for the additional taxes that a phantom equity arrangement creates compared to true equity.

The judicious use of equity arrangements, whether genuine or phantom, can go a long way toward making non-family employees feel well protected and fairly treated. By removing the perceived disadvantage of not receiving equity in a company that is, or someday may be, publicly traded, these compensation packages do not just level the playing field; they may tilt it in favor of the family business. Corporate managers come and go, and public corporations can change ownership or management on little more than a moment's notice. A successful and well-managed family business can offer stability and security that public companies often cannot match.

Beyond compensation, employees want to work for people they respect. Nepotism is not a practice that engenders respect. Yet in any family business, nepotism is another significant potential problem. Like equity-based compensation, however, it can be managed.

There is nothing inherently destructive about bringing family members into a business that relies on non-family employee talent. If the family members prove themselves to be able and pleasant co-workers, they will usually be accepted. This is even more likely to occur if the owner makes certain of a few key points:

- Make it obvious that the family member has earned, and is qualified for, any promotion or responsibility he is given. Inexperienced relatives of the boss should enter the business at entry-level jobs.

- Make it clear to non-family employees that their own career paths are unaffected.

- If you are determined to keep the top decision-making positions inside the family, do this as a means of maintaining the firm's mission and values. Don't do it to ensure that the highest-paid slots go to relatives. Make sure that every employee, family and non-family, is paid everything he or she is worth to the business, but not more.

This last point, the matter of owner compensation, warrants further discussion. Everyone who works at a business gets paid for his or her labor. But owners also have a right to be paid for something else, which is their capital invested in the business (even if it is only "invested" through the equity they created, bought or inherited). Shareholders of public companies get paid dividends though they contribute no labor at all. Dividends are a return on their capital.

Owners of family businesses, especially the founders, are not accustomed to thinking of their own compensation as either wages or dividends. They think of "profits." In many businesses, the owner takes no salary. Employees get paid their wages, and the various vendors to the business get paid for what they provide. Profit is what is left over. The owner keeps all of it, or reinvests some to grow the business.

But the owner should think of things this way: His work has a certain value, no matter who performs it. If the owner prefers to stay home and watch television all day, he can, but he might need to hire someone else to work in his place. How much would he have to pay someone else to do the same work at the same level of skill? That is what the owner's job is worth.

If profits exceed the value of the owner's job, this is the equivalent of a dividend. The excess is what the owner gets to keep by virtue of the fact that he owns the business. If, on the other hand, profits are less than the value of the owner's job, then the owner is, in effect, paying for the privilege of being his or her own boss.

Why would a self-employed person stay in business if he or she could make more money working for somebody else? There are many reasons, some valid, some not so valid. The expectation (or at least the hope) of making up the economic shortfall through future profits or future equity value is one of the better reasons. Some people also value the greater ability to control their working conditions, such as by setting their own hours or working from home, which often comes with being self-employed. Some individuals just have trouble taking direction and prefer to be their own bosses. In certain professions, such as journalism, there may be more income security in doing freelance work for multiple customers than in working for a single organization that might cut you loose in the next round of layoffs.

A wise business owner would turn the question upside-down and ask: Why should my employees choose to work for me, rather than for somebody else or for themselves? The best way to satisfy your employees is to start by understanding what they value most.

Most working people are employees, not business owners. Many simply do not possess the capital or the skills to run their own businesses, or they work in fields where doing so may not be practical. If your passion is automotive design, for example, it is certainly a lot easier to go to work for a car company than to start one of your own.

Even individuals who could work for themselves typically choose not to do so. Almost any lawyer could set up shop for herself, yet most will go to work for an established law firm. Such firms offer training and guidance from more-experienced practitioners, a ready-made client base, a bank account with money to cover the next paycheck, and all sorts of infrastructure, from office space to desks to reference materials. Just as important, going to work for an established company allows the lawyer to focus on her major interest – the law – without having to worry about extraneous matters like computer security, balky air conditioners or which telephone system to acquire.

Working for somebody else provides far more structure than a small business owner typically enjoys. Chances are that employees of the family business value that structure – as long as they know the structure is fair to them. Fairness is paramount.

A rule that says "nobody can earn more than me, because I am the owner" is unfair and ultimately self-defeating. You might have an employee whose work is worth more than yours. If you don't pay that employee what her work is worth, she may soon leave.

A rule that says "Nobody can run the company except me or my children, because I am the owner" is likewise unfair and self-defeating. As the owner, you are entitled to the profits of the business, but there is no law of nature that says you should always be in charge – and even less so for your kids, who may not have your skills and experience. If you want your heirs to step into your shoes, they must be prepared to fill them.

## Planning an Orderly Exit

If you are 55 or older, you are more likely to be thinking about leaving a business than about starting one (not that there is anything wrong with someone in this age bracket starting a business; we address this in Chapter 19). Succession planning is one of the most vital and most difficult aspects of managing a family business. Among financial and business advisers, the generally accepted rule of thumb is that only 3 in 10 family businesses successfully transition to a second generation, and only 3 in 10 of those that survive to a second generation make it to a third. Crunching these numbers leads to the widely repeated statement that more than 90 percent of family businesses do not successfully make it to a third generation. (30 percent of 30 percent is 9 percent, the share of businesses presumed to survive through three generations.) I will not attest to the accuracy of these statistics, but the bigger truth is indisputable: Transferring a family business to new management is a perilous task.

I believe there are two principal reasons for this. First, most business founders consider themselves indispensable, forgetting the adage that "the graveyards are full of indispensable men." Picture a typical organizational chart with the CEO at the top, the heads of various key functions – sales, production, personnel, finance – reporting to the boss, and different sub-functions (for example, purchasing, treasury and payroll within the finance function) reporting to the head of that discipline.

## Corporate Organizational Structure

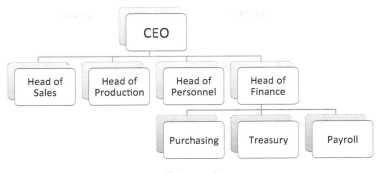

Figure 1

Now picture the classic organizational structure of the entrepreneurial business. Everyone reports to the CEO, who is also the founder. There might or might not be a head of finance, but the boss has a tendency to stick his or her nose into everything. The second-in-command of a $65 million a year business once told me that his staff hid invoices from the chief executive, who would otherwise question the need for, and price of, every desk and photocopier the company bought. Nobody, least of all the boss, had time for that much micromanagement.

## Entrepreneurial Business Structure

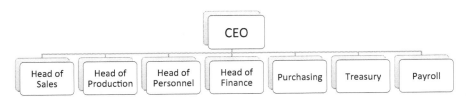

Figure 2

A founder who believes nobody else can run the business is not likely to prepare early or well for the inevitable transition.

Anyone who starts a business has a unique chance to grow as the enterprise grows. Things tend to start small and get bigger, to start simple and become more complex. Along the way, the founder builds relationships with employees, customers, suppliers, landlords, bankers and all the other parties that make an enterprise successful. As the business expands, the founder also has the most detailed knowledge of how the enterprise operates. Eventually a founder may not know everything or everyone, but as head of the business, he or she should know everything that the boss needs to know.

An effective successor is usually one who is well-groomed – and we are not talking about fashion sense. The transition from one generation of leadership to the next should be planned far in advance. The future boss, especially a younger relative of the founder, must have the right skills and personality to command respect from everyone who comes in contact with the business – employees, customers and vendors alike. The future leader should receive the right training and gain the right experience. Often, it is a good idea to have that individual work his or her way up through the organization, building relationships with peers who are about the same age and who will help the new leader carry the business forward.

Simply designating a son or daughter as the future chief executive is not enough. The business owner has to be open-minded enough to recognize the situation if, in the process of preparing the successor, it becomes evident that the heir is not up to the job. Nobody's interest is well served by putting the wrong person in charge.

Most of all, the departing leader has to be truly prepared to let go of the reins. It helps a lot to have another activity – a new venture, a charitable foundation, a personal hobby – that beckons. It is important to let the new chief step out of the shadow of the old one.

In some cases, it helps for the founder to establish a board of directors or an advisory board well before the leadership transition. Don't choose board members who are beholden to the founder, such as the company's lawyer or accountant. Don't use people who are afraid to disagree with the boss. Look for experienced, knowledgeable individuals who have relevant expertise, and who will be forthright when they disagree with the CEO, yet who also know how to collaborate. Putting a competent board in place can make a big difference when a new chief has to take over. Even before the transition, a good board can help build a stronger business.

It is important, too, for the outside world to recognize that the departing boss is not the embodiment of the company, and that life will go on under the new regime. When I launched my own business, I was just Larry M. Elkin, CPA, CFP®. I did business as Larry M. Elkin & Co. once I began hiring employees. But less than a decade after I launched my firm, I settled on the name "Palisades Hudson" because I wanted outsiders to recognize my firm as something distinct from, and more than, myself. It was a way of signaling that the enterprise could go on without me, as indeed I intend it to. The name change was one of the early steps in my succession plan. I was not yet 45 years old when I took it.

An effective plan for business succession must answer three key questions:

1. Who is going to own the business?

2. Who is going to control the business?

3. Who is going to run the business?

If a succession plan fails, it will most likely be because it failed to address one or more of those questions, or because the answer it provided was unworkable.

Here is a classic and all-too-common situation. A CPA who specializes in tax work has been in practice for 30 years, employing an experienced assistant, when he suddenly dies. The accountant's spouse, who is not a CPA and knows nothing about taxes, concludes that she has no option other than to sell the business. But the experienced assistant has never signed a non-compete agreement or any other employment contract with the firm.

If the CPA had sold the firm himself, he probably would have stayed with the practice temporarily to smooth the transition to new management. But the CPA is gone. If the experienced assistant has formed good relationships with the clients, maybe the assistant will stay and ensure the transition to new ownership — but the assistant is perfectly free to solicit those clients and go into business for himself. The spouse is then left with nothing to sell. Alternately, the assistant might demand a big raise or a large bonus from the new owners, who in any case are unlikely to pay much money up front while they wait to see if the clients stick around. Any retention bonus paid to the assistant is likely to come out of the surviving spouse's share.

I encountered a real-life situation like this some years back, but the facts were even worse. Not only was there a poorly motivated assistant, but the practice's files were a shambles and its technology was a wreck. The late CPA's wife had called to see if I was interested in buying the practice. Needless to say, I wasn't.

What might the CPA have done differently to put his wife in a better position?

First, since the owner of a tax preparation business does not need to be a CPA, he could have organized his practice in a business entity that would be more easily transferred to his wife as part of his estate. Or he could have put that entity into a trust that would continue to exist after his death, so that no transfer would have been necessary. The trustee might have been his wife, or it might have been someone with more business experience who would have been comfortable operating the firm.

Second, the CPA would have entered into valid employment and non-compete agreements with his key employee. This would not have guaranteed that the employee might not try to leave and take the clients on his way out the door, but it would have made it less likely. Retaining the assistant to serve the CPA's tax clients would have required that he have as much tax knowledge as the CPA. The CPA might have invested in additional training for his assistant.

The accountant also might have acquired life insurance on behalf of the business as well as his wife. The business could have used insurance proceeds to provide a "golden handcuff" deal to the employee, in the form of a retention bonus. Insurance money also would have provided an opportunity for the business to make up for any drop in revenue as some clients inevitably left following the loss of their longtime tax adviser. With good management and marketing, new business could have been found to replace that which was lost.

The accountant also could have made his wife's life much easier if he had established a prior arrangement with another firm prepared to buy his practice. These arrangements are called "practice continuation agreements." The CPA could have continued to practice independently, but he would have identified a future buyer. Typically, the acquiring firm is somewhat larger than the practice being acquired, but is located in the same area and with a similar clientele. The future acquirer is given an opportunity to become familiar with the target firm's work, technology and files. (This would have given the CPA a strong incentive to get his workplace in order, rather than leaving the disarray in which I found it.)

A practice continuation agreement will typically establish a formula to determine a selling price, and it can also provide for temporary service to the target firm's clients in the event the target firm's operator becomes sick or injured. Every sole practitioner in a professional service industry ought to consider entering into such an agreement – to protect clients as well as the business – and small companies in other industries can probably adapt this model to their needs as well.

As bad as this situation was, things can often be much worse when the founder's children are involved.

My experience has been that most business owners, like most other parents, want to be fair to all their children. They usually interpret fairness to dictate that the children receive equal inheritances – at least equal in value, and often as equal as possible in the specific assets the children receive. When it comes to the family business, however, even-steven is not always a formula for fairness. Just as often, it is a recipe for disaster.

Consider the hypothetical case of a construction company owner who is divorced and who has three daughters, one of whom is well-trained and who works in the business, and the other two of whom are uninvolved and who know little about the firm and nothing about the industry. Think about what happens if the owner dies abruptly, bequeathing the company stock equally to all three children. The daughter who is active in the business will now find herself working not for her father, but for her siblings.

Sometimes that is not a problem. Often it is.

If the active daughter is prepared to assume her father's responsibilities, she will likely want a raise. At the very least, she will expect to receive more money from the business than her sisters, who are free to spend their days elsewhere. But her sisters may believe that no raise is warranted because their father wanted them treated equally. They may believe all the business earnings should be paid out as dividends or distributions to owners, not partly as salary to an owner-manager like their sibling. (Presumably the sisters did not read my explanation earlier in this chapter of the distinction between being paid for labor and being paid for capital. The active daughter is entitled to be paid for both; her sisters are not.)

Some potential conflicts are even worse. What happens if the active daughter believes she is qualified to take over from Dad, but her sisters disagree? There might be a non-family employee in whom the two sisters outside the business have more confidence. Maybe the two siblings are right and maybe they aren't, but either way, there could be a lot of awkward silence or worse around the family's Thanksgiving table.

An even more extreme, though not uncommon, disagreement could arise if the two uninvolved sisters decide they want to sell the business, while the active sister argues that their father intended to keep it in the family under her management. Many an enterprise has passed from family control in these situations. Many more have been torn apart, their value permanently diminished or destroyed, by the conflict.

In these cases, effective succession plans are often built around the idea of using multiple classes of equity. Family members may receive preferred stock with a stated dividend rate, so they can count on a regular stream of income – a return on capital. These dividends can be reduced or interrupted, however, if the business lacks earnings or cash flow to support the payments. Sometimes the plan goes a step further, giving the children who are active in the business – or other trusted parties – voting control. This does not guarantee that there will not be conflict among heirs who have different objectives or opinions, but it can place control in the hands of the individuals that the founder believes are best equipped to make good decisions.

There are other techniques for getting cash flow to non-involved family members while allowing only those who are active in the business to have a say in how it is managed. One method is to put certain key assets of the business, such as a factory, a distribution center, or even intellectual property such as patents or trademarks, in a separate entity. The business pays rent or royalties to the separate entity, which can distribute these cash flows to the non-involved relatives. The relatives get an income stream, while equity in the business goes to the individuals who work at building its value.

Another approach is to divide business assets among multiple heirs, giving each heir control over his or her own domain. I have seen this technique implemented in various ways. In one manufacturing company, the founder's three sons were given equal allocations of stock, but different responsibilities over the business. One son was put in charge of production, a second took control of finance, and the third is responsible for sales and marketing. The founder retired to Florida, and the business has prospered under the sons' management.

In another instance, a man with sizable timber holdings wanted his two children to share equally in its value, but he wanted to avoid triggering conflicts in case they disagreed over how to manage the trees or whether to sell any of the property. He divided his holdings into two LLCs, gave each child a 50 percent interest in both LLCs, and gave each child one of the LLCs to manage. Each of his offspring can make decisions about half of the holdings without consulting the other, but all of the proceeds must be split 50-50.

All of these arrangements transfer equity in the family business to younger family members. How do you make certain the equity stays in the family after the transfer? Younger family members can get divorced, run into financial trouble, or just decide they want to cash out and do something else with their inherited wealth. This can inject non-family members who have different priorities and values into the business.

If the succession plan aims to keep things in the family, it will usually include provisions to restrict transfers to others. Common measures include the use of trusts, the establishment of buy-sell agreements or rights of first refusal, or simply organizational limits on transfers, such as requiring consent of all owners before any interest can be sold or given away.

## Estate Tax Complications

For larger family businesses, another key consideration is how to minimize gift and estate taxes when ownership passes to younger generations, as well as how to provide the cash to pay whatever taxes are due. In the U.S., these wealth transfers are generally taxed at 40 percent by the federal government after a cumulative lifetime exemption – $5.34 million in 2014 – which is indexed for inflation. Some states have additional taxes and lower exemption amounts. Taxes are typically not due on transfers between spouses, except when the recipient spouse is not a U.S. citizen. With proper planning, a married couple can pass total wealth of more than $10.6 million to children and other heirs, free of at least federal taxes. This protects most family businesses, but not the largest and most valuable.

Taxpayers often get into disputes with the IRS about the value of nonpublic businesses. Publicly traded companies are usually simple to value, because their share prices are quoted daily on major stock exchanges. But valuing an enterprise whose ownership interests seldom, if ever, change hands is a subjective and controversial exercise. In particular, taxpayers and tax authorities often lock horns over how much a non-controlling minority interest in an enterprise is worth.

Once the tax on a gift or inheritance that includes a family business has been computed, where does the money to pay it come from? Federal estate taxes are due nine months after the owner's death. There are provisions in the tax code to delay the payment in certain situations, usually when the business makes up a large share of the decedent's estate. But this deferral comes with interest charges and is not always applicable.

Capital gains taxes are typically easy to pay, because the sale of a stock or other capital assets that triggers the tax provides the necessary cash. But an inheritance is not a sale and does not generate cash. Sometimes a business might need to borrow money itself to lend to the decedent's estate so it can pay the taxes. The resulting debt can jeopardize the company if business conditions deteriorate. Sometimes the founder's executor might need to sell other, more liquid or less desirable assets to raise the necessary cash. In the worst cases, the business itself might need to be sold, passing out of family control.

It is a sad result when taxes alone are the reason a family must sell an enterprise. It is not always the wrong answer, however. Good succession planning for a family business does not always require that the business remain in the family's hands.

If no family member has the aptitude or desire to run the business, the only sensible thing to do is to put somebody else in charge. Promoting a capable non-family employee to CEO can give the business its best chance to prosper while it remains in the family. Alternatively, selling the company can allow the family to diversify its assets and possibly generate better long-term returns at lower risk.

Sometimes, the best buyer for an enterprise may be the employees who already work there. The business itself can provide the funds for the sale through a leveraged buyout structure. There are other possible vehicles as well, such as tax-favored Employee Stock Ownership Plans (ESOPs). In other cases, outside investors or similar companies in the same industry (so-called "strategic buyers") are the most logical prospective buyers.

The Mennen family's handling of The Mennen Company is an example of a succession plan that worked very well over an extended period. Three generations of family members ran the company for more than a century after Gerhard H. Mennen founded the business. Eventually the family turned over day-to-day management to non-Mennen executives, even though family members continued to hold the stock. This entitled the family to collect dividends, though as a private company Mennen did not need to publicly disclose if it paid any. This structure also left family members in control of whether to keep or sell the company. In 1991 they decided that Mennen was too small to compete with such rivals as Procter & Gamble and Colgate-Palmolive, and the following year they consummated the sale to Colgate.

Did Gerhard Mennen expect the talcum powder business he established in Newark, N.J., would someday sell for more than $600 million? It is hard to imagine that he did; such sums were almost inconceivable when he lived, in the late 19th and early 20th centuries. Did he dare to hope that his business would employ some of his children and grandchildren, launch one member of the family to political prominence (G. Mennen Williams, known as "Soapy" for the family business, was Michigan's governor from 1949 through 1960 and later chief justice of the Michigan Supreme Court), and provide financial security for generations to come? I suppose he might have, in his wildest dreams.

It goes to show that with good planning, a family business can make even the wildest dreams can come true.

# 5

## ESTATE PLANNING
### David Walters, CPA, CFP®
### Melinda Kibler, CFP®

---

Estate planning, much like getting an annual physical or doing your taxes, is an essential activity that most people would rather avoid. While it's easy to put it off indefinitely, having a concrete estate plan will not only give you greater peace of mind, but will save your family and loved ones considerable work and stress later.

Many people think of estate planning as something only for the affluent, but everyone can benefit from estate planning to some degree. If you have a spouse, dependents or children young enough to need guardians, it is important to make sure your loved ones are provided for as you would like. For those with a spouse or partner of the same sex, the tangle of state and federal laws makes careful planning to this end even more essential. Additionally, if you wish to leave specific items to particular beneficiaries, or if you have charitable objectives, proper planning can ensure your wishes are honored in an efficient, tax effective and straightforward manner.

This chapter will cover the basics of estate planning considerations and assist you in compiling your important documents. For those with an estate plan in place, it will be a good reminder to review your current plans and ensure they are still up-to-date.

## Get Organized

The first step in creating a useful estate plan is to give careful consideration to your objectives. You should think about what you would like your estate plan to accomplish. Your primary focus may be ensuring the transfer of your assets is efficient, costs are minimized, and that certain assets pass to specific beneficiaries. Or your goals may be to reduce or eliminate estate taxes on your assets, to secure an efficient succession in a family business, to avoid or simplify probate, or to arrange for charitable gifts. Any and all of these are excellent goals, and it is not uncommon for an individual to have multiple objectives in mind. Once you have your goals set, and have considered their priority, you will use them to shape your estate planning decisions.

Additionally, you likely want to take the concerns and wishes of your family and beneficiaries into account. While you have the final say in the disposition of your assets, open communication with your spouse, adult children, or other beneficiaries can help avoid surprises or disagreements in the future. Presumably, you don't wish to leave assets to those who don't want or can't use them. In addition, clear communication will give you a better sense of your beneficiaries' capability and responsibility, which may also shape your choices. (See Chapter 2 for more information on financial discussions with your adult children.)

After establishing your goals, the next step is to compile important personal documents and information. While you don't have to put all of the documents in the same place, you should have a master list, or table of contents, with the current location of everything. To be safe, you should provide at least two trusted people (such as your spouse, financial adviser, or adult child) with the master list.

- ✓ **Estate Planning Documents**: First you'll want to collect your original estate planning documents. Your will is the primary one. If you don't yet have a will, see the section on wills later in this chapter. These documents may also include trusts you have created, an advance medical directive or durable power of attorney for health care (see Chapter 3), a living will, a durable power of attorney, and a personal property memorandum. You will want to keep documents related to your estate plan in a safe but accessible place.

- ✓ **Memorial Instructions**: Consider drafting explicit instructions for your memorial. These won't go in your will, but having them recorded in writing can be very helpful to whichever loved one will organize such arrangements. It may be helpful to compile a list of people who should be notified, especially if you have family or friends who live far away or with whom you do not speak regularly.

Other questions to consider: Do you want a funeral or ceremony of any kind? If so, what religious tradition, if any, should preside, and where should it be held? Who should be invited? Would you prefer a donation to a cause or charity instead of flowers? You should also specify your wishes for your remains, if any, such as burial, cremation or donation. These are unpleasant things to think about, but the more choices you can make in advance, the fewer will be left for those mourning you in the midst of a time when the number of decisions they face can seem overwhelming.

✓ **Personal Records**: You should also assemble or note the location of your birth certificate, marriage certificate, divorce or separation documents, pertinent death certificates, adoption papers, citizenship documents and military records. It is also wise to make copies of your driver's license or state-issued ID, Social Security card, health insurance and Medicare cards, and any organ donor cards or information.

✓ **Other Personal Items**: If there are any important family items, such as heirlooms or photograph albums, that would not be readily evident, you can also leave a list of the location of such items.

✓ **Legal and Financial Documents**: Legal and financial documents should also be readily available. Legal documents can include prenuptial or postnuptial agreements, employment agreements, LLC or corporate documents, and leases or partnership agreements. Financial documents should include copies of your recent bank, credit card and investment account statements; your original life insurance policy; original stock and bond certificates; real estate documents, including deeds, mortgages and title insurance policies; retirement accounts such as 401(k)s and IRAs; titles to cars, boats or planes and corresponding insurance policies; liabilities, such as mortgages and student loans; tax returns; and copies of any recent inventories or assessments.

✓ **User-IDs and Passwords**: It is also wise to take a moment to create an updated list of usernames and passwords or PINs for important websites, such as your primary email account or your online banking portal. If you store passwords in your browser, most will allow you to export your saved list that can be opened in a spreadsheet program. If you have wishes as to who should be responsible for shutting down your various online presences, you should consider including these wishes in your estate plan.

Once you have assembled all the relevant documents, you should create an accompanying contact list of any relevant individuals. This list should include the person's full name, their relationship to you, a current address, phone number and email. This list can include personal contacts, such as your current and former spouses, parents and step-parents, children and grandchildren, siblings, and close friends in the area (especially if family members are far away) as well as professional contacts, such as your attorney, accountant, investment adviser, stockbroker, insurance agent or trust officer.

Your contact list and documents should be stored in a secure place, such as a personal fire- and waterproof safe. If you choose to store any or all of them in a safe deposit box, make sure the key is accessible and that someone has a durable power of attorney or is on the list of those who can access the box. Should the need arise, you will want someone to have immediate access.

You may also want to consider arranging for an inventory of your assets. A property inventory catalogs what you own so nothing is forgotten, by you in your estate plans or by your beneficiaries later. An inventory can also assist you in tax planning, help you keep track of fluctuating values for pieces such as art or antiques, and allow you to create very specific wills or trusts. However, if you have minimal physical property, or if you intend to bestow your estate in its entirety to only a few individuals, an inventory may not be necessary.

When proceeding with an inventory, group your assets by type. Categories could include:

- Bank accounts/money market accounts/certificates of deposit

- Personal belongings, such as jewelry, artwork and furnishings

- Real estate, including your primary residence

- Retirement accounts

- Stocks and brokerage accounts

- Business interests, including digital assets such as websites or domains

- Patents, royalties and copyrights

All of this preparation is important, but perhaps the most important step – and often the hardest – is initiating a discussion with your family or loved ones. While some may be resistant to making such plans, it's important that they be able to discuss your wishes with you while you're still in a position to communicate clearly. The more normal such discussions become, the easier they will be in the future should things change or need to be revised. Don't wait for your loved ones to ask; the burden is on you to begin these conversations.

---

## Melinda's Advice

---

### How much should you disclose in discussing your estate plans with family?

It is important to discuss your estate plan, but the amount and type of information you divulge may depend on the relationships you have. If you have reservations about sharing details, consider simply providing an overview so your heirs understand your goals. You can offer more details to a select few with whom you are more comfortable sharing information. At least two people, preferably including your executor or other fiduciaries, should know the location of important documents and should have access to logins and passwords.

-MK

---

## Types of Property Transfer

Once you have prepared your lists of property, you can begin to consider how you would like to go about transferring the assets to your heirs. Generally, your assets will pass through probate, a process in which the court validates and then oversees the operation of your will or, if no valid will is found, applies the law to distribute your assets. However, certain non-probate events can bypass this process.

Being able to transfer property or assets without going through probate has several advantages. It will generally save time and expense. Additionally, it will keep your affairs private – probate proceedings expose assets to public scrutiny.

## Avoiding Probate

*Joint Tenancy With Right of Survivorship*

What, then, are some common ways to avoid probate? One of the most common is joint tenancy with right of survivorship (sometimes just called "joint tenancy" or JTWROS). In this form of property ownership, all tenants have an equal right and an equal liability to the owned asset. At the death of one of the tenants, the property passes directly to the other tenant(s) without being subject to probate. While many spouses use this form of property ownership, it's important to realize the potential downsides. Your co-tenants can block your wishes for the property, whether by obstructing a sale or ignoring your wishes after your death without legal ramifications. Your fellow tenants should be not only people you wish to benefit, but people who are also responsible and with whom you communicate well.

*Tenancy By the Entirety*

In some states, property may be owned as tenants by entirety. This type of titling is specifically for married couples and allows them to own the property as a single legal unit. When property is owned under such titling, creditors of an individual spouse may not go after an interest in the property unless they are creditors of both spouses. Similar to joint tenancy with right of survivorship, the property passes directly to the surviving spouse without being subject to probate at time of death. Note that only 26 states currently allow for this type of titling and of those 26 states, some allow for tenants by entirety ownership only for real estate, not bank and investment accounts.

*Revocable and Irrevocable Trusts*

Another common method of avoiding probate is the use of trusts. While trusts have a colloquial association with only the wealthiest tier of society, they can be a useful tool for any individual who might choose to exercise greater control over the way assets are transferred. A revocable living trust allows you to avoid probate, while giving you, as the grantor, significant control and flexibility. This is because transferring property into a revocable trust puts the assets under the trust provisions, but still allows you, as the grantor, to reclaim the property and change the beneficiaries at any time while you are alive. When you die, the trust provisions will determine the beneficiaries of the trust property without involving probate. However, for tax purposes, the property is still included in your estate as though it were owned by you personally, potentially creating an estate tax liability. An irrevocable trust provides a greater tax shelter, but at the cost of a revocable trust's flexibility. Once an irrevocable trust is created and you transfer assets into it, you may not retrieve those assets. By transferring property into an irrevocable trust, the assets are no longer considered to be owned by you personally, and are therefore usually not part of your estate for tax purposes (although you may have to pay gift tax, or use your lifetime gift tax exemption, when assets are contributed to an irrevocable trust).

*Other Trusts*

Depending on precisely what you want to achieve, there are many different types of trusts and they can be written to meet your specific needs. Certain types may be relatively expensive to draft or administer, so you should consult a professional when deciding what trust is most appropriate for your situation, as well as during the organization process. Trusts are useful, but they can also be complicated. In some circumstances, other probate-avoiding vehicles may be more suitable.

It's also good to bear in mind that not all trusts result in non-probate transfers. For example, testamentary trusts are trusts created by a person's will. They take effect at the time of death. With testamentary trusts, assets are subject to probate; hence, a testamentary trust would not be appropriate if your goal is to avoid probate.

*Direct Beneficiary Designation*

Another way to avoid probate is through property that allows you to designate a beneficiary directly. A life insurance policy generally allows you to appoint specific individuals. Similarly, you can designate beneficiaries for retirement accounts, shielding the assets in the account from probate. A medical savings account (MSA) or health savings account (HSA) will also allow you to name a beneficiary, should you die with money still in your account. If this beneficiary is your spouse, the money is transferred not only out of probate, but also tax-free.

You can also set up a payable-on-death (POD) account or transfer-on-death (TOD) account in order to avoid probate. These are more or less the same; POD accounts are usually bank accounts while TOD accounts are usually investment or brokerage accounts. With these accounts, you are given the option to name a beneficiary who receives the balance of your account upon your death without having to go through probate. Until that time, the beneficiary has no rights to the account. You can name multiple beneficiaries, provided you include percentages for how the assets should be divided. Additionally, the beneficiary can be changed at your discretion but it must be done directly; it can't be accomplished in your will. For POD and TOD accounts, rules vary by state so be sure to research thoroughly before proceeding.

Whenever you name a beneficiary for your account, you should be mindful of common errors to avoid. Though this may seem simplistic, don't name a beneficiary who is impossible to identify or contact. Specify the beneficiary's full, legal name, and make sure that the contact information for that person stays current. You should also avoid simply listing a beneficiary "as per my will." Though this may seem a handy way to make sure your beneficiary designations stay up-to-date, many custodians are reluctant to accept it, and it can create confusion should your will be unavailable or otherwise unusable. This practice can also force your assets into probate, which is what you presumably hoped to avoid in the first place. In cases where you have more than one beneficiary on the same account or property, specify percentages, not amounts. If the asset's value changes, the specified amounts may not add up to 100 percent of the asset, which can lead to lopsided distributions or conflicts between beneficiaries. You should also be sure you understand all legal requirements, especially on the state level. For example, children under the age of majority cannot be retirement plan beneficiaries, but the age of majority varies from state to state. Don't forget to consider the tax consequences for yourself and your beneficiaries, especially if you select a beneficiary who is not your spouse. Finally, remember to review your choices periodically to be sure the listed beneficiaries are who you wish them to be, and that their contact information is still current.

## Life Estate

If you wish to transfer real property without going through probate, you also have the option to establish a life estate. A life estate is a kind of joint ownership, where you retain the right to live in or control the property during your lifetime and the property passes to your intended heir (called "the remainderman") at your death. The downside is that this arrangement, once set up, is irrevocable, and your life estate generally cannot be transferred to anyone else.

## What Else to Know About Avoiding Probate

With all of these strategies for avoiding probate, you should remember that assets not included in probate can still be included in your gross estate for determining tax liability. There are some exceptions. For example, only 50 percent of JTWROS accounts are included in your estate if the only other tenant is your spouse, and there is ordinarily no estate tax on the included portion if your spouse is a U.S. citizen. However, if the joint tenants have a relationship other than marriage, the surviving tenant must prove he or she made contributions to the account or contributed to the purchase of the property. If he or she cannot, the entire value counts toward the deceased tenant's total estate. It is important to keep these types of rules in mind for each account when formulating estate tax strategies. (For more information on transfer taxes, see Chapter 6.)

As previously mentioned, state regulations play a large role in the treatment of property. For example, community property states are states in which assets acquired during marriage are automatically considered joint, unless the owner can prove the separation of ownership (such as a car purchased in one individual's name, prior to the marriage). As a general rule, any income earned by one spouse is considered to be half earned by the other spouse. Oddly, unless right of survivorship is specified by law by using the titling "community property with right of survivorship," community property is typically subject to probate, even if the property is bequeathed to the decedent's spouse. Currently, the following states are considered community property states: Arizona, California, Idaho, Louisiana, Nevada, New Mexico, Texas, Washington, and Wisconsin. In Alaska, couples may opt-in for community property law, or may follow common law as used in other states.

## Wills

Why are wills so important? As discussed earlier, your will is the primary document that directs how your assets will be distributed via the probate process. A person with no valid will is "intestate," which means that since you have no will it is the probate court's responsibility to distribute your assets according to law. This is generally a very undesirable scenario, as the intestate laws that dictate how your assets will be distributed can often be very different from your actual desires.

The specifics of how this is accomplished vary from state to state, but all states have intestacy laws. Many states base their statutes on the 1990 Uniform Probate Code, which specifies that close relatives are recognized prior to distant relatives in roughly the following order:

1. A surviving spouse

2. Children or direct descendants

3. Parents

4. Descendants of parents (siblings, nieces or nephews)

5. Grandparents

6.  Descendants of grandparents (aunts or uncles, first cousins)

Adopted descendants are usually treated as equal to biological descendants for probate purposes. If none of these relations exist or can be
found, the deceased's property goes to the state; none will go to unrelated
beneficiaries or to charity. Even if your loved ones know your wishes,
intestate succession applies unless a valid will can be produced.

If there is a living spouse, he or she is usually entitled to all or most
of the net estate – the amount left after all debts, taxes and administrative expenses have been paid. However, even if you intend to leave your
entire estate to your spouse and have relatively simple financial affairs, it
is still recommended that you leave a will to avoid complications in the
probate process and reduce expenses.

The first major choice to make when creating a will is whether you will
write the will yourself or hire a lawyer to draft it for you. If your estate is
very simple, or if you plan to leave everything to only a few beneficiaries,
you can probably write your own. Books and software are both widely
available to help you create a legally sound document. For a complex
estate, or if you have very specific objectives to accomplish, consulting a
professional can be worthwhile to ensure your wishes are honored legally
and without contest.

Whether you write your own or hire a professional, you will want to
know what is usually included in a will. For starters, remember clarity and
specificity are usually best.

**Your will should:**

• Establish your identity and domicile (see Chapter 14 for more information on domicile)

• Revoke any former wills

• Name an executor

• Name guardians for any children who are minors

• State your preference for how to pay any debts or taxes owed by the
  estate

• Provide for any pets*

• Confirm your wishes for any established living trusts

**Your will should not:**

- Include conditions for your gifts (e.g. "I leave my primary residence to my son provided he is employed at the time of my death")**

- Include detailed instructions for your memorial service or final arrangements

- Express wishes regarding non-probate assets, such as a POD account or an IRA

- Arrange directly for the care of a beneficiary with special needs***

* You cannot leave assets or property directly to a pet. However, you can name a new caregiver, and then name that person a beneficiary for assets used to take care of the pet.

** Placing conditions on your bequests is legally complicated, and usually leads to problems. Certain conditions, including marriage, divorce or a change of religion, are legally prohibited. If you want bequests to be subject to such conditions, you may want to consider an incentive trust.

*** If you have a beneficiary with special needs, it is generally safer to set up a special needs trust.

There are also a few steps you can take to make sure your will stands up in court. In some states, certain steps are mandatory, but doing more than required makes the document even more legally sound. For example, you should type your will. In some states, handwritten wills are invalid, but even if they are permissible, they can be hard to read and easy to misconstrue. Once your will is complete, sign and date it. Have two witnesses sign as well. The witnesses do not need to know the will's contents unless you wish them to, and can be any competent adults (though usually they cannot be beneficiaries named in the will). Though having your will notarized is optional in most states, including a self-proving affidavit signed by a notary public will help your will's legal standing. For your will to be valid, it should also be clear you are of sound mind and acting of your own volition, without undue influence or fraud.

Once you have a valid will, it is important to keep it up-to-date. If there has been a major change in your personal life, such as a marriage, a divorce, the death of a loved one, a move to a new state or abroad, or a major change in financial circumstances involving you or one of your beneficiaries, you should make sure your wishes reflect these changes. You should also review your will if there has been a change in tax law, estate law, or the laws governing probate or trusts. And, of course, if you simply change your mind about the distribution of your assets, you should change your will promptly to reflect your new decisions.

---

# David's Advice

---

## How should my will address my digital estate?

As part of your estate planning documents, you should include a list of all online accounts and passwords for your executor. Your will can stipulate what should be done with email and other online accounts at your death. Absent that, it may be very difficult for an executor to deal with digital vendors. As of this writing, only seven states have laws addressing online estate planning, so in most cases the service contract between the deceased and the online vendor will dictate what powers an executor may have over an online account.

-DW

---

## Fiduciaries

A fiduciary is a person or institution that you grant the power to act on your behalf, or to administer your affairs according to your wishes. Fiduciary duty is a fiduciary's legal obligation to act on your behalf in good faith. In your estate plan, you will likely have several people or institutions that fall under the category of fiduciary.

### Executor

Perhaps the most important fiduciary is your executor. This individual, sometimes also called a personal representative or an administrator, is the person responsible for administering your estate in accordance with your will. Assuming you name an executor in your will, a probate judge will honor your wishes unless there is a reason the person cannot legally serve or is disqualified through legal contest. If you die without a valid will, the probate judge will designate an executor according to the state's statutes.

### An executor has many responsibilities, which may include:

* Locating and proving the validity of your will

- Finding and contacting beneficiaries

- Filing all required documents with the probate court

- Locating and protecting probate assets

- Obtaining appraisals for probate assets

- Determining and overseeing the payment of debts

- Assessing tax liability for income and estate taxes; filing related returns

- Gathering date of death values for non-probate assets (if your estate is subject to tax)

- Paying estate expenses until the estate is closed

- Investing the estate's assets until they can be distributed to beneficiaries

- Overseeing the distribution of the net estate to beneficiaries

As you can see, serving as executor entails a great deal of responsibility and work, so choosing an executor is a decision to which you should give serious consideration. You should choose someone who you know to be trustworthy, fair, honest, and capable of fulfilling the entire fiduciary duty. Your executor should also be practical and organized. The executor's tasks will involve a great deal of paperwork and important deadlines, and you don't want to select someone who will find the job completely overwhelming. The executor need not be a financial or business expert, however. Executors are entitled, and usually are well served, to obtain advice from legal and financial counsel and other experts. A good executor is someone who knows how and when to seek such advice, and to follow it.

If possible, you may also want to choose someone who lives nearby, or at least in the same state. Some states require your executor be a resident, but even for those that do not, your executor will probably need to remain available to conduct estate business for quite some time. Selecting someone who lives near you can save your executor both stress and travel.

It is best to think of the position of executor not as an honor you bestow but rather a request you make of someone close to you. You are handing the person you select a large and complicated task. As such, you shouldn't simply designate a spouse or a favorite adult child without thought, and you should certainly discuss your choice with whomever you ultimately select. If you pick a family member or a friend, it is also wise to make sure you put your future executor in contact with your adviser or attorney. Give your adviser or attorney the name and contact information of your selected executor as well. If the executor decides to hire legal help, he or she will then have the option of approaching someone you trust, who already understands your affairs.

You also have the option to name more than one executor. This has some advantages. The executors can serve as checks and balances against one another's potential errors or inclination to secrecy, or can offer complementary skills or knowledge. Having more than one executor also relieves each individual of some of the burdens they would otherwise face. However, be cautious with this decision. If the executors disagree, you risk deadlock or, in a worst case, litigation. This is particularly the case when the executors are potentially adverse parties, such as a surviving spouse and a child from a prior marriage. Disagreements can lead to added time, and poor communication can lead to mistakes. Having more than one executor can also result in added expense in the form of fees.

It is also possible to name an institution, such as a bank with a trust department, as your executor. Some people choose this route because institutions offer expert management that an individual executor may not be able to provide. Since they must be licensed, they are held to a high fiduciary standard. Also, an institution is more likely to be neutral and unaffected by the emotions of various beneficiaries. The downside to an institution as executor, however, is that they can be inflexible and generally have no historical knowledge of family dynamics. They will be rigid in their interpretation of your will, and are very likely to be expensive. In certain cases, it can also lead to long delays due to a committee approach to decision-making or because of legal requirements that would not bind an individual executor.

Ultimately, the selection of an executor rests on your particular situation and priorities. Once you've selected an executor, it is wise to discuss your choice not only with the future executor and your attorney, but also with family members and loved ones. It is better to cut the element of surprise for those close to you, so that when the time comes, emotions can stay in check and no one contests your wishes during probate.

Besides an executor, you may need to select other fiduciaries in your estate planning process. Perhaps the most important for parents of young children is selecting an alternative legal guardian. Guardians will have the legal authority to care for your children after your death. If you do not select a guardian and one is necessary, the probate court will assign a guardian for you (usually a close family member if one is able to serve). However, this is not a decision you will want to leave to chance. Your children's guardians should be willing to serve; you should also be sure that they are physically, financially and emotionally able to properly care for your children. You may also want to consider geographical factors such as how far your children would need to relocate.

## Key Responsibilities of an Executor

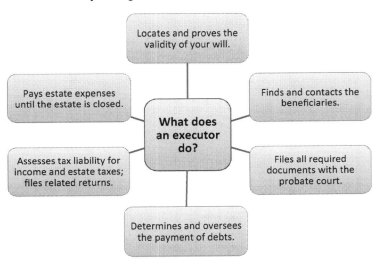

Locates and proves the validity of your will.

Finds and contacts the beneficiaries.

Pays estate expenses until the estate is closed.

**What does an executor do?**

Files all required documents with the probate court.

Assesses tax liability for income and estate taxes; files related returns.

Determines and oversees the payment of debts.

If you choose to set up one or more trusts, you will need to select trustees. For a minor child's trust, this is often the same person you select to be the child's guardian. Regardless, a trustee should be reliable, and you should know he or she is willing and able to carry out the trust's terms. The trustee should also be financially responsible. Depending on a trust's size, an institution or an individual with professional financial experience may be the best choice. However, as with selecting an executor, trusted family members or friends are often better choices than institutions as they can be more flexible and cognizant of family dynamics.

Others who have a fiduciary duty in your estate plan may include legal or financial advisers and your health care proxy or attorney in fact (see Chapter 3). These individuals may be people you appoint, or they may be people you choose to hire, but you must select them in one way or another. You should make your choices carefully.

There are several requirements a person must meet before he or she can serve as an individual fiduciary. He or she must be an adult; depending on the state, this can mean over the age of 18 or over 21. Your family members are almost always allowed to act as fiduciaries, but friends may or may not be, depending on state law. Executors may need to be U.S. citizens, depending on the requirements of their position and your location.

Also, an executor may not be a convicted felon. Professional advisers, such as an attorney, accountant or financial planner, can generally serve as executors, though they sometimes choose not to because of increased costs (increased liability insurance, for example) or due to real or perceived conflicts of interest. Institutional executors can generally serve in any state in which they are licensed. Some trusts may have further specific fiduciary requirements, so you should make sure your fiduciary choices fulfill them to avoid having your selections barred from serving on legal grounds.

Fiduciary compensation will depend upon the fiduciary's role, among other factors. For an executor, you may specify or restrict compensation in your will. For intestate estates, the probate court will determine the appropriate executor's fee. Some states provide specific rules about compensating an executor, while others simply provide guidelines. If the fee is set by state law, an executor may be entitled to an extraordinary fee for services above and beyond what is generally expected. The fee may also be affected by whether there is more than one executor, or if the executor is an institution. If your executor is also your attorney, he or she may only charge one lump sum, though whether this is allowed varies by state. Generally, executors are also entitled to reimbursement if they pay fees or expenses out of pocket while administering the estate. Note however, that one should give careful consideration if you are going to be overly restrictive in allowing fiduciaries to be properly compensated for their services in your estate planning documents, as this could limit the parties who are willing to accept such responsibilities when it comes time for them to serve.

## Conclusion

While this chapter cannot exhaustively cover a subject as complex as estate planning, it should provide a solid foundation on the issues you should consider and the initial steps you should take. Further information is available to the layperson through books and the Internet, and for complex affairs or large estates, a trustworthy attorney and financial planner is invaluable. Whatever your estate plan, once you have recorded your wishes and set up the appropriate vehicles, be vigilant about keeping them up-to-date. You should revisit your plans often, if only to make sure that they still reflect what you want.

A good estate plan is both comprehensive and flexible. Not only will it protect and provide for the people and causes most important to you, it will give you peace of mind.

# 6

## TRANSFER TAXES
### David Walters, CPA, CFP®

Estate, gift and generation skipping transfer taxes have received a lot of media attention in recent years because of the legislative uncertainty surrounding the topic. As it stands today, most Americans will not be directly affected by estate or gift taxes, but individuals and families that are subject to these levies could lose substantial wealth. This puts a premium on smart and timely planning.

Unfortunately, a lot of people, even those with substantial wealth, can find the entire topic of transfer tax planning daunting, to the point of paralysis. This is hardly surprising, given that these taxes can be notoriously complex. But good planning is well worth the cost and effort, and with good advice, any diligent individual can manage these taxes effectively.

### How Do Transfer Taxes Work?

A good understanding of the broad framework for transfer taxes can be helpful in your personal planning and in talking with your accountant or financial planner about your gift and estate plans. Gift and estate taxes are the two major elements of the "unified" federal gift and estate tax.

The gift tax exists, in large part, so that taxpayers cannot avoid estate taxes by simply giving away assets prior to their death. Since the taxes are really two sides of the same framework, it's important to understand them in concert with each other as well as individually.

## Federal Estate Tax

The federal estate tax is determined by the value of your estate at the time of your death (or six months after your death, if your executor makes an alternate valuation date election). Your gross estate consists of everything you own, or have certain interests in, on the date of death. The calculation of the gross estate includes the fair market value for these assets; your original acquisition price isn't relevant. It's also worth noting that your gross estate generally includes non-probate as well as probate assets. (For more on the difference, refer to Chapter 5.) Your taxable estate is the gross estate minus certain deductions, which will be discussed later in this chapter.

If your taxable estate is lower than the personal exemption (also known as the "unified credit amount"), generally no estate tax will be due at your death. The personal exemption is set by Congress, and has varied by a fairly large margin in recent years, but as of this writing in 2014 it was $5.34 million. However, if your gross estate is greater than the personal exemption, your executor must file an estate tax return even if your estate ultimately owes no tax. If you are married, your executor may want to consider filing a return even if it is not required, in order to secure the portability election for your spouse; see more on this later in the chapter.

An estate tax return must be filed within nine months of the individual's date of death. Your executor or tax preparer can request a six-month extension, as long as he or she submits the request prior to the nine-month deadline. In this case, the estate must still pay the estimated amount of tax prior to the nine-month cutoff. Depending on your circumstances, your estate may also need to file an income tax return.

It is a good idea to involve professionals when handling estate taxes, since it can be a complicated area. When planning, it is a good idea to involve, at minimum, an attorney and a tax professional, such as an accountant or enrolled agent. If circumstances allow, putting your executor in contact with the professionals who helped develop your estate plan can make the process run much more smoothly.

## Federal Gift Tax

Federal gift tax applies to any gifts that do not meet the requirements for a non-taxable transfer. For the IRS, a gift is any transfer for which you receive either nothing or something less than fair market value in exchange for the asset in question. Fair market value is the price at which an asset would sell between a willing and knowledgeable buyer and equally willing and knowledgeable seller. If this sounds a little vague, that's because it is. For anything other than cash or publicly traded securities, it is hard to know with any certainty how the IRS will assess an asset's value after you report having made a taxable gift. The best option is to have a professional appraise the asset's value and proceed accordingly, keeping in mind that the IRS may disagree. To count as a completed gift, the transfer must also be irrevocable, and the giver must totally cede control of the asset.

There are certain sorts of gifts that are not subject to federal gift tax. Gifts smaller than a set value, called the annual exclusion amount ($14,000 per donee in 2014), are not subject to the tax at all; neither are gifts of any value to your spouse, as long as your spouse is a U.S. citizen. You can pay another person's tuition or medical bills in any amount without triggering the tax, as long as you pay such bills directly. You may also give as much as you wish to political organizations (within limits set by campaign finance rules) and to certain qualifying charities.

If a gift is taxable, the giver is generally responsible for paying the tax. Under certain circumstances, the recipient may arrange to pay the tax, but both parties should consult a tax professional if they mutually agree to handle the tax this way. If you make a taxable gift, you must file a gift tax return, which is due the same time as your federal income tax return for that year. However, until it is exhausted, your personal exemption will prevent otherwise taxable gifts from triggering an immediate tax liability. Any personal exemption amount that remains unused at your death will shelter assets in your taxable estate from estate tax.

## Generation Skipping Transfer Tax

Some gifts may also trigger the Generation Skipping Transfer (GST) tax. The GST tax applies when you make a gift to a skip person – a recipient two or more generations below your own. Commonly, this is a grandchild or great-grandchild, but it can also be a non-lineal descendant, such as grandnieces and nephews or non-family members. For non-lineal descendants, a recipient two generations younger translates to a recipient at least 37.5 years younger than the transferor. The tax can apply to lifetime gifts or to bequests. GST tax exemption is equal to the basic exclusion amount ($5.34 million), so it changes as the personal exemption does. Like the personal exemption, the GST tax exemption is linked to the taxpayer rather than to the recipient.

Generation skipping transfers may be direct or indirect. A direct skip is a gift you make to the skip person directly or to a trust that is solely for the benefit of skip persons. For example, if you write your granddaughter a check or give your great-grandnephew a beach house, both of those would count as direct skip transfers.

An indirect skip is usually accomplished with a gift to a trust that could benefit both skip and non-skip beneficiaries. These skips fall into two subtypes: taxable terminations and taxable distributions. A taxable termination occurs when the interest of the last non-skip beneficiary of a trust terminates. For example, say you set up a trust for your son with the condition that, on your son's death, any remaining property continues to be held in trust for the benefit of your granddaughter. At your son's death, the cessation of his interest in the trust, which is the last non-skip interest, constitutes a taxable termination. This triggers the GST tax even though no funds are distributed from the trust. Taxable distributions are distributions from a trust directly to a skip person. In this example, a distribution from the trust to your granddaughter while your son is alive is a taxable distribution.

## David's Advice

### Can a trust for children and grandchildren avoid wasting GST exemption?

Yes. A trust can be subdivided into two separate portions: one that is primarily for children and a second for grandchildren or other skip persons. GST exemption can be applied only to the portion for skip persons. This exempt portion is generally not subject to GST no matter how large it grows, while the non-exempt portion would be subject to GST if skip persons eventually benefit from it.

-DW

The timing of when you apply your GST exemption can make a very big difference in your family's ultimate tax bill. If you establish a trust for your children and grandchildren, contribute $5 million to this trust and immediately apply $5 million of your GST exemption, the entire trust will be exempt from GST tax no matter how large it ultimately grows. Your grandchildren might inherit $10 million or $20 million from this trust at some point in the future, free of GST tax. But if this trust ultimately ends up distributing all its assets to your children, who are not skip persons, you will have wasted that $5 million of GST exemption that might have been better used elsewhere in your estate plan.

To prevent this waste, you might wait until some point in the future to apply your GST exemption. If you wait until the trust holds $10 million and then apply $5 million of exemption, you can only exempt half the trust from GST tax.

In addition to federal transfer taxes, some states also have their own additional estate tax. As of this writing, 14 states (Connecticut, Delaware, Illinois, Maine, Maryland, Massachusetts, Minnesota, New Jersey, New York, Oregon, Rhode Island, Tennessee, Vermont and Washington) and the District of Columbia have state-level estate taxes. These estate taxes generally have lower rates than the federal tax, but in many cases they apply at a much lower threshold. State estate tax regimes are each unique and can be just as complex as the federal estate tax system. In some cases they are based off of the federal estate tax laws. Discussing each state estate tax regime is beyond the scope of this chapter, but residents in these states must give careful consideration to the impact of state taxes when planning their estates.

Some states also have a separate inheritance tax. Unlike estate tax, inheritance tax is an obligation that affects the beneficiary, not the estate. A spouse is always exempt, and, typically, close relatives such as children are totally or partially exempt as well. In some cases, bequests to charitable institutions are also exempt. As of this writing, inheritors for decedents in Indiana, Iowa, Kentucky, Maryland, Nebraska, New Jersey and Pennsylvania may face inheritance tax, even if the inheritors themselves live in other states.

Also unlike estate tax, the estate's size is usually irrelevant in determining inheritance tax. For non-exempt beneficiaries, the tax is generally triggered by bequests over a certain threshold; some states determine their own, and some link them to federal estate tax thresholds, adjusting when federal law changes. If inheritance tax is due, the estate's executor is responsible for overseeing the filing; there is only one return, regardless of how many beneficiaries are involved.

As of this writing, Connecticut is the only state to levy a state-level gift tax. If you live in a state that imposes gift, inheritance or estate taxes, the same techniques to reduce potential federal estate taxes may apply at the state level. Of course the simplest solution is to move to a state that does not impose estate or inheritance tax. However, if you spend substantial time in more than one state, estate tax might be one of several factors to consider when deciding where to establish your domicile. See Chapter 14 for more information.

In recent years, the estate and gift tax system has been a source of uncertainty for estate planners and individuals alike. The American Taxpayer Relief Act of 2012, passed at the start of 2013 to resolve the "fiscal cliff" debate, set estate taxes at 40 percent for taxable estates over $5 million, indexed for inflation. Inflation adjustments have since brought this exemption to $5.34 million. Importantly, this law included no built-in end date, as the most recent previous legislation had. For the time being, the estate tax is permanent, at least by legislative standards.

## Tools for Minimizing and Managing Transfer Taxes

The primary reason that very few taxpayers will have to worry about federal gift or estate taxes is the personal exemption. In other contexts, this exemption is sometimes called the unified credit. Under either name, the exemption applies to the unified gift and estate tax, and is the amount under which an estate, less any lifetime gifts that were applied, is exempt from federal transfer tax.

### Personal Exemption

It works like this: Assume a personal exemption of $5.34 million. Jane made three taxable gifts during her lifetime, in the amounts of $100,000, $500,000, and $50,000. At the time of the gifts, she had available unified credit that was applied to all three gifts. Her gross estate, at the time of her death, is $4 million. Since her estate and the gifts together only take up $4,650,000 of Jane's personal exemption, her executor will not have to pay any federal estate tax.

However, if Jane had made taxable gifts totaling more than $1.34 million during her lifetime, she may or may not have to pay, depending on her other deductions and credits. Either way, her executor would need to file an estate tax return in this case, since her gross estate exceeded her $5.34 million personal exemption.

Using your personal exemption, however, is not the only way to avoid the federal gift tax on every gift you make. There is also an annual exclusion amount, which applies to each person you may make a gift to over the course of the year. The annual exclusion amount for 2014 is $14,000, so you can give up to $14,000 to each of your adult children (or any other person, for that matter) in a given year without having to pay any gift tax or use a portion of your lifetime exclusion, no matter how many children you have.

Further, if you and your spouse give away jointly owned property, you are each entitled to take up to your full annual exclusion on the gift, letting you give double what you could give alone. Spouses also have the option of "gift splitting" when making a gift. Gift splitting is an option to count the gift as coming half from you, half from your spouse, regardless of which spouse actually made the gift. You and your spouse must file gift tax returns to document your mutual agreement to split the gift should you decide to do so, even if you owe no tax. Gift splitting is a commonly used method for taxpayers to maximize their ability to make gifts without tapping into their lifetime exclusion.

## Other Gift Tax Exemptions

Another gift tax "freebie" is payments made on behalf of another individual for tuition or medical expenses. If you make payments for these expenses directly to the institution or service provider, such payments are exempt from gift tax, regardless of amount.

Additionally, property in any amount given to a spouse during your life or bequeathed to a spouse at your death is tax-free, as long as your spouse is a U.S. citizen. A spouse who is not a citizen can receive up to $145,000 tax-free in 2014 (this annual amount generally changes each year). Tax-exempt charities can also receive unlimited amounts without triggering a transfer tax. Bequests to either spouses and qualifying charities are deducted when calculating your estate's taxable value.

## Deductions

In addition to these exempt gifts, there are other deductions that will reduce the value of your estate for tax purposes. These deductions include mortgages and other debts, costs for your funeral and estate administration, casualty losses to estate property incurred during the administration period, and state death tax deductions related to any state-level estate or inheritance taxes paid out of your estate.

Individuals recognized as married by the federal government also have the option of using their portability election. A relatively new feature of the federal estate tax, portability allows the unused portion of one spouse's personal exemption to roll over upon his or her death to the survivor. This effectively gives the couple a joint exemption worth twice the individual exemption, which they can then apply in whatever way provides the best tax benefit.

To make use of the portability election, the executor of the first spouse's estate must file an estate tax return, even if no tax is due. This preserves portability as an option for the surviving spouse, allowing him or her to decide how to use it in the future. If the surviving spouse has more than one predeceased spouse – for example, if a widow remarries and then survives her second husband – the unused exclusion is limited to the lesser of the personal exclusion limit ($5.34 million) or the unused exclusion of the most recently deceased spouse.

Beyond the features built into the law, there are a few options for those who wish to make large lifetime gifts or who think their taxable estates will exceed the exemption. Careful estate planning can minimize or eliminate the taxes on such wealth transfers.

**Trusts**

*Irrevocable Trust*

The primary tool for achieving such aims is an irrevocable trust. By giving to an irrevocable trust, you remove those assets from your estate. In turn, any growth in those assets' value after they have been put in trust also passes outside your estate, increasing the value you can leave to your heirs. If the trust is structured correctly, the beneficiary and the trustee can be the same person, putting your heir in a position to control his or her own gift. In many cases, a trust can also protect assets from creditors. If the beneficiary leaves assets in the trust, those assets will also pass outside of his or her estate, subject to certain rules. For more information on irrevocable trusts and their varying forms, see Chapter 5 on Estate Planning.

Of course, estate and gift tax concerns are not the only reason to consider trusts in estate planning. Trusts can be especially useful for blended families, or for planning related to gifts that might otherwise trigger a GST tax penalty. I will discuss a few types of trusts in more detail, but the following section is not exhaustive. Depending on your specific needs, another trust may be the most logical option.

*Credit Shelter Trusts*

Prior to the portability election, credit shelter trusts (also known as bypass trusts) were a common way to allow spouses to take advantage of their full personal exemption, even when leaving all or most of their estates to one another. Prior to the portability election, leaving the bulk of your estate to your spouse meant that your personal exemption went unused, since the marital deduction meant that none of the bequest to your spouse would have been taxed anyway. When your spouse died, however, the property you had left him or her would then raise the value of the sole remaining estate and risked triggering or increasing the federal estate tax.

*Marital Share / Family Share*

To avoid this result, credit shelter trusts divide your estate into two portions: the marital share and the family share. The marital share can either pass to your spouse outright or remain in trust – a good option if you want to shield assets from creditors or avoid probate. In either case, the marital share is meant to provide income to the surviving spouse during his or her lifetime. The entirety of the family share, meanwhile, remains held in trust and is generally made available to the surviving spouse for support if the marital share is exhausted. The portability of a spouse's exemption has reduced the need for credit shelter trusts in some cases, but they are still commonly used.

### AB Trust

An alternative way to secure both spouses' personal exemption is the AB trust. In an AB trust, both spouses leave their property to an irrevocable trust, rather than bequeathing it directly to each other. After the first spouse dies, the survivor receives income from the trust, and under some circumstances has access to the principal; after the second spouse dies, the couple's children usually inherit the remaining property, though you can select other beneficiaries if you prefer.

Like credit shelter trusts, AB trusts were more common prior to the portability election, though they do still have uses. While recent federal rulings recognize same-sex marriages that are performed in those jurisdictions that authorize them, couples who live in states not yet recognizing same sex marriage may want to consider this estate planning tool. It can also be useful for those who want to be sure their children ultimately receive their property, even if their spouses remarry, or if the children in question are from a previous marriage. Further, if you set the trust up as an AB disclaimer trust (a trust which would receive assets disclaimed by the surviving spouse at the first spouse's death), the surviving spouse can decide at the time of the first spouse's death whether or not to create the trust. This flexibility allows you to adapt to changes in the law.

At the same time, it's important to consider the drawbacks of an AB trust. It will place restrictions on the survivor's use of the property; he or she may lose the option to sell trust property, for example. Setting up a trust can also be expensive, both at the outset and through increased recordkeeping and paperwork, such as an annual tax return for the trust. And, like most irrevocable trusts, an AB trust is hard to change or revoke outright should your situation – or the law – change between the time you set it up and the time it would go into action.

### Qualified Terminable Interest Property Trust

Another option is a Qualified Terminable Interest Property (QTIP) trust. Such a trust puts conditions, or "strings," on your property. This can allow you to be quite specific with your bequest, for example, providing for a spouse and also children from a previous marriage. It also allows some flexibility for an executor, letting him or her decide how much, if any, of the property earmarked for the trust should actually be held that way. Depending on your situation, this executor may be your spouse, an adult child or a neutral third party. Similarly, you must name a trustee who can be any of the above. See Chapter 5 for advice on selecting a fiduciary.

When the first spouse dies, his or her executor must make the QTIP election on the estate tax return (meaning that, even if the estate owes no tax, a return should still be filed). The election allows the executor to specify how much, if any, of the assets set aside for the QTIP will actually go into the trust. This mechanism allows for flexibility if your financial situation or tax laws have changed since you planned for the trust. If the executor chooses only some assets, it's called a partial QTIP election.

Assuming assets go into the trust, the surviving spouse will receive a life estate. The survivor is entitled to any income produced by the assets held in trust. If the assets include real estate, the survivor is also entitled to use the property. The survivor cannot, however, sell or give away the assets. After the surviving spouse dies, the trust assets go to the "remainder beneficiary" named in the trust – often, but not always, the grantor's children.

## Quick Notes:
## Some basics about Qualified Terminable Interest Property Trusts

| Qualified Terminable Interest Property (QTIP) Trust | What does it do? | It puts conditions, or "strings," on your property. This can allow you to be quite specific with your bequest. |
|---|---|---|
| | Who can be the trustee? | The trustee may be your spouse, an adult child or a neutral third party. |
| | What happens after a spouse dies? | When the first spouse dies, his or her executor must make the QTIP election on the estate tax return. Assuming assets go into the trust, the surviving spouse will receive a life estate. The survivor is entitled to any income produced by the assets held in trust. |

A QTIP trust doesn't eliminate estate tax, but it does postpone it until your spouse's death. To get this benefit, your marriage must be federally recognized, and your spouse must be a U.S. citizen, since the deferral is contingent upon the marital deduction. It can, however, be a useful way to set up a bequest within parameters more specific than simply leaving property to your spouse alone might allow.

### Irrevocable Life Insurance Trust (ILIT)

If you own (or intend to own) life insurance, you may also consider an Irrevocable Life Insurance Trust (ILIT). If your life insurance policy is substantial, removing it from your estate by transferring it to an irrevocable trust can give you protection and control you wouldn't receive otherwise. Insurance policies owned by you at your death will be included in your estate as taxable assets for estate tax purposes. However, policies held in an ILIT are generally excluded from a decedent's estate. For this to work as an estate-reduction strategy, the trust must be irrevocable; you cannot be a trustee; and a policy you transfer to the trust must have been in the trust for at least three years prior to your death. You can still pay the premiums on the policy once it has been placed in trust by making additional future gifts to the trust, which it can then use to pay annual policy premiums. Or, if you have an ILIT in mind from the start, you can buy a single premium policy, so the trust doesn't have to manage payments.

While setting up a trust is more expensive and complicated than simply giving your policy to another person, it does have benefits. You can use the terms of the trust to control who the beneficiary or beneficiaries will be, how the premiums will be paid, and when and how the beneficiaries will receive payment. If you choose to set up an ILIT, however, it's important to build in flexibility through donor powers, beneficiary powers, trustee powers or provisions within the trust document itself. Such flexibility will allow you, your trustee or your heirs a way to respond to a changes in your family situation, or to new tax and non-tax laws.

### Qualified Personal Residence Trust

If you want to transfer property, another option to consider is a Qualified Personal Residence Trust (QPRT). This sort of trust is designed to hold a primary or secondary residence, allowing you to continue to live there for a set amount of time. This is called a retained income period. After this predetermined period of time, the property passes fully to your beneficiaries. You can continue to live in the home after this transition, as long as you pay fair market rent to the new owner or owners.

This strategy has several advantages. The transfer is treated as a gift to the ultimate beneficiaries for federal gift tax purposes, though it is valued at a reduced rate from full market value, since your beneficiaries will not have immediate, full use of the property. It removes the value of the property from your estate while you continue to live there. In addition, if you stay after the transfer, your rent payments are not considered gifts, which will allow you to further transfer value to your beneficiary, and reduce your estate, without incurring gift tax. One drawback to the QPRT, however, is that you must outlive the trust term. Otherwise the trust assets will still be included in your estate, as if the trust was never created in the first place. Accordingly, one would not want to make the trust term so long as to make it likely that the grantor will die before the trust concludes.

You can also use a charitable trust to reduce your estate, if planned properly. See Chapter 18 for more information on charitable trusts.

## Basis Step-Up

Trusts are not the only tool available to you as you plan for federal estate taxes. There are a variety of other steps which may be helpful to you. Note, for example, the use of basis step-up in transferring value to your heirs. If you bequeath assets and the beneficiary sells them, the seller's tax cost for capital gains tax purposes is the fair market value of the assets on the date of your death (or, in a few cases, six months after) – not the original value of the assets when you acquired them. If the sale happens soon after your death, there is usually little or no gain to tax, as opposed to the tax you would have faced if you had sold the assets before transferring them. Note that basis step-up only applies to bequests at your death. Lifetime gifts generally retain the donor's original cost basis.

At times when market values are depressed, it also may make sense to transfer investments that have lost value. This allows you to count the value at the time of transfer for gift tax purposes, allowing you to give your donee any future appreciation tax-free. You can also take advantage of a low interest rate environment, when one exists, by using vehicles such as grantor retained annuity trusts (GRATs) or selling assets to a trust in exchange for an interest-bearing promissory note, either of which will allow you to transfer most of the future increase in value without incurring gift tax, while reducing the value of your taxable estate.

## What to Avoid When Facing Federal Transfer Tax

*The "Sweetheart" Will*

There are also some common pitfalls you should avoid if you are concerned about facing federal transfer tax. One of the most common is an "I love you" or "sweetheart" will, which is a will that simply leaves the entirety of your estate to your spouse outright. Often, spouses will both leave everything to one another, compounding the problem.

Even if you want to leave all or most of your estate to your spouse, there may be better ways to go about it. A sweetheart will offers your spouse no protection from creditors or liability; it also doesn't protect assets in a divorce, should your spouse remarry and then separate without a prenuptial agreement. Such a will can also shut out your adult children, or other family members, especially if your spouse does remarry.

Further, a sweetheart will doesn't allow for tax law uncertainty. Congress could revoke portability, or the personal exemption could shrink between the time you make your will and your death. While a will is a good idea for everyone, individuals who suspect they may trigger the federal estate tax especially may want to consider whether leaving everything to their spouse is best.

## Conclusion

Estate tax planning can also be complicated by cash flow worries and the resulting reluctance to make irrevocable transfers. As you can see from the trusts and techniques discussed in this chapter, there are a variety of ways you can make gifts and still maintain some level of control over how or when those gifts are made. Some trusts even provide an income stream back to you, though you've irrevocably given away the assets. Your financial planner or accountant can help you to meet both your current liquidity needs and your future estate tax planning needs at once; they needn't be mutually exclusive.

Estate planning "paralysis" is not uncommon when faced with the uncertainty surrounding transfer tax issues and the complicated questions that can arise. Financial market turbulence and political wrangling can make it seem impossible to make and stick to an effective estate plan. It is important to sort out your emotional reactions to uncertainty, and to realize that a good estate plan is both thorough and flexible, allowing you and your advisers to react to changes in the law or economic conditions. It is important not to let fear of making wrong choices keep your from taking any action at all. It's just as important to work with your advisers to build in flexibility to your estate plan so that you can adjust it as your needs and priorities change.

Finally, once your plans are in place, you should review them periodically. Check regularly to be sure your beneficiary designations on your retirement accounts, and the contact information for those beneficiaries, are up to date. Review paperwork for any trusts to ensure they are up-to-date and error-free. Such a review should be a part of your larger estate plan, but it's especially important not to neglect such details.

While transfer taxes affect relatively few American taxpayers, it's important that you educate yourself and stay alert to any changes. For those who are affected, the impact is significant but with proper planning, estate, gift and generation skipping taxes need be no more intimidating than any other tax.

# 7

## GRANDCHILDREN
### Rebecca Pavese, CPA
### Anthony D. Criscuolo, CFP®, EA

F or most people with children, those children's financial futures figure heavily into long-term wealth management goals and strategies. The extent to which such plans include grandchildren varies much more widely.

Many older adults look forward to their children having children. In many cases, the joy of having a new addition to the family is amplified by the joy of having a new baby that you do not have to feed, change, or care for directly. The doting grandparent figure is a stereotype for a reason – it's only natural to enjoy seeing your children building a future for a new generation in the same way you did for them, and it's just as natural to want to provide the best possible life for all of your family members.

If you have grandchildren already, anticipate grandchildren soon, or even if you see the idea as a vague possibility on the horizon, planning for your grandchildren early can be a significant advantage, especially if you want to provide financial as well as moral support. While the impulse to include your grandchildren in your financial plans is admirable, it is especially important to plan carefully in order to do so effectively. There are numerous potential tax consequences for gifts, especially large gifts to generations younger than your children. There are many ways you can end up transferring less than you intended, but these hazards can be avoided or lessened with forethought.

## Gifts to Grandchildren: The Basics

Making planned gifts to grandchildren is increasingly common, especially for individuals with a substantial amount of wealth who want to eliminate estate tax liabilities currently looming over their assets. Even if they do not anticipate estate taxes, many grandparents want to give gifts of cash or future financial support to their grandchildren, whether through college funding or providing a nest egg for their future. Simply writing a check, though, may not be the most effective option once gift tax, estate tax and generation-skipping transfer tax come into play.

Some grandparents may not be aware of these tax pitfalls; others may find them a complete discouragement. You should not conclude that gifts aren't possible, or that giving to grandchildren is not an effective way to reduce the size of your estate. Options for making an effective transfer do exist. Some strategies require careful planning and the help of a financial planner or attorney, while others are less complicated.

### Outright Gifts and the Annual Exclusion

The federal government, and many state governments, attempt to tax gifts you make during your lifetime and the estate you leave behind at your death in a variety of ways. (See Chapter 6 for a more in-depth discussion of transfer taxes and strategies for minimizing them.) A thoroughly planned, well-considered approach is the best way to make sure these taxes do not unnecessarily reduce the size of your intended gift.

Taking advantage of exclusion gifts is one of the simplest ways to avoid gift tax. Annual exclusions – $14,000 per recipient as of 2014 – allow taxpayers to make numerous gifts tax-free. Furthermore, if you make large gifts while your spouse makes none, you can elect to combine your individual exclusions. (More technically, you will split the gift as if it came equally from each of you, thus taking advantage of both exclusion amounts.) If your annual gifts stay below the threshold, transfer taxes need not be a concern.

Individuals can also make use of a lifetime exemption amount for large gifts. While always subject to change based on the prevailing political climate, the lifetime exemption for 2014 was set at $5.34 million. This amount is indexed for inflation, so it will increase over time. The lifetime transfer tax exemption applies to both estate and gift tax, meaning that any amount allocated to gift taxes during your life is deducted from the exemption available for estate tax purposes at your death. Gifts that fall under the annual exclusion do not count as taxable gifts and therefore do not eat into your lifetime exemption amount. You can make gifts of amounts up to the annual exclusion each year for decades and still have your full lifetime exemption amount available to offset your estate tax at your death. This is why annual exclusion gifts can be such a powerful wealth transfer tool.

You can pay certain bills or expenses on your grandchild's behalf without incurring gift or transfer taxes at all. For example, you can pay for an unlimited amount of your grandchild's medical or health care expenses completely free of gift tax, as long as you make the payments directly to the hospital or doctor providing the care. You can also cover tuition expenses without transfer taxes, which we will discuss later in this chapter.

## Anthony's Advice

**Can I pay for my grandchildren's health insurance tax-free?**

Yes, the tax code allows for unlimited gifts to pay for another person's health care costs free of gift and GST tax. Health care costs include health insurance premiums and payments directly to doctors or hospitals. Payments must be made directly to the health care provider; you may not claim this exclusion if you reimburse your grandchild for health care costs after they have been paid.

-AC

## Gifting Through Trusts

If you have a sizeable estate, gifts up to the annual exclusion may not be enough to reduce the size of your estate as fully as you might wish. You may also not be comfortable making a large outright gift to your grandchildren, especially if they are still young and not ready to handle significant wealth. If your grandchildren are older, you may want to protect assets from their potential creditors. Making gifts through a trust can be a solution to all of these concerns.

The basic idea of a trust is to create a legal relationship in which one party will hold assets for the benefit of someone else. The trustee acts as fiduciary and manages the trust assets according to the rules and guidelines stated in the trust document as well as relevant state law. The trust document can ensure the trustee only makes distributions for certain purposes, such as your grandchildren's health or education. The trust document can also expressly state that the assets in the trust may not be used to satisfy any debt of the beneficiary; such a provision will protect the trust assets from your grandchildren's creditors.

Gifts to a trust will qualify for the annual exclusion so long as the beneficiaries have a "present interest" in the trust. A present interest means the beneficiaries must have some right to withdraw the assets, at least for a short period of time. Such a withdrawal right is often referred to as a "Crummey" power. The term comes from a taxpayer named Clifford Crummey, who won a case in 1968 against the Internal Revenue Service, creating the precedent for using the present interest exclusion on contributions to trusts.

Trusts are most commonly used when making large gifts, though the Crummey power provision means they can be useful even when gifts are relatively modest. Besides providing financial support to the named beneficiaries, large gifts to a trust during your lifetime are also an effective estate freeze strategy that can help minimize the estate tax liability at your death. All future income and appreciation on assets you give to the trust will be outside of your estate and free of estate tax at your death. In this way, you can make a more valuable gift to your grandchildren than they would realize if you simply held the assets and transferred them upon your death.

## Quick Notes:
### Some basics about trusts

**Trusts**

| | | |
|---|---|---|
| **What do they do?** | Create a legal relationship in which one party will hold assets for the benefit of someone else. | |
| **Who manages the trust?** | The trustee acts as fiduciary and manages the trust assets according to the rules and guidelines stated in the trust document as well as relevant state law | |
| **What are they commonly used for?** | Most commonly used when making large gifts, though the Crummey power provision means they can be useful even when gifts are relatively modest | |

While an excellent strategy for many grandparents, trusts do have several disadvantages. In order to realize the estate tax benefits, you must generally structure the trusts to be irrevocable, meaning that you cannot dissolve the trusts and recover the assets for yourself. Trusts also need to file their own tax returns and to pay their own taxes. Because the tax brackets for trusts are more compressed relative to individuals, the total tax liability paid by a trust can often be larger than the tax would have been if the assets in it were held by an individual. This problem can often be avoided if the grantor making the trust drafts the document in such a way as to retain responsibility for the income tax applicable to the trust assets (technically referred to as an intentionally defective grantor trust). Thus the grantor, not the trust, will continue to pay the income tax liability, generally at a lower rate. The tax paid by the grantor on the trust income is not considered an additional gift. Therefore, this structure allows the grantor to pay the taxes, which leaves more assets inside the trust to accumulate and ultimately benefit your grandchildren.

Forming a trust properly is also relatively expensive. In addition to legal fees at the outset, a trust may incur annual accounting fees, tax compliance fees, and trustee fees. Ultimately, whether an outright gift or a gift through a trust is right for you will depend on a number of factors based on both your situation and that of your grandchildren.

## Custodial Accounts

If your grandchildren are still minors, you can also consider giving them financial support through a custodial account. Like an irrevocable trust, a custodial account contains money that is legally no longer yours; once the child reaches adulthood (usually age 18 or 21, depending on the state law and the type of account), he or she gains full legal control of the account. Until that time, a custodian (usually the child's parent) oversees the account, but a custodian is legally prohibited from using the account for purposes other than the child's benefit. Custodial accounts can thus offer some assurance that the gift will benefit your grandchild while leaving that benefit flexible to meet future or unanticipated needs.

The two main types of custodial accounts are structured under the Uniform Gifts to Minors Act (UGMA) or the Uniform Transfers to Minors Act (UTMA). Chapter 8, Education Funding, discusses both types of accounts in more depth, but custodial accounts are not restricted to educational expenses. As with trusts, you can transfer amounts up to the annual exclusion without tax consequences.

Your grandchildren will gain control of the funds in a custodial account at a relatively young age, and custodial accounts can result in a more complicated tax situation. The so-called "Kiddie Tax" rules mean that minors who earn investment income above a certain threshold ($2,000 in

2014) may be taxed at their parents' ordinary income tax rate. It is also important to remember that, since the assets will belong directly to your grandchild, custodial account balances can potentially reduce need-based educational financial aid.

Given the potential complications, it is important to discuss setting up a custodial account with your children before taking action. It is also wise to involve a financial adviser, who can guide you toward the most beneficial way to set up such accounts.

## Generation-Skipping Transfer Tax

In addition to regular gift and estate taxes, the federal government imposes special taxes on taxable wealth transfers to a "skip person." A skip person, simply put, is a gift recipient two or more generations below the person making the gift. In most cases, a grandchild would be considered a skip person for their grandparent's gift, though there are exceptions if the grandchild's parent is deceased. If not planned carefully, this generation-skipping transfer (GST) tax can quickly erode the value of gifts you planned to leave to your grandchildren. You should consult with your financial adviser or attorney before you make sizeable gifts of any kind to grandchildren, in order to make sure you understand your potential tax obligations and plan the sort of gift that will most effectively benefit your recipients. (See Chapter 6 for more details about how this tax works.)

## Intra-Family Loans

Not every grandparent is in a position to make large, outright gifts to a grandchild. This need not prevent you from offering financial support. You may be able to help your grandchildren by making a loan. If they need funds to attend college, pay for a wedding, or make a down payment on a home, you can lend the funds that you don't need currently but are not ready to give away on a permanent basis.

This strategy entails some risk. Your grandchild may be unable or unwilling to pay you back, or setting up the formal provisions of the loan may cause strain between family members. You are the best judge of whether this sort of transaction would work for your family. If it seems like a good fit, it can be a huge help to your grandchildren, while also providing a benefit to you.

In order for the IRS not to treat the loan, or any foregone interest, as a gift, you should properly document and respect the loan terms, including payment of interest at a rate at least equal to the Applicable Federal Rate. This rate is always lower than the interest rate the local bank would charge. You may choose to charge a higher rate that is still advantageous to your grandchild, if you wish.

Such formal loans, which should be drawn up and agreed upon in advance, generally involve reasonably large sums of money. You may also decide to help your grandchildren in smaller ways, with the additional goal of helping to teach them financial responsibility. For example, say your granddaughter plans to go on a two-week study abroad trip that costs $2,000. Your child told your granddaughter she was responsible for funding 50 percent of the trip. Your granddaughter has saved some birthday money and pursued babysitting jobs, but is still $500 short of her $1,000 payment. You can lend her the $500 under prearranged terms. This will help her take her trip while also teaching her the basics of how loans work.

Help from grandparents doesn't need to be strictly monetary. Spending time with your grandchildren, helping working adult children accommodate busy schedules through child care or help around the house, and sharing the joys and trials of your grandchildren's lives are qualitative ways to help provide for them. Don't underestimate the value of what you can provide in these non-financial ways.

## College Funding

One of the most common areas in which grandparents provide support is with money for educational purposes. As the cost of college climbs, it is only natural to want to help your children and grandchildren afford the best education possible.

Avoiding tax liabilities for educational expenses is far easier than for many other types of gifts. The law allows you to make tuition payments directly to a school on behalf of your grandchild (or anyone, for that matter) in unlimited amounts, gift-tax free. The important rule to remember is that the payment must be made directly to the school or college, not to the individual student, even if the student uses those funds to pay for their education. If your grandchild attends a private university where tuition costs hundreds of thousands of dollars, you will be able to pay the costs directly to the school completely free of gift tax. Note, however, that this exception does not apply to room and board, activity fees, book fees, and similar expenses.

### Section 529 Savings Plans

Section 529 savings plans are among the most popular options for funding educational expenses, and not without reason. These plans are specialty investment accounts, operated by a state or university, intended to build wealth to be used towards tuition and other qualified education expenses. (There is a second type of 529 plan, a prepaid tuition 529; these plans operate differently.) There are many special rules and regulations surrounding 529 plans, which we cover in greater detail in Chapter 8.

Anyone can set up a 529 savings account for a named beneficiary; in this case we will assume a grandparent is setting up an account for a grandchild. The grandparent invests funds in the account for future growth and all earnings and capital gains within the account are tax-free. 529 savings plans are similar to IRAs but are designed for saving for education, rather than retirement. Withdrawals from the account are not taxable as long as they are used to pay for qualified education expenses such as tuition, room and board, student activities fees, and the like). Many states provide an income tax deduction for contributions made to 529 plans.

Contributions to 529 plans are considered gifts made to the named beneficiary. The annual exclusion is available to reduce the amount of any gift that is taxable. However, with college costs rising, many grandparents may want to contribute more than the annual exclusion. Contributing when the beneficiary is young will allow the maximum time for the funds to grow tax-free, taking greatest advantage of the account. Because of this, 529s offer a unique feature which permits contributors to make a lump-sum contribution of up to $70,000 and then elect to spread the gift evenly over the subsequent five years. Provided you make no other gifts to the same beneficiary in the five-year period, you will avoid triggering federal gift and GST taxes.

### Equalization

Assume that you have multiple grandchildren of varying ages, and that you have been giving each of these grandchildren gifts of varying sizes since birth. Operating on this principle, it is only natural to then assume that the amounts you have given over the years are not perfectly equal.

Depending on your point of view, this may or may not be inherently problematic. Your grandchildren are different ages, and presumably have different wants and needs. If they are cousins rather than siblings, they may have different levels of support from their own parents. Some of them may live farther away, so you may give them larger gifts on fewer occasions compared to the grandchildren who live nearby.

The process of balancing gifts is known as equalization. Although equalizing gifts doesn't mean very much to some people, it means a lot to others. Only you can make the decision to equalize gifts to your grandchildren but if you choose to, it is important to strategize. Some people who did not originally care about equalizing gifts may begin to feel they should as they near the end of life. If one grandchild received $100,000 over 10 years while another has only received $10,000, the impulse to equalize is not surprising.

If you have made cash gifts to your grandchildren over the course of their lives and want them to end up with similar levels of cash upon your death, using a portion of your lifetime exclusion amount can be a way to transfer large amounts without incurring large gift tax liabilities. However, this strategy will reduce the amount of your exclusion that can be applied to your estate, so the logistics should be carefully considered in the context of your overall estate plan.

Another option is to stop giving to the grandchildren who have received more until the grandchildren who have received less catch up. For grandparents who are relatively young and in good health, with a long expected lifespan, this approach can be very successful.

Often it is necessary to consider the premise that fairness is not always the same as equality. You should consider the wealth certain grandchildren may inherit from their own parents and the chances your grandchildren have to be successful with their own abilities. You may have three children, two of whom are just making ends meet and one who has enjoyed enough financial success that she has already amply provided for her own children. In this scenario, you could make transfers to all of your children but only to the grandchildren whose parents have not had financial success. Your financially successful child will have the option to disclaim his bequest from you and, if she does, the gift will legally pass to her children. In the end, all of your grandchildren will be recipients of your wealth, but not necessarily to the same extent. Whether this seems more satisfactory than giving each grandchild an equal dollar amount is a personal decision, and one you should consider carefully.

Whether you want to equalize gifts to grandchildren or not is a decision only you can make. If you choose to take strides towards making gifted amounts equal, begin as early as possible and talk to your financial adviser about the most effective ways to pursue this goal.

## Quick Tips:
You may want to consider equalizing your gifts if one grandchild has substantially more than the other.

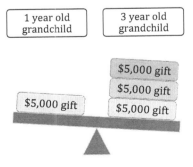

**Future Grandchildren**

Even if you already have grandchildren, more grandchildren – or great-grandchildren – could be on the way. Part of the challenge of financial planning for grandchildren is planning how and to what extent to provide for those who haven't been born yet. Though you can always alter your financial plans to provide for new grandchildren during your life, you may want to consider how to handle any grandchildren born after your death.

---

## Rebecca's Advice

---

### What happens if circumstances change after my death?

Your will cannot be changed after your death, but you can give your family some leeway by including a tool known as a special power of appointment in your estate documents. This tool grants your spouse, child or another individual the power to change the terms under which assets pass to your grandchildren via trust. Special powers provide flexibility to deal with a grandchild who may have special needs or who faces divorce or other financial problems.

-RP

---

Legally, after-born children are children born after the creation of a will, trust or other document, while posthumous children are those born after the death of a parent. While not a topic frequently considered before the advent of reproductive assistance, these situations and the planning complexity they engender are becoming more and more common.

The topic was first broached at the U.S. Supreme Court in Astrue v. Capato, a 2012 case that centered on a woman who conceived and gave birth to twins after her husband's death from cancer, using sperm donated and frozen by the husband after he was diagnosed with the illness.

The Social Security Administration denied survivor benefits to the posthumous children. In the state of Florida, where the couple resided, inheritance in such cases is only permitted if the beneficiaries are named in a will. In this case the husband's will did not specifically acknowledge children conceived with his sperm following his death, so they did not qualify. However, as the judge presiding over the case was quick to indicate after providing his ruling, this situation may have had a very different outcome in states with less specific laws regarding inheritance.

Planning for future children is complex enough, let alone future grand-children. As grandchildren do not have the direct beneficiary rights that children do in some states, there is an extra layer of distance. And while grandchildren born after their grandparent's death are nothing new, there are few legal mechanisms in place that automatically provide for their inheritance. Thus, provisions in your will that apply to all your grand-children are unlikely to extend to any grandchildren who may be born after your passing. Depending on the timeline, your estate may have been entirely distributed before their birth, unless the executor had a reason to set part of it aside.

This does not mean that you cannot make provisions for any grand-children who might be born after your death, should you wish to do so. When it comes to considering financial and estate planning for grandchil-dren, the idea of "specific language" is central. Being as specific as pos-sible about any current and future beneficiaries will clarify your intentions and help make sure your wishes are carried out.

Inheritance laws vary widely from state to state, and in some places, it may not be practical to provide for after-born grandchildren simply through direct bequests in your will. In these cases, establishing a trust can be very effective. Trusts can be established in a variety of ways to ad-dress the needs of current and future generations, including beneficiaries who are not yet born.

### Adopted Children

Planning for future grandchildren becomes even more complicated when adopted children enter into the picture. In some states, there is no legal distinction between adopted and biological grandchildren; in other states, this can be complicated if the adoption is open (meaning the child's biological parents still have contact and certain rights). Thus special planning may be necessary if you have adopted grandchildren.

If an individual, such as a grandchild, is named in your will, he will have a legal right to whatever is bequeathed to him. The matter becomes more complicated in cases where the grandparent is intestate (which you can prevent by making a legal will) or in cases where the child is adopted after the grandparent's death (which is obviously out of your control). One solution may be to establish a trust designating your grandchildren as the joint beneficiaries and include special language in the trust document in order to ensure that adopted grandchildren are not excluded from an inheritance. Since state law varies drastically, employing the assistance of a financial planner and an estate planning attorney is essential in creating the right kind of plan to include adopted grandchildren. If you have rea-son to believe one or more of your children may one day wish to adopt, it is worth discussing your options with a professional.

## Children Conceived and Born Unconventionally

While egg donation, sperm donation, and in vitro fertilization have existed for many years, these forms of reproduction were once uncommon and seen as a last resort for infertile couples. As the modern family evolves and as technology improves, more and more parents-to-be are considering alternative means of reproduction.

According to the Centers for Disease Control and Prevention, over 1 percent of all infants born in the United States each year are conceived using assisted reproductive technologies, or ART. In 2011, ART use resulted in 61,610 infants in the U.S. While wonderful for couples who want children but who cannot conceive unassisted, there are many legal issues that have come to light in this emerging trend. For example, legally, who is the father of a child whose mother pursued sperm donation? Does this child have a father? Does the biological father have rights towards his child? When a biological mother who used a sperm donor dies, is the sperm donor eligible to seek custody, possibly in lieu of the child's grandparents?

Over the years, many of these questions have been addressed in court cases, prompting decisions on both the state and federal levels. The Uniform Probate Code has been expanded to discuss parentage of children born through artificial means, including posthumous children whose parents die intestate. For example, there is usually a time limit on the birth, meaning that the children must be born within three or four years from the time a deceased passed away.

The Uniform Parentage Act, on the other hand, has established rules (in states that have adopted it) regarding parents who die with a will but who had children artificially. While only applicable in several states, this act seeks to determine a child's legal parent in cases involving sperm donation, surrogacy, in vitro fertilization, and egg donation. As these rules vary, it is always advisable to consult a lawyer with estate planning expertise to make sure your estate plan keeps up with the reproductive technologies of the times.

## Conclusion

As a grandparent, it is only natural that you love your grandchildren. After all, they are the children of your children and a continuation of your family tree. It is also natural to want to provide financial support for your grandchildren to the extent that you can. Whether you wish to provide the occasional treat, a substantial nest egg, or college tuition, it can be deeply satisfying to help your grandchildren achieve their goals. No matter what you have in mind for your grandchildren, planning appropriately takes the same level of dedicated care as every other aspect of your financial and estate plans. The results are worth the extra time and energy.

Grandparents are free of the "responsibilities" that come along with being a parent, and grandchildren are free of the pressures and expectations they may feel when dealing with their parents. The bond is a special one. Enjoy every minute and know your children take pleasure in the happiness they see in both generations' eyes.

# 8

## EDUCATION FUNDING
### Thomas E. Walsh

---

Education is important. It is also expensive, and it is unlikely to get cheaper any time soon.

There are a variety of reasons education funding may remain a priority for those over 55. You may have had children relatively late in life, or married a younger partner who brought children to the marriage. You may have young nieces or nephews. You may wish to help fund your grandchildren's education. Perhaps you are interested in going back to school yourself, for personal enrichment or to start a new career after retiring from your old one.

No matter the reason, the best strategy in paying for higher education is to start saving as early as you can. Over the past decade, tuition prices have increased substantially faster than inflation. If current trends continue, today's infants will face college costs at more than triple current rates. The earlier you start planning for these expenses, the more options you will have.

It is tempting to think that any shortfalls can be made up through student loans. Today, most students do need some sort of financing to afford college, especially when pursuing four-year degrees. However, exhausting other options before taking out educational loans can keep student debt levels to a minimum and allow students to graduate with a smaller sum to pay back and less interest to cover.

The "sticker price" of a given institution is not always the most useful information when deciding what is or is not affordable. Two-thirds of college students receive some form of grants or scholarships, the College Board reported in 2013. And highly ranked schools are generally those most likely to offer merit scholarships, regardless of need. A strategic combination of scholarships, aid and savings can put many schools in reach, even for students who wish to avoid or minimize debt.

If you are saving for someone other than yourself or your child, you may think it is simplest to give the future student an outright gift. However, depending on the amount, you could trigger federal or state gift taxes. A direct gift is also more likely to impact the student's eligibility for need-based financial aid, as I will discuss later in the chapter. While a direct gift may sometimes be appropriate, it is worth considering all your options first in order to decide what is most beneficial for both you and the student.

## Education Funding Options

There are a great many ways to pay for educational expenses. This section presents the most common methods.

A Section 529 plan, occasionally called a Qualified Tuition Program or QTP, is an educational savings plan operated by a state or educational institution. It is designed to help families set aside funds for future college costs, encouraging such savings through tax benefits (much as IRAs reward saving for retirement). There are two types of Section 529 plans: prepaid tuition plans and college savings plans.

### Prepaid Tuition Section 529 Plans

Prepaid tuition 529 plans allow savers, usually but not always the future student's parents, to pay for future tuition expenses at present tuition rates plus a small premium. Some plans cover tuition and fees only; some also cover qualified educational expenses, such as books, supplies, equipment and, in some cases, room and board. Once the account holder has paid down the price of the 529, it becomes the plan's obligation to deliver the promised benefits. In this way, the account holder locks in current tuition rates, which are almost certainly lower than the future rates will be.

There are various types of prepaid 529 plans, whose rules are determined by the state or institution offering them. Contract plans allow you to prepay tuition for a set number of years or semesters at an in-state, public institution. Generally, such plans cover both two- and four-year programs. In unit plans, you purchase fractional tuition units, typically 1 percent of one year's tuition. These units are redeemable based on average tuition rates at a target group of schools. Voucher plans allow you to prepay a specific percentage of tuition for the beneficiary at participating schools.

Some states offer more than one of these types of plan. You are not limited to participating in your home state's plans, though some states offer residents additional benefits such as tax breaks that out-of-staters cannot access. Before you decide on a plan, research what your state (or your beneficiary's state, if it is not the same) offers. For any plan you consider seriously, it is essential that you read the official enrollment materials. Much like a health insurance plan, a 529 plan will often have different rules for "in-network" (that is, participating) colleges and "out-of-network" colleges. Your prepaid dollars generally will be worth less at schools not specifically covered by the plan, meaning that if the beneficiary wants to go to a school out-of-state or outside the plan's parameters, they – and you – will get less for your money.

The advantage of a prepaid 529 plan is that there is no risk to the principal you contribute, except, perhaps, for the risk that the beneficiary will choose a non-participating school. In addition, contributions to such accounts build tax-free, as long as the money is not withdrawn for any purposes other than tuition or approved educational expenses. Many states also give resident account holders an income tax break on 529 contributions.

However, a prepaid 529 plan can have significant downsides. The most alarming is the ongoing trend of states running into trouble funding obligations, due to both state budget troubles and the fact that education costs are rising faster than investments can grow to keep up with them. It is essential that you take the time to find a well-managed plan before investing. Look for plans backed by the "full faith and credit" of the state issuing them, or by participating colleges, and consider the current state of the plan's funding.

If the beneficiary wishes to go to a private college, even in-state, the prepaid 529 may not be enough, as most of these plans are aimed at in-state public tuition. Moreover, some plans are limited to tuition and fees, meaning the beneficiary will need separate funds in order to cover room, board and expenses such as textbooks, even at an in-state school.

Additionally, the return on investment may be weaker in a prepaid 529 plan than it would be in another instrument. Families with financial savvy or professional financial advisers may be better off investing the funds themselves. A prepaid tuition 529 plan also typically caps maximum contributions sooner than a 529 savings plan will. 529 savings plans can preserve the tax advantages of a 529 prepaid plan without many of these downsides.

**Quick Notes:**
Key advantages and disadvantages of prepaid tuition
Section 529 plans

| Advantages | Disadvantages |
| --- | --- |
| • They allow payer to pay for future tuition expenses at present tuition rates (plus a small premium).<br><br>• Contributions to such accounts build tax-free as long as the money is withdrawn for tuition and approved educational expenses.<br><br>• Many states give resident account holders a tax break on 529 contributions. | • Plan investments may not keep up with benefit obligations.<br><br>• They may not cover private college tuition cost. Most plans are aimed at in-state public tuition.<br><br>• The return on investment may be weaker in a prepaid 529 plan than it would be in another instrument. |

**College Savings Plans**

*Section 529 Savings Plans*

529 savings plans do not lock you into today's tuition at prepaid rates. Instead, such plans are tax-exempt college savings vehicles with the added benefit of minimal impact to the beneficiary's need-based financial aid eligibility.

The owner of the 529 plan makes contributions into a designated investment account and, using investment vehicles offered by the plan, grows the funds tax-free for use to pay qualified education expenses. Some 529s are self-directed, while others offer predetermined allocation strategies depending on the saver's needs. Much like an IRA, a 529 savings plan is not itself an investment, but rather a vehicle for allowing investments to grow for a specific purpose.

The 529 savings plan's owner can be anyone interested in the beneficiary's educational well-being. However, if the beneficiary does not attend college, the account owner can only change the beneficiary to another member of the initial beneficiary's family. Anyone can contribute to the plan on a beneficiary's behalf. Friends, colleagues, extended family or even strangers could theoretically contribute to a child's educational savings. As noted in the previous section, contribution limits are also generally higher than in a prepaid tuition 529 plan. Most 529 savings plans currently accept contributions until all account balances for a beneficiary reach around $350,000. In some plans, the limit exceeds $400,000 per beneficiary. These limits are expected to increase as the cost of education continues to rise.

Though qualified educational expenses vary from plan to plan, they usually include tuition, fees, books, supplies and equipment required for enrollment or attendance at an eligible college or university. Computers are considered "supplies" only if the school specifically requires students to bring their own computers. Room and board are, for the most part, only included for students who are enrolled at least half-time; such expenses are limited to what the school charges students who live in campus housing or to the school's budget figures for students housed off-campus.

529 savings plans do entail risk. Investments are always subject to market conditions, and there is no guarantee that your savings will be sufficient to cover all college costs outright. However, with this added risk comes the opportunity for greater returns, stretching your contributions further. Most 529 savings plans offer adaptive asset allocation strategies, based on the age of the beneficiary or the number of years between opening the account and the anticipated educational start date. Plans tend to start off with aggressive, higher risk investments far from matriculation, and gradually become more conservative as the beneficiary nears college age.

A 529 savings plan offers many advantages that make it one of the most attractive ways to save for education expenses. The account owner controls the money in the plan, not the beneficiary. If the beneficiary decides not to attend college, he or she cannot access the funds for other uses. An account owner can also change the beneficiary, as long as the new beneficiary is an extended family member of the old beneficiary, without incurring a tax penalty. For example, if your oldest grandchild decides not to attend college, you can transfer the account to benefit his younger sister, or even to his cousin. Many plans have no maximum beneficiary age, so you can be the beneficiary of your own account. There is no date by which the funds in a plan must be used.

Once a year, the account owner can roll over the funds in a plan to a different 529 plan, or he or she can change the investment strategy. The plans generally offer flexible investment options, such as age-based asset allocation strategies and risk-based asset allocation strategies, depending on the account holder's needs and preferences. Many plans offer a choice of professionally managed funds and index funds. As with prepaid 529 plans, the money grows tax-free as long as it is withdrawn for qualified expenses, but many states also offer resident account holders a tax break on contributions for 529 savings plans.

In addition to investment flexibility for the account holder, 529 savings plans typically offer substantial choice to the beneficiary. The future student can typically choose any accredited post-secondary educational institution without penalty, and neither the beneficiary nor the account holder must live in a state to choose that state's sponsored plan. Generally 529 plans have low impact on a student's need-based financial aid eligibility, because assets in the plan are attributed to the account owner rather than to the beneficiary, which can help make up any gap between the account balance and the school's sticker price.

Section 529 savings plans can have some drawbacks. Choosing to use a 529 plan for saving also limits your investment options, and some states charge excessively high sales loads or management fees. As with any investment, more aggressive investment options offer greater potential return and, in consequence, greater risk – including loss of principal.

In certain cases, a 529 plan can complicate your tax situation. State tax benefits may be limited to that state's section 529 plan. State tax consequences on withdrawals may arise for residents of certain states, even if used for qualified expenses, although a majority of states impose no tax. If you need to withdraw funds for any non-qualified expenses, the earnings portion of such withdrawals is taxed as ordinary income, plus an additional 10 percent tax penalty. Should the beneficiary die or become permanently disabled, this 10 percent tax penalty is waived. In the event that the beneficiary receives a scholarship, the penalty is waived on distributions up to the amount of the scholarship. States may also assess additional penalties on non-qualified distributions in order to recapture any tax benefit the taxpayer received at the time the contribution was made. This is true for both prepaid and savings 529 plans.

529 account holders should also keep in mind that contributions are considered gifts, creating the potential for gift tax exposure. However, 529s offer a unique feature. Contributors can make a lump-sum contribution – up to $70,000 in 2014 – and elect to spread the gift evenly over five years. Provided you make no other gifts to the same beneficiary in the five-year period, you will avoid triggering federal gift tax. Account holders should also note that if they change the beneficiary to someone of a younger generation than the original beneficiary – for example, from a child to a grandchild – the transfer could expose the account to generation-skipping transfer tax unless handled correctly.

Because you can open a 529 savings plan in any state, it can feel overwhelming to try and decide which plan is best. The College Savings Plans Network, which offers tools for comparison shopping, listed 88 separate Section 529 savings plans as of this writing. As with any other investment strategy, it makes sense to proceed methodically.

Consider the plan's fees, the investment options the plan offers, and what tax breaks, if any, it will offer you. Fees and expenses are deducted from your investment returns, so you should work to keep those costs as low as possible. Also, make sure you understand what you would be paying for; some plans' management fees include the underlying funds' expenses, while other plans break these fees out individually. Enrollment fees and administration fees vary.

Investment diversification is also important. The plan you select should offer flexible mutual fund and exchange-traded fund (ETF) investment options that will allow you to diversify your holdings, not only across asset classes but among geographic regions. Tax breaks will vary depending on your situation, but note that some states allow you to deduct contributions to a 529 savings plan. New York, for example, allows you to deduct up to $5,000 if you are a single filer, or $10,000 for a married couple filing jointly.

### Quick Notes:
### Key advantages and disadvantages of Section 529 savings plans

| Advantages | Disadvantages |
|---|---|
| • The account owner can change the beneficiary, as long as the new beneficiary is an extended family member of the old beneficiary, without incurring a tax penalty. | • Choosing to use a 529 plan for saving also limits your investment options, and some states charge excessively high sales loads or management fees. |
| • Once a year, the account owner can roll over the funds in a plan to a different 529 plan, or he or she can change the investment strategy. | • A 529 plan can complicate your tax situation. |
| • Plans generally have a low impact on a student's need-based financial aid eligibility. | • If the account owner changes the beneficiary to someone of a younger generation than the original beneficiary – for example, from a child to a grandchild – the transfer could expose the account to generation-skipping transfer tax. |

At Palisades Hudson, we often recommend the Utah Educational Savings Plan (UESP), the Connecticut Higher Education Trust (CHET), the College Savings Plan of Nebraska and, for New York residents, New York's College Choice Tuition Savings Program. Consider discussing your situation with a financial adviser or professional, who can help you find the right balance of features for your needs.

*Coverdell Education Savings Accounts (ESAs)*

A Coverdell Education Savings Account (ESA) is another type of tax-advantaged savings vehicle. It allows you to save up to $2,000 per year on behalf of a qualified beneficiary, such as your child or grandchild, for qualified education expenses. Unlike 529 plans, an ESA's qualified expenses can also include certain elementary or secondary school costs. Beneficiaries must be younger than 30 for Coverdell ESAs.

For a time, ESAs were out of favor, since many of their most attractive provisions were set to disappear along with other Bush-era tax cuts, first in 2010 and then in 2012. The American Taxpayer Relief Act of 2012 (ATRA) locked in the enhanced benefits of ESAs that were established on a temporary basis a decade earlier. By removing uncertainty about the duration of these features, ATRA made ESAs more attractive to savers.

Besides the wider range of qualified education expenses, the other advantage offered by an ESA is greater control of investments than is typically available in a Section 529 plan. Account holders can use the same investments that are typically available in any brokerage account. ESAs can be invested in mutual funds, ETFs, or even individual securities, if desired. These accounts are often used alongside 529 plans, and like 529s, ESAs allow contributions to grow tax-free. Distributions are not taxed as long as they go toward qualified educational expenses. Also like a 529 plan, an ESA counts as the account holder's asset, not the beneficiary's, when calculating financial aid eligibility.

ESAs are similar to 529 savings plans, but have more drawbacks. Unlike contributions to a 529, contributions to an ESA are neither recoverable nor transferable by the account owner if the beneficiary does not attend college; they are for the sole benefit of the beneficiary. Any funds remaining in the account when the beneficiary reaches age 30 must be immediately distributed, subject to tax and a 10 percent penalty if there are no qualified educational expenses that year. Some ESA custodians allow you to transfer unused funds to an eligible family member under 30, but this varies, so it pays to read the ESA agreement carefully. Unlike 529s, ESAs do not allow account holders to realize state tax deductions on contributions.

Additionally, high earners face an income phase-out for ESAs that does not apply for 529s. Though this can be worked around by making a gift to the beneficiary and having him or her make the contribution, most high earners find it simpler to solely use a 529 instead. When using a 529 savings plan and an ESA side by side, the benefit of the ESA's larger number of investment options shrinks as the 529's balance grows. The larger the 529 balance, the less sense it makes to hold some of the savings in an ESA.

ESAs also offer less account control. After the beneficiary reaches legal age, he or she is the only one who can change the account to benefit someone else. It's also important to note that the $2,000 annual limit is per beneficiary, not per contributor. And once the beneficiary reaches age 18, no one can make new contributions.

**Quick Notes:**
Key advantages and disadvantages of Coverdell Education Savings Accounts

| Advantages | Disadvantages |
|---|---|
| • Unlike 529 plans, an ESA's qualified expenses can also include certain elementary or secondary school costs. <br><br> • ESAs offer greater control of investments than what is typically available in a Section 529 plan. <br><br> • Like 529s, ESAs allow contributions to grow tax-free and distributions are not taxed as long as they go toward qualified educational expenses. | • Beneficiaries must be younger than 30. <br><br> • Any funds remaining in the account when the beneficiary reaches age 30 must be immediately distributed, subject to tax and a 10 percent penalty if there are no qualified educational expenses that year. <br><br> • ESAs offer less account control. After the beneficiary reaches legal age, he or she is the only one who can change the account to benefit someone else. |

You can transfer funds from an ESA to a 529 as long as the beneficiary remains the same. However, you cannot go in the other direction, from a 529 to an ESA. You can – and many people do – have both types of accounts for the same beneficiary if you wish, though as noted above, this is not always the most beneficial way to save.

*Custodial Accounts (UGMA and UTMA accounts)*

Custodial accounts are much closer to direct gifts than the vehicles previously discussed. The Uniform Gift to Minors Act (UGMA) established a simple way for a minor to own securities without the need for an attorney to prepare trust documents or for the court to appoint a trustee. The terms of an UGMA trust are established by state statute, rather than by a trust document. The Uniform Transfer to Minors Act (UTMA) is similar, but it allows minors to own other types of property, including real estate, fine art and intellectual property. UTMA also made it possible for the transfers to occur through inheritance and offered somewhat more flexibility than UGMA. However, for the purposes of this chapter, UGMA and UTMA accounts are similar enough to discuss together.

Much like traditional trusts, custodial accounts have custodians, or trustees, with the fiduciary duty to manage the money prudently on the minor's behalf. These custodians are usually the beneficiary's parents, but any adult can set up a custodial account for a child under 18. The assets in the custodial account belong to the minor, but they are controlled by the custodian until the minor reaches the adulthood. This age can vary from 18 to 21, depending on the state and on whether the account is an UGMA (which usually ends at 18) or an UTMA (which usually ends at 21).

Unlike 529s or ESAs, there is no contribution limit at all on custodial accounts, though gifts beyond the annual exclusion are subject to gift tax. UGMAs and UTMAs offer a wide variety of investment options and a certain level of favorable tax treatment. For beneficiaries younger than 19, or 24 if they are full-time students, a set amount of income is tax-free if they file as part of their parents' tax returns. Another set amount is taxed at the child's tax bracket, and anything above those amounts is taxable at the parents' rate.

The major downside of custodial accounts for educational gifts is that these accounts are not tax-advantaged, so annual taxes will be due on any generated income or capital gains. Contributions are irrevocable and can only be used for the child's benefit, nor can the beneficiary be changed, by either the child or the gift-giver. Once the child reaches the account's age of majority, he or she will have complete control of the funds, and there is no requirement that they be used for educational expenses. As you might imagine, this means that financial aid calculations consider UGMA and UTMA accounts the property of the child, which creates a substantial impact on financial aid eligibility.

While custodial accounts were popular college savings vehicles before the advent of ESAs and Section 529 plans, they are best deployed carefully to meet the specific needs of both the giver and the beneficiary. The potential disadvantages of this method can often outweigh the increased flexibility it offers.

## Quick Notes:
## Key advantages and disadvantages of custodial accounts (UGMA and UTMA accounts)

| Advantages | Disadvantages |
|---|---|
| • There is no contribution limit at all on custodial accounts. | • Gifts beyond the annual exclusion are subject to gift tax. |
| • UGMAs and UTMAs offer a wide variety of investment options and a certain level of favorable tax treatment. | • UGMA and UTMA accounts are not tax-advantaged, so annual taxes will be due on any generated income or capital gains. |
| • For beneficiaries younger than 19, or 24 if they are full-time students, a set amount of income is tax-free if they file as part of their parents' tax returns. | • The child obtains complete control of the funds upon reaching the account's age of majority. Eligibility for financial aid can be substantially affected. |

### Federal Grants

Supplementing educational savings can help reduce the net cost to college to something less than a school's sticker price. One of the most appealing of these methods is applying for federal grants.

Grants, unlike loans, do not need to be repaid. A student's eligibility is determined by the results of his or her Free Application for Federal Student Aid (FAFSA). Many schools use the FAFSA as well, in order to calculate need-based aid.

The largest and most popular of the federal grants is the Federal Pell Grant. The maximum award varies from year to year, and depends on the program's funding levels. For the 2013-2014 academic year, the maximum grant was $5,645, though students may receive less. The size of a student's award is determined by the FAFSA, in conjunction with the school's cost of attendance. Pell Grant recipients may be eligible for additional merit grants too, including the Academic Competitiveness Grant and the National Science and Mathematics Access to Retain Talent (SMART) Grant.

The Department of Education also offers need-based grants to students with exceptional financial need (Federal Supplemental Educational Opportunity Grants), students who plan to become teachers (TEACH Grants), and students whose parent or guardian died during military service in Iraq or Afghanistan (Iraq and Afghanistan Service Grants).

### State, Institutional and Private Scholarships

Scholarships can help make school more affordable for all sorts of students. Scholarships offered by institutions can generally be sorted into "need-based" and "merit" funding. (Often, need-based aid is called a grant and merit-based aid is called a scholarship, but terminology varies from institution to institution.) Need-based aid is usually based on the FAFSA, sometimes in combination with the more-detailed CSS/Financial Aid PROFILE form. The PROFILE, which is mainly required by private colleges, is more detailed than the FAFSA. Merit scholarships are awarded regardless of need.

Merit-based aid can cover a large portion of education expenses, though full rides are very rare. Examples of merit funding include athletic scholarships, artistic scholarships, and academic achievement scholarships. Increasingly, colleges and universities use merit scholarships in order to attract high-achieving, often affluent students to apply. This helps to boost the schools' selectivity rankings and to entice students and families who will be able to pay the remaining tuition balance. The exception is the highest tier of elite schools, such as Ivy League institutions, many of which do not offer merit-based aid at all.

Many states have formulas for scholarships and grants that depend on factors such as a student's grades or test scores. Certain states also offer help to students if they choose to stay in-state to attend college, even if the in-state school is private. Many websites and directories exist to help point students toward scholarships for which they qualify, including state-level aid.

Scholarships are often available from other sources too, including community organizations, religious groups, private companies and others. Some scholarships require essays or other demonstrations of skill, while some simply ask that qualified students go through a simple application process. Students in science, technology, engineering and math (STEM) fields may also find a number of scholarships geared to their needs. Though awards tend to be relatively small, they can add up. Many of these scholarships are need-blind, and many are regional or local, which keeps the applicant pool smaller.

Be aware that some schools, such as Cornell and Dartmouth, have practiced what is called "aid displacement." Aid displacement is the practice of reducing financial aid packages of students who receive third-party scholarships and grants. Their outside aid effectively "displaces" their aid from the school, meaning that the time and effort students spent applying for outside aid was essentially for the school's benefit rather than that of the student. Third-party scholarships can also sometimes reduce federal aid or need-based aid eligibility, depending on the student's situation and the way in which the award is disbursed.

*Work-Study*

When calculating student aid packages, many schools include a work-study portion. Schools that participate in the federal work-study program provide part-time jobs for students with financial need in order to help them pay for educational expenses. Though it is a federal program, the work is offered and overseen by the school. In addition to on-campus work, some schools arrange off-campus employment with a private non-profit or a public agency; rarely, work-study may be with a private, for-profit employer if the job relates to the student's field of study.

Student workers must be paid at least once a month, and must earn at least the federal minimum wage, though some workers may earn more. Schools pay students directly, except in cases where students request the school use the money to defray the cost of institutional charges such as tuition and fees. The amount a student earns in a school year cannot exceed the total work-study award in his or her financial aid package, which will limit the student's hours. However, unlike an outside job, work-study income is exempt from the student contribution portion of the FAFSA, keeping financial aid eligibility higher than it would be if the student earned the same amount at a non-work-study job.

## Student Loans

Loans are used to fill any gap between college expenses and the resources available to the student through savings, grants and scholarships. Students at four-year colleges or universities, community colleges or vocational schools can apply for federal financial aid, including loans. Like federal grants, most federal student loans are granted based on need, so students will need to submit a FAFSA.

*Federal Student Loans*

Unlike grants, federal student loans must be repaid, with interest. New federal student loans are funded through the Federal Direct Loan Program (FDLP). FDLP loans are either originally borrowed from or owned by the Department of Education. There are several types:

Stafford Subsidized Loans

These loans are available to undergraduate students who demonstrate financial need. They are used to help cover the educational costs of a college or career school. The loan will not start accruing interest until the student finishes his or her education; the federal government pays the interest as long as the borrower is a student.

Stafford Unsubsidized Loans

Unsubsidized Stafford loans are available to undergraduate, graduate, and professional students. Students do not have to demonstrate financial need in order to be eligible. Interest is charged from the time the loan is disbursed until the loan is completely paid off, though you do not have to start repaying the loan until after you graduate.

Direct Parent Loans for Undergraduate Students (Direct PLUS Loans)

Direct PLUS loans are for graduate or professional students, or for the parents of undergraduate students who are their dependents. Such loans are intended to help pay for educational expenses that other forms of financial aid do not cover. Unlike Stafford loans, a modest credit check is required.

Federal Perkins Loans

These loans offer a fixed interest rate. The lender is the college or educational institution. Rather than lending directly, the government gives the college the money, and the college then takes responsibility for distribution.

Direct Consolidation Loans

As the name implies, these loans allow students to combine their eligible federal student loans into a single loan with a single loan servicer, typically after the student graduates.

Before taking student loans, it is important to understand that federal student loans are not automatically discharged if the borrower files for Chapter 7 or Chapter 13 bankruptcy. Instead, the bankruptcy court will consider whether repayment would impose undue hardship on you and your dependents. The courts use a three-part test to determine hardship:

- You would not be able to maintain a minimal standard of living if forced to repay the loan;

- There is evidence that the hardship would continue for a significant portion of the remaining loan repayment period;

- You made a good-faith effort to repay the loan prior to filing bankruptcy (usually this means you have been in repayment for a minimum of five years).

Courts are reluctant to discharge student loan debt. Undue hardship is decided on a case-by-case basis, but should not be counted upon in advance. Considering the cost of interest and the long-term obligation involved, students should borrow only what they need, even if the school offers a greater loan amount as part of the financial aid package.

## Thomas' Advice

### Is it worth borrowing money to attend an elite college?

It depends on how much you plan to borrow and what you (or your student relative) will do after graduating. If you pursue a degree in engineering or business, you may be able to repay your loans within a reasonable amount of time. But if your heart lies in a field like film or journalism, or if you anticipate graduate school, the prestige of an elite university is likely not worth the stress of starting a career, or financing another degree, with tens or even hundreds of thousands of dollars of debt. Since flagship state universities can be regarded as highly as many private schools, those are sometimes the best bets for academically gifted students who want to position themselves for success.

-TW

While your loans may not be easily discharged, as of mid-2014, some students can qualify for the Pay As You Earn Repayment Plan. This plan is designed for borrowers whose student loan debt is high relative to their income. To qualify, the borrower must have partial financial hardship, defined as a case where the monthly required payment on eligible federal student loans under a 10-year standard repayment plan is higher than the monthly required payment would be under Pay As You Earn. Qualified loans include Federal Stafford Loans (subsidized and unsubsidized), Federal PLUS loans for graduate students or professional students, and federal consolidation loans that did not repay any parental PLUS loans. Private education loans or parent PLUS program loans are not qualified. Other factors may impact a borrower's eligibility on an individual basis. A similar but somewhat less generous program is Income-Based Repayment. Under both programs, unpaid loan balances may be forgiven after a period of time (generally 10 or 20 years for PAYE and 25 years for IBR). Most loan forgiveness will count as taxable income.

Federal loans offer some additional advantages that many private loans do not, such as deferred repayment while you are a full-time student; no requirement for a credit check or a co-signer in most cases; no prepayment penalty fees; and potential tax deductions for some or all of your interest on the loans. Whether your loan is federal or private, you should be sure to carefully read and understand the terms of the student loan before signing, just as you would with any other loan or contract.

*Private Student Loans*

As the result of growing demand for secondary education and costs that have outpaced inflation, private student loans are becoming increasingly pervasive. Outstanding student loan debt in the United States passed the $1 trillion mark in 2011. Most private student loan interest rates are quoted as LIBOR (a benchmark short-term interest rate) plus a percentage. The best loans offer rates of LIBOR plus 2 percent. These loans will usually require a creditworthy cosigner. Often, but not always, this will be a parent. The loans' total amount and interest rate can vary widely not only between servicers, but between applicants, depending on their financial situations.

As a rule of thumb, students should exhaust all their options, including federal student loans, before applying for private loans. Private loans tend to have the highest interest rates, and applicants often cannot review the full terms of the loan until submitting their applications. Bank fees can also dramatically increase the overall cost of private student loans.

For students considering private student loans, comparing lenders is essential. You will want to consider the loan's interest rate, whether fixed or variable, as well as its Annual Percentage Rate (APR), which better reflects the actual expenses. Be sure not to neglect investigating other parameters too, such as when you must begin repayment, whether there is a penalty for early repayment, and the price of administrative fees. Take the time to comparison shop. Several websites, including SimpleTuition and Overture Student Loan Marketplace, offer comparison tools for students and parents.

It is worth noting that, from a purely financial perspective, taking on significant debt to fund education is not always the wise choice. Consider the future earnings potential you expect the education to provide. Some families may want to send their student to an expensive school, regardless of their future career plans. This choice is personal, but students and families should consider such a choice a form of consumption, rather than an investment that will yield tangible results. While a student may have a personally enriching experience at a pricey university, an education from a less expensive school could yield similar career opportunities at a much lower cost, making it a sounder choice from a purely financial point of view.

## How Financial Need Is Calculated

In several of the previous subsections, I have mentioned the impact of a given funding method on a student's financial need. A student's resources and, to a lesser extent, the resources of the student's parents, will determine eligibility for certain types and levels of aid. Eligibility is calculated using the FAFSA form, and is specifically affected by one figure: the Expected Family Contribution (EFC).

The EFC is a formula used to determine the amount of financial support a student and his or her family is expected to provide annually, whether through savings or loans. The following factors determine a student's EFC on the FAFSA:

- 20 percent is determined by the student's own assets (cash, investments, business interests, real estate, etc.)

- 50 percent is the student's income (less certain allowances)

- 2.6 to 5.6 percent is determined by the assets of the parent or parents (based on a sliding income scale and less certain allowances)

- 22 to 47 percent is the parent or parents' income (again, based on a sliding income scale and less certain allowances)

Certain assets are left out of EFC altogether, including retirement accounts, equity in a primary home, family-owned businesses, non-custodial parent income, insurance policies and annuities. Only an estimated 7 percent of families will have enough income and assets to make them outright ineligible for need-based aid. If you have more than one child in college at the same time, EFC will drop further.

You can now see one of the most appealing features of a 529 account or an ESA; these accounts are included in the parental asset section, which is a small portion of total EFC, rather than in the much larger student asset portion. If grandparents own the account, the portion included in the calculation goes down to nothing. Even if the dependent student, or the dependent student's custodian, owns the account, it is reported as a parental asset regardless (as of the 2014-2015 academic year). Withdrawals for qualified educational expenses do not show up in the income portions, either, as they are excluded from federal income tax. Note, however, that if grandparents or other third parties own the accounts, the distributions must be added back on the FAFSA.

Custodial (UGMA or UTMA) accounts are considered student assets for the purposes of computing EFC. This means that such accounts have a high, direct impact on need-based financial aid eligibility.

If your EFC is high, your eligible aid as determined by FAFSA will be low. You should seek out merit-based scholarships to supplement your savings. Conversely, a low EFC will qualify you for more need-based aid. Apply first for federal grants, then for subsidized federal loans to take best advantage of your eligibility.

When students and their families consider colleges, it can be difficult to determine how affordable a given school will be, since some schools with high tuition costs may offer a great deal of aid and others will not. Federal regulation requires any college or university that receives federal funding to publish a Net Price Calculator for prospective students. Though these tools can help, they vary in reliability and usefulness; calculators that ask many questions tend to be more reliable than those that ask few. The College Board also provides information about schools' past scholarship practices and offerings, allowing an educated guess about which schools are likely to offer financial aid and what type.

Families should also factor information about schools' four-year graduation rates into their decisions, as a fifth year of school adds an additional year of costs.

## Education Funding Strategies

Both personal circumstances and goals shape good financial choices, and educational funding is no exception. You will most likely employ some combination of the options discussed earlier, but which options you pursue – and in what order – will change depending on your starting point.

If the student's EFC is high and he or she is therefore unlikely to qualify for most forms of need-based aid, the best option to pursue is merit scholarships. After that, saved educational funds from a Section 529 plan, ESA or custodial account should be used to the fullest extent available. If the student is able and willing to earn some of the necessary funds by working, consider making up some of the shortfall with part-time or summer employment, including work-study opportunities if available. If any gap remains, only then turn to loans: federal first, then private when all other options are exhausted.

For students who have a minimal EFC and will almost certainly qualify for need-based aid, federal grants and need-based scholarships are the best choice for educational funding. If the student needs to take loans after using aid and any saved educational funds, federal subsidized and unsubsidized student loans should be the first option to explore.

Many students may find themselves somewhere in the middle, with an EFC that is high but not prohibitively high. For these students, often the smartest move is to take steps to minimize expected family contribution, in order to increase need-based aid eligibility.

As previously mentioned, EFC weighs student assets and income much more heavily than those of the student's parents. This is one of the reasons that 529 plans are so attractive. On the surface, it may seem that if it is good for parents to own such accounts, it is even better for grandparents to own them, since grandparents' assets are not considered in EFC at all, but be careful. Distributions from the 529 plan are reported as untaxed income to the beneficiary. This makes it student income, with the potential to severely reduce need-based aid eligibility the following year. For this reason, students should wait until after they have filed their last financial aid application before withdrawing funds from grandparent-owned 529 accounts. For four-year students, this usually happens during the second semester of the third (junior) year.

If your resident state offers a tax break on contributions to its own state-sponsored 529 savings plan, but the plan features are otherwise unattractive, consider opening two 529 accounts – one in your resident state and one in a state that better fits your objectives. Contribute to your state's plan to receive the maximum allowable tax benefit, and then place any excess contribution in the non-resident state's plan. Further, if you find that the 529 account balances will more than cover the student's educational expenses, be sure to take qualified withdrawals from the account with greater earnings and appreciation. This minimizes the undesirable tax consequences of taking non-qualified withdrawals once the student no longer has use for the funds.

When minimizing EFC, parents who have saved money for education using traditional UGMA or UTMA accounts should consider liquidating the accounts and rolling the money over into a custodial 529 savings plan instead. This will move the custodial account from the child's assets to the much lighter-weighted parental asset category. This change significantly improves the child's eligibility for need-based aid. 529 plans only accept cash contributions, so you can't transfer the securities held in an UGMA or UTMA directly into a 529 plan. You will need to sell the securities first, which could possibly result in a tax liability. The new 529 account must be used solely for the minor's benefit and, unlike most 529 accounts, you lose the option to change the account's beneficiary. The beneficiary of the account will receive control of the 529 plan at the age of majority specified by law of the state governing the account. Because of these limitations, you should open a separate 529 if you roll over custodial accounts in order to escape the carried-over provisions. Further, you should exhaust the assets in the custodial 529 savings plan account before taking any distributions from any non-custodial 529 accounts and prior the point when control of the custodial account transfers to the beneficiary.

Parents should max out contributions to retirement accounts in order to shield assets from the EFC calculation. If the student has saved throughout childhood, this is an ideal time to teach him or her the benefits of a traditional or Roth IRA and the importance of saving early for retirement. Not only will the contributions grow tax-free, the funds will no longer be considered a student asset for financial aid eligibility.

Whatever methods you choose, it is wise to start saving as soon as possible. Longer time horizons allow for more aggressive investment and offer more potential for your savings to grow. With college costs continuing to rise, the odds are that even students who receive some financial aid through grants and scholarships will need to supplement that aid with savings, work, loans or some combination of the three.

Though this chapter has focused mainly on adults helping their children or grandchildren to handle education costs, many of these strategies can be adapted for helping your nieces and nephews, godchildren and children of friends, or yourself in affording the costs of a degree. Education is a priority for many. With some foresight, you can make sure your savings reach as far as possible in securing it for whomever you would like to assist.

# 9

## LIFE INSURANCE
### Shomari D. Hearn, CFP®, EA
### Anthony D. Criscuolo, CFP®, EA

At some point when you were in your 20s or 30s, someone probably told you that you ought to buy life insurance. "What would happen to your loved ones if they suddenly had to survive without your income," this relative, friend, salesperson or financial planner likely asked. How would your spouse keep up with mortgage payments? Who would pay for your children's college tuition?

If your household is like 70 percent of those in America, you agreed and have some form of life insurance today. But do you still need it? And is the policy you have still the right one?

Most arguments for life insurance are aimed at young income-earners with dependents. As you approach or move into retirement, and as your children establish themselves on their own, you may begin to wonder what, exactly, you are insuring against. After all, insurance is typically a way of protecting against financial losses, and if you are no longer collecting a salary, you no longer have any earnings at stake. It may be time to celebrate making it through your income-earning days by killing off your life insurance policy. However, if you have amassed wealth that you want to someday transmit to your heirs, you may have new uses for that life insurance policy. In this chapter, we will look at how life insurance can play a role in the next stage of your life.

## Life Insurance: What Kind, How Much, for How Long?

In attempting to determine if they need life insurance — and if so, what kind, how much, and for how long — many people jump quickly to the numbers. However, it's impossible to calculate your life insurance needs without first looking at why you might need the insurance. Life insurance is generally used for one of four main purposes.

1. Personal Income Protection: This is the traditional use of life insurance and the one that you were probably most concerned with when you first began to think about life insurance, early in your career. Life insurance used for income protection provides a way of replacing income in the event of your premature death to protect and provide support for your dependents.

2. Business and Partnership Income Protection: While this use is less common, life insurance can serve the same income protection function for a business as it can for a family. Life insurance is used for this purpose when a business would suffer significantly due to the death of a key manager, generally one who is responsible for the growth and income generation of the business. In this case, the protection is for the business and the surviving owners, and the business is generally both the owner and the beneficiary of the policy.

3. Estate Tax Liquidity: Life insurance can serve a specialized purpose for individuals who own illiquid assets, such as businesses or real estate, and expect their estates to be subject to estate tax. Since taxes must be paid with cash, the estate may be forced to sell all or a portion of the illiquid assets in order to pay the estate tax. Often such assets must be sold at a discount to their true fair market values. A life insurance policy in the appropriate amount can be used to provide the estate with cash to cover the tax bill and allow the heirs to preserve the illiquid assets.

4. Wealth Transfer: Life insurance can also be an effective means to transfer wealth to younger generations. When life insurance policies are set up properly for this purpose, proceeds are generally free of both income and estate tax, maximizing the value passed on. Life insurance can also play a role in financing long-term care, as discussed in the next chapter, by guaranteeing a base level of inheritance for heirs even if other assets are depleted by health care or other costs.

This is particularly useful for those whose heirs will be dependent on inherited assets for support, such as a spouse, domestic partner or disabled child.

After you determine the purpose your life insurance would serve, the questions of whether you need it, how much you need, and how long you will need it become far easier to answer. If it is for income protection, whether for your family or your business, you need insurance only for as long as your family or business is reliant on your income, and you need enough to take the place of that income until such replacement is no longer necessary. Insurance for estate tax liquidity, on the other hand, continues to be necessary as long as you have a large proportion of illiquid assets to pass on and insufficient cash to pay the associated taxes, and insurance for wealth transfer usually must remain in place for your entire life in order to accomplish its purpose.

The amount of life insurance you need for estate tax liquidity purposes can usually be calculated precisely based on the expected tax on your estate. However, when Congress changes the estate tax laws frequently (as has been the case in recent years), such precision becomes more difficult. For wealth transfer purposes, deciding how much to transfer through an insurance policy needs to be part of your overall investment and estate plan. If you are concerned about guaranteeing a particular amount for heirs who will be dependent on your estate for support, however, you may be able to calculate fairly accurately what the value of your policy needs to be.

| Life Insurance Protection | | | |
|---|---|---|---|
| **Personal Income Protection** | **Business Income Protection** | **Estate Tax Liquidity** | **Wealth Transfer** |
| **Do you need insurance?** Would your dependents suffer from the loss of your income? | Would your business suffer from the loss of the income/sales you generate? | Might your heirs need to liquidate businesses or property to pay estate taxes on them? | Does a life insurance policy fit into your overall investment/ estate plan? Or, do you need to guarantee a certain amount for your heirs? |
| **How much do you need?** Enough to replace your income for as long as your dependents will be reliant on it | Enough to replace your earning power for as long as the business will be reliant on it | Enough to pay the estate tax that will be due on the businesses or property you are leaving to your heirs | As much as fits with your overall investment/estate plan or as much as you need to guarantee for your heirs |
| **For how long do you need it?** As long as your dependents are reliant on your income | As long as the business is reliant on the income/ sales you generate | As long as you have business interests or property to transfer to your heirs and expect that your estate will be subject to tax | As long as you continue to have assets you want to transfer to your heirs and as long as an insurance policy continues to be the best means of doing that |

Chart 1

## What Kind of Life Insurance? Term vs. Permanent

The type of life insurance you need also depends on its intended use. While there are a wide variety of policies on the market, with an assortment of provisions and riders, life insurance can generally be divided into two main categories: Term insurance and permanent life insurance.

### Term Insurance

The defining characteristic of term insurance is that it provides coverage for only a certain time period, or term. A term insurance policy can have a term of just one year, called an annual renewal policy, or a term lasting a longer period, ranging from five to thirty years, called a level term policy. Premiums generally remain the same throughout the term. While term insurance policies can usually be renewed for additional terms, premiums increase with each renewal, as the insured ages and the likelihood of death rises. Some policies may not be renewable at all after a certain age, often 70 or 80.

The time limitation allows term insurance to work like any other form of insurance; for a relatively low but certain cost, the insured can avoid the possibility of a high but uncertain cost associated with an unlikely event — in this case, early death. Traditionally, insurance can protect against only rare events; otherwise, premiums would need to be nearly as high as the costs associated with the events themselves. While death is obviously certain, death within a particular timeframe is not. Premiums on term policies increase with age because the probability of death occurring in any given year likewise increases.

Because premiums rise rapidly with advancing years after middle age, term insurance works best if you are concerned with a particular time-span — most likely the time when your dependents must rely on your income. Term insurance, therefore, fits neatly with the purposes of personal and business income protection. In some term policies, increasing premiums are replaced with decreasing benefits. With these policies, premiums remain level, but the amount of coverage decreases as the risk of death increases. This sort of policy can be particularly useful for those whose needs will decline over time, as they pay off a mortgage or as their children become self-sufficient, for example.

**Permanent Insurance**

Unlike term insurance, permanent insurance is designed to last until it pays out – meaning until your death. However, because such policies can eventually be redeemed, permanent life insurance cannot run on the same simple, pure insurance model as term insurance. Instead, permanent life insurance policies are typically built around the accumulation of cash value, which is used to fund death benefits when they are eventually paid. Permanent life insurance is often described as a combination of a term policy and a tax-sheltered savings or investment account. Earlier in life, individuals pay higher premiums than they would with a term insurance policy. The insurer invests the excess on behalf of the policyholders. When the savings or investment account in a policy reaches the promised death benefit, that policy is said to be "endowed." Essentially, the insurance portion of the policy is the insurer's promise to pay the full death benefit if the insured dies before the policy endows. After the policy endows, there is no more risk for the insurer, and the policy becomes more like an investment product than an insurance product.

Because of the cash value component of permanent life insurance, policyholders can usually "cash out" policies, reclaiming the amount that has been invested, which is known as the surrender value. Generally, policyholders also have the option of taking loans or withdrawals from their cash balances. It's important to note, however, that because a portion of premium payments goes toward paying death benefits for those who die before their policies endow, the cash value of a policy at any given point is typically lower than the sum of premiums paid and interest earned.

Since permanent life insurance is guaranteed to pay out (so long as premiums are paid) and accumulates cash value, it works well as a means of providing money to heirs after death. This can be either just enough to cover estate taxes or a larger sum that you intend to pass to your heirs. Because of the saving or investment component, however, permanent life insurance is generally far more expensive than term insurance early in life, and it is therefore a poor choice for those who want to protect against loss of income for only a set time. In that case, a term policy is most appropriate.

Obviously, insurance needs change over time. A 20- or 30-something is unlikely to think about the possible estate planning uses of permanent life insurance. Fortunately, most term policies can be converted to permanent life policies. Usually, conversion is only available until the policyholder reaches a certain age. However, for most term policies, new evidence of insurability or health is not required for conversion within that window.

## Types of Permanent Life Insurance

Because of the combination of the insurance component and the investment component, there are a number of variables to consider in selecting a permanent life insurance policy, and there are a myriad of policy types that combine these variables in different ways. The most important difference between policy types is how much risk the insured takes on, which ultimately affects the policy's cost. Some policies focus on guaranteeing benefits, whereas others emphasize the investment aspect of permanent life insurance, allowing the insured to direct how their cash value is invested and to adjust premiums and benefits based on needs and performance.

### Traditional Whole Life Insurance

These policies generally guarantee both premium levels and benefit levels, and therefore involve the least risk to the insured. The insurance company takes on the task of calculating expected investment returns and mortality rates, and uses these calculations to guarantee to each policyholder that his or her policy will accumulate enough value to cover the death benefit or the insurance company itself will pay the difference. The primary disadvantage of traditional whole life insurance is that, in exchange for the guarantees it offers, policyholders must give up flexibility. With these policies, it is usually not possible to change coverage levels or to decrease or increase premiums. Policyholders also have no say in how their premiums are invested, and the interest earned on the cash value in these policies is often lower than could be obtained elsewhere. Because of the added risk the insurer takes on in guaranteeing premiums and benefits, these policies are also generally more expensive than other options.

While premiums are locked in when you purchase the whole life policy, there is often some element of choice as to the payment schedule. There are three main options:

- Whole (Ordinary) Life: A level premium is paid for life or to a high age, such as 100.

- Limited Pay Life: All premiums are paid at a level rate up to a certain age, such as 65.

- Graded Premium Whole Life and Modified Life: Premiums start off lower, but then increase and level off.

*Universal Life Insurance*

In universal life insurance policies, the insurance component and the investment component are unbundled. This creates added flexibility, because the policyholder has the ability to manage how earnings from the investment component are used. Specifically, investment earnings can generally be applied to premium payments for the insurance component of the policy, giving policyholders the option of temporarily stopping or reducing their out-of-pocket premium payments while maintaining coverage. The death benefit can also usually be adjusted. As with traditional whole life insurance, however, policyholders cannot direct how their cash balance is invested, and earnings are often relatively low.

*Variable Universal Life Insurance*

In addition to the flexibility offered by universal life insurance, variable life insurance policies also allow policyholders to decide how their cash balances are invested by choosing from a variety of different investments, such as mutual funds. This added flexibility, however, comes at the cost of added risk assumed by the policyholder. If the value of the cash account drops dramatically, the policyholder may be required to pay additional premiums to keep the insurance portion of the contract in force and protect the guaranteed death benefit. Variable universal life insurance policies can be a good option for those who are willing to accept the degree of risk that selecting investments carries. The expenses associated with variable universal life insurance investments are generally higher than those associated with other, non-insurance investments, but the policies offer the additional benefits of tax-deferred growth and access to a guaranteed death benefit.

| | Type of Insurance | | | |
|---|---|---|---|---|
| | | Permanent Life | | |
| | Term | Traditional Whole Life | Universal Life | Variable Universal Life |
| Purposes | Personal or business income protection | Personal or business income protection, *and* estate tax liquidity or wealth transfer | Personal or business income protection, *and* estate tax liquidity or wealth transfer | Personal or business income protection, *and* estate tax liquidity or wealth transfer |
| Pros | Most cost-effective way to protect against loss of income for a limited time | Guarantees premium and death benefits for life | Offers opportunity to adjust premiums and death benefits while still offering a guaranteed interest rate | Offers the most flexibility: opportunity to adjust premiums, benefits *and* investment choices |
| Cons | Premiums increase with age, resulting in most people letting the coverage terminate at the end of the policy term instead of extending the term or converting to a permanent policy. If the insured is still living at the end of the policy term, the beneficiaries do not receive a death benefit. No cash value. | Most expensive. Limited flexibility. | No option to direct investments and earnings may be relatively low. | Highest risk. No guaranteed rate of return. |

Chart 2

## Purchasing and Monitoring Life Insurance Policies

Of course, determining what kind of life insurance you need is only the first step. The second step is actually purchasing that insurance. Fortunately, there are plenty of people — insurance agents and financial advisers — eager to help you with step two.

Working with a life insurance agent is often viewed as the worst part of the process of purchasing insurance. The public perception is usually one of a pushy salesperson trying to sell the most expensive and complicated insurance products possible. This leads to mistrust and confusion within the marketplace. It's important that you find a good agent that you can trust. Usually a referral is best, but if that is not an option, you should always shop around and speak with a few agents before moving forward. Almost all insurance agents receive a commission for selling you a policy, so be mindful of what they are recommending and how it affects their own compensation. But know that most agents are also honest, and they must uphold high ethical standards imposed by the state in which they practice and the company for which they work.

## Anthony's Advice

**Do I have to monitor my life insurance and what red flags should I be looking for?**

Monitor your insurance as you would monitor an investment. If the policy's performance falters, consider it a red flag. Request updated policy illustrations under adverse assumptions and ensure your policy is not at risk of lapsing. A company that experiences higher-than-expected mortality costs or a large number of lapses, in which healthier policyholders seek coverage elsewhere, is not likely to perform very well. Be especially wary if the insurer's financial strength ratings are downgraded.

-AC

It is often a good idea to involve an independent financial adviser when considering life insurance. Involving an objective third party in the process will ensure that your interests are not overlooked. A fee-only financial adviser, who is usually paid a flat fee by you, can assist in the process and advise you as to how much life insurance you need and what type of policy will best meet those needs. The adviser will also be able to review policy documents and policy illustrations to ensure that your agent is presenting you with fair and reasonable expectations. The financial adviser can play a key role, too, in ongoing monitoring and evaluating of your life insurance policies and needs.

Regardless of who you go to for advice on your insurance needs, you should also have a general sense of the broad considerations involved in picking an insurance company.

## Picking a Company

### Mutual vs. Stock

There are two main types of companies from which you can buy life insurance: mutual companies and stock insurance companies. In a mutual insurance company, the owners of the company are also the policyholders. Profits are returned to policyholders in the form of dividends or reduced premiums. Stock insurance companies, on the other hand, are owned by outside investors.

Like any company, management should strive to maximize value for its owners. In the case of a mutual insurance company, its owners are also the policyholders, which aligns the interests of everyone involved. A regular stock company is owned by outside investors, so management will try to maximize value for its shareholders and not necessarily for its customers. Any good business manager, however, will recognize that building value for customers will lead to higher value for owners, so stock insurance companies are not automatically a bad option. When selecting an insurance company, it is important to know the difference between the two types and always to look for a good management team with a solid track record of building value for both owners and policyholders. Like any investment, you want an insurance policy from a company that is run well and is financially strong.

### Evaluating Financial Strength and Claims-Paying Ability

Evaluating the financial strength of a carrier is in some ways the most important and in other ways the least important part of selecting an insurance provider. It is the most important because, were your insurer to fail, your benefits could be at risk. There is no national equivalent to the Federal Deposit Insurance Corporation (FDIC) for insurance companies. Instead, each state maintains its own guaranty association to protect benefits. Like the FDIC, however, these state associations cap the level of coverage they offer. The limits vary by state, but generally death benefits are protected only up to around $300,000, and cash surrender values are protected only up to around $100,000.

Insurance company failures are extremely rare. From 1987 to 2009, the National Organization of Life and Health Insurance Guaranty Associations, which includes all 50 state guaranty associations as members, was involved in only 74 failures of multi-state insurance carriers. Because of this low rate of failures, the chances that your claim will not be paid because of company failure are small. However, you do not want to gamble when selecting an insurer, considering that the purpose of obtaining coverage is typically to protect against risk of loss. Your chances of avoiding a potential failure are even better if you take the time to conduct some basic research.

While your financial adviser, if you are working with one, will likely perform his or her own assessment of the strength of the carriers you are considering, he or she will also likely look at the assessments done by the major rating agencies, which provide snapshots of different aspects of a carrier's financial position. The four major rating agencies are:

- A.M. Best: A.M. Best focuses on consistent growth and profits by line of business. Its ratings take into account some qualitative considerations but are primarily based on hard statistics.

- Standard & Poor's (S&P): S&P focuses on the "claims paying ability" of insurance companies. It primarily looks at a company's liquidity, management strategy, business profile, earnings, investments, capitalization and financial flexibility.

- Moody's/Fitch: Moody's/Fitch focuses on the carriers' ability to generate consistent profits, as well as the quality of their management and assets.

- Weiss Ratings: Weiss Ratings differs from the others in that it only uses publicly available data and is not compensated by the insurers it rates. Its ratings are generally aimed towards the general public rather than financial professionals, who are the other agencies' primary audience.

Generally, you should look for a carrier with ratings of at least A+ from A.M. Best (its second highest rating), AA- from S&P (its fourth highest rating) and Aa3 from Moody's (its fourth highest rating).

There are some limitations to the value of credit ratings, including an inherent conflict of interest, since carriers are the ones who pay for the ratings (except for ratings from Weiss). Rating agencies also do not always respond immediately to changes in a carrier's financial position and may fail to downgrade carriers whose financial strength has deteriorated. Because of this, a financial adviser can help you to better understand both the ratings and other factors that go into evaluating a carrier's strength.

One of those other factors is the carrier's risk-based capital ratio, or RBC. The RBC compares the carrier's total assets, minus liabilities, to its level of risk to determine if the carrier has enough cash to meet possible needs of paying out death benefits. A carrier with a low RBC is said to be inadequately capitalized. As with ratings, the RBC ratio does not provide a complete picture of a carrier's financial strength, but it serves as an important metric of financial stability.

*Evaluating Financial Performance*

While knowing that your insurance carrier is unlikely to fail is important, you also want to look for a carrier that is likely to give you a good return on your premium dollars, and ideally one that pays dividends beyond the guaranteed minimum rate of return. The best carrier, in terms of financial performance, is the one that generates the largest death benefits and greatest cash values for a given amount of premiums, taking into consideration the time value of money.

There are four primary factors that affect insurance carriers' performance: mortality risk (the rate at which claims must be paid), investment risk, lapse risk (the rate at which customers abandon policies) and expense risk (the general costs of doing business). If you are working with a financial adviser, he or she will look at several metrics that capture these factors. These measurements include:

- Historical Investment Performance: The old caveat that past performance does not guarantee future results is as true in evaluating insurance carriers as it is in evaluating any other investment. Looking at performance trends, however, is usually the first step in assessing a carrier's current position and its future prospects.

- Ratio of Non-Performing Assets to Asset Valuation Reserve (AVR): To get a more detailed view of where the company stands, your financial adviser will likely look at the actual composition of the carrier's investments, examining the ratio of non-performing assets, such as bonds in and near default, non-performing mortgages and real estate, and real estate recovered through foreclosure, to what is known as the "asset valuation reserve" (essentially a reserve kept to protect against risk from non-performing assets).

- Three-Year Lapse Rate: While lapses, or cancellations, might seem good for insurers, since policies that lapse represent claims the insurer won't need to pay out, in reality lapses hurt insurers in two ways. First, policies often lapse before the insurer has recouped the initial costs associated with making the sale. Second, lapses fuel a problem known as "adverse selection." People who don't expect policies to pay out any time soon (that is, people in good health) are more likely to let their policies lapse, which leaves insurers with a higher proportion of their customers who expect policies to pay out soon (i.e. those in poor health). A higher lapse ratio means a higher level of risk among the customers who are left. The saying goes: "Sickies never cancel."

- General Expenses and Commissions to Total Income: Like any type of company, insurers must pay administrative expenses in addition to the actual costs of providing benefits. Their cost-to-income ratio offers a measure of efficiency. However, this ratio may sometimes be skewed by temporary factors. For example, an insurer with increasing sales might have particularly high commission costs for a given year, increasing its cost-to-income ratio even though, ultimately, the cost of the commissions will be made up by the premiums the new policies generate.

- Return on Equity: The Return on Equity (ROE) provides a basic overall measure of a carrier's financial performance and economic efficiency. As with the expense ratio, however, it may be distorted by temporary factors. If the ROE is low or negative, your financial adviser will likely look more closely to see whether this is a sign of fundamental problems.

**Picking a Policy**

Evaluating a particular policy involves more than just deciding what type of insurance is best and what company to buy from. You or your financial adviser should also look at the specifics of the individual policy. Before you purchase an insurance policy, the insurer will provide you with what is known as a "policy illustration," which lays out the particulars of the policy and shows how it will perform over time, based on different assumptions. Essentially, the policy illustration should answer all of the "what if" questions you might have about a prospective policy. State laws and regulations based on standards developed by the National Association of Insurance Commissioners control what information insurers are required to put in these illustrations. One of the things insurers must include is a "worst-case" scenario, showing the minimum guaranteed results. Generally, the illustration will also include a "current" scenario, based on the assumption that key metrics will remain level. You or your financial adviser can, and should, request additional illustrations based on various assumptions, such as higher or lower interest rates.

### Monitoring Existing Policies

You may be inclined to put your life insurance policy out of your mind as soon as you sign the contract, but the process shouldn't end there. If you have a permanent policy, you should treat that policy as part of your investment portfolio and include it in any periodic reviews of your overall financial situation. While most people recognize the need to continually monitor and reevaluate investments such as stocks or mutual funds, many overlook the importance of regularly reassessing life insurance policies.

In monitoring your policies, you should pay attention to the same key factors that you considered when purchasing a new policy. If you find that your insurer's financial position appears to have deteriorated, you should look closely at the specific cause of the change. As mentioned before, decreases in certain measures of financial performance can be signs of growth, rather than decline, but it is important to dig deep enough to find which cause is likely at play.

## Shomari's Advice

### Are there significant drawbacks to canceling a life insurance policy?

If you still need life insurance but you surrender an existing policy before obtaining a new one, you may find that you do not qualify for new coverage or must pay unfavorable rates due to health reasons. Get a replacement before you cancel your old policy. Also, you may trigger taxable income if the policy you cancel has a cash surrender value that exceeds the total premiums paid. The difference is taxed as ordinary income, not capital gains.

-SH

If you do decide that you are dissatisfied with your current policy's performance, there are three factors to consider before you jump ship. The first is how changes to your health might impact premiums if you were to enroll in a new policy. If you were significantly younger than you are now when you enrolled in your current policy, or if you have since experienced changes in your health, you may find that you are unable to obtain your current level of coverage for similar premiums elsewhere. Therefore, you will want to obtain the replacement policy before allowing your current policy to lapse. Second, a new policy comes with significant upfront costs, which you paid on your existing policy and will not recoup; you will want to consider whether a switch is worth the additional cost. If you have a permanent life insurance policy, the third consideration is the income tax implications of surrendering the policy. If the cash surrender value exceeds the amount of premiums that have been paid on the policy, the difference is treated as ordinary income and is subject to federal and state income tax. Note, however, that you can avoid incurring income taxes by conducting a Section 1035 exchange, swapping your existing permanent life insurance policy for a new permanent policy.

Even if you decide to keep your current policy, you may want to change the way in which you pay premiums. As discussed earlier, with universal life and variable universal life policies, you typically have the option of using dividend payments to cover future premiums, allowing the policy to become self-funding. Whether you want to do this will depend on the financial performance of the policy, or the amount of coverage your premium dollars can buy, and the amount you could earn by investing the would-be premium payments elsewhere. A financial adviser can help illustrate a variety of scenarios, based on different actions on your part and on variables outside your control, such as your lifespan and the rate of return on your investments, to assist you in making this decision.

## Taxes and Planning Considerations

The purpose of a life insurance policy is to provide your heirs with assets — not liabilities. But without proper planning, the beneficiaries of your policy can end up with a substantial tax burden. Assets in life insurance policies accumulate free of income tax, and proceeds are also income-tax-free. However, if you own your life insurance policy, the death benefit will be included in the value of your gross estate. If your estate is already over the exemption level for the federal (or state) estate tax, or if the death benefit from your life insurance policy puts it over that level, your estate will have to pay estate tax, which will reduce the total value of assets passed to your heirs. This is true even if you name a beneficiary other than your estate, so long as you are still the one in control of the policy at the time of your death.

The solution to this problem is not to own your life insurance policy. You can either have someone else, such as a relative, own the policy, or you can place the policy in what is known as an Irrevocable Life Insurance Trust (ILIT). When you put a policy in an ILIT, the trust itself becomes the owner and beneficiary of the policy. You must select a trustee to take on the responsibility of managing the policy once it is in trust. The trustee can be either an individual or a corporate fiduciary, such as a bank or trust company. Generally, the trustee should be an impartial representative, such as a close relative who is not a beneficiary of the trust, a trusted friend or an adviser. You can have a trust beneficiary serve as the trustee if you wish.

It is important to note the word "irrevocable" in the term "Irrevocable Life Insurance Trust." When you put your policy into an irrevocable trust, you permanently give up the freedom to make changes to the policy or to the provisions of the trust agreement, including the ability to change the named beneficiaries of the trust. Depending on state laws, your appointed trustee may still be able to make some changes. Even when changes can be legally made, however, there is a risk that a change might trigger the taxes the trust is designed to prevent. In addition to giving up the right to make changes, you also surrender your ability to personally borrow against the policy. Again, the trustee may, in some cases, be able to take out loans, but only if doing so is in the interest of the named beneficiaries.

Of course, no matter how much control you surrender to the trustee, in most cases he or she is unlikely to want to pay premiums out of pocket. It is important, therefore, to have a way to fund the trust. But since the trust is for the ultimate benefit of your heirs, money you put into it for the purposes of premium payments can be considered gifts and might trigger gift taxes. Fortunately, you are permitted to give a set annual amount, $14,000 per recipient as of 2014, without triggering gift tax. The catch is that to qualify for the annual exclusion, the gift must be of a "present interest" to the recipients. For gifts to be of a "present interest," recipients must be able to access them immediately, without restrictions. Common sense suggests that contributions to a trust containing a life insurance policy would not apply. However, by giving the beneficiaries of your policy the option to withdraw the money immediately, you can take advantage of the exclusion, even if the beneficiaries decide not to actually withdraw the money. This is known as using "Crummey" powers. The term comes from a taxpayer named D. Clifford Crummey, who won a case in 1968 against the Internal Revenue Service, creating the precedent for using the "present interest" exclusion on contributions to trusts.

To use "Crummey" rules and ensure that money you give to your trust to pay for policy premiums qualifies for the annual gift tax exclusion, your trustee must notify the trust's beneficiaries of their right to withdraw the money you wish to give the trust. Generally, the beneficiaries are granted a set amount of time, such as 30 or 60 days, to make withdrawals, after which the money becomes available for the trust's use. If you explain the situation to them, beneficiaries are likely to understand the advantages of not exercising this right and instead allow the money to remain in the trust. Once the withdrawal window expires, the money can be used for premium payments. It is important that contributions be timed so that the money is, in fact, available for the entire withdrawal window, even if you already know that the beneficiaries will not exercise their withdrawal rights and that the trustee will use the money to pay premiums.

If you decide that an ILIT is right for you, the best option is to create the trust first, and then have the trust take out the insurance policy. If you already have a policy that you want to move into a trust, you can still create the trust and then transfer the policy. However, for the first three years following the transfer, any benefit from your policy will still be taxed as if the policy were held in your name.

Similar considerations apply if you decide to make another individual the owner of your policy. Whether you transfer a policy to a trust or an individual, you need to be sure to give up any so-called "incidents of ownership," or signs of control, over the policy. This means that you should not retain any legal right to change beneficiaries, borrow against the policy, surrender or cancel the policy, or select beneficiary payment options.

## Collecting Benefits

The purpose of a life insurance policy is to provide for your loved ones after your death. To do that, you need to take the time to understand what your beneficiaries must do to collect the benefit and you should leave everything in order to allow them to do so as easily as possible. Life insurance companies try to make benefit collection easy. After the insured dies, the executor of the estate or the beneficiaries of the policy should notify the insurance company of the insured's death. The insurance company will generally provide a claims package with paperwork to be completed and returned along with a certified copy of the insured's death certificate. After processing the documents and approving the claim, the company will distribute the death benefit to the beneficiaries. It is best to keep your insurance records in good order and to ensure that someone close to you knows where they are located, as well as how to contact the beneficiaries.

If an insurance agent asked you the same questions today that may have prompted you to purchase life insurance decades ago, your answers would likely be different. You may no longer have any earnings to protect or any dependents to support. But if you have assets you intend to pass on to heirs and are looking for a way to do so while minimizing your tax obligations, life insurance can continue to be an important tool.

# 10

## FINANCING LONG-TERM CARE
### Anna K. Pfaehler, CFP®

Americans today are living longer than ever. These added years offer new opportunities—to spend time with grandchildren and perhaps even great-grandchildren, to develop hobbies, and, in some cases, to launch new business ventures, as discussed in Chapter 19. However, it is important to realize that, in these extra years of life, your needs may change, as basic tasks such as bathing, dressing and moving from place to place, or daily chores, such as housework and preparing meals, become challenges. Many people, as they age, eventually require assistance with these tasks. This assistance is called long-term care.

Unlike other health care, long-term care focuses largely on support beyond direct medical attention and is generally provided by professionals who are not doctors or nurses, but it is critical to ensuring continued health and well-being. Long-term care addresses both essential personal care tasks, known as "Activities of Daily Living," or ADLs, and other daily chores, known as "Instrumental Activities of Daily Living."

Around 69 percent of people over the age of 65 will require some sort of long-term care. On average, someone who is 65 today can expect to need long-term care of some sort for three years. Women generally need care for longer than men do—3.7 years, compared to 2.2 years—and one fifth of people will need care for longer than five years.

## Long-Term Care Needs

**Activities of Daily Living**
- Bathing
- Dressing
- Eating
- Transferring between bed and wheelchair
- Using the toilet
- Taking medications

**Instrumental Activities of Daily Living**
- Housework
- Preparing meals
- Shopping
- Managing money

Source: Adapted from Department of Health and Human Services,
National Clearinghouse for Long Term Care Information
Figure 1

The rise in long-term care needs is particularly tied to the prevalence of dementia, as many people who are still physically healthy, or who can manage their physical ailments, develop neurological conditions that prevent them from caring for themselves. A 2007 study found that 13.9 percent of people in the U.S. older than 71 were affected by dementia. Among those over the age of 90, 37.4 percent were affected.

As life expectancies increase, more and more people can expect to live to 90 and beyond, meaning that dementia and the long-term care it necessitates will become increasingly salient concerns.

Given these statistics, long-term care needs are an important consideration for anyone planning for the later stages of life. As with so many of the topics in this book, the time to begin thinking about long-term care is long before it is actually needed. This is especially true because long-term care is not only common, but also expensive.

## How Much Does Long-Term Care Cost?

The cost of long-term care depends largely on what kind or kinds of care you ultimately need. By the time you begin to contemplate your own future long-term care needs, there is a good chance that you will have already gone through the process of evaluating long-term care options for a parent or other aging relative. It may be useful, however, to quickly review the types of care available with your own possible needs and circumstances in mind.

## Life Expectancies

| Year | At Birth | | At 65 | |
|---|---|---|---|---|
| | Male | Female | Male | Female |
| 1980 | 70.0 | 77.4 | 14.1 | 18.3 |
| 1990 | 71.8 | 78.8 | 15.1 | 18.9 |
| 1995 | 72.5 | 78.9 | 15.6 | 18.9 |
| 2000 | 74.1 | 79.3 | 16.0 | 19.0 |
| 2005 | 74.9 | 79.9 | 16.8 | 19.5 |
| 2006 | 75.1 | 80.2 | 17.0 | 19.7 |
| 2007 | 75.4 | 80.4 | 17.2 | 19.9 |
| 2008 | 75.6 | 80.6 | 17.3 | 20.0 |
| 2009 | 76.0 | 80.9 | 17.6 | 20.3 |

Source: Centers for Disease Control and Prevention

Chart 1

Generally, the types of care are grouped by whether individuals remain in their own homes or move to a specific facility where care can be delivered.

## Home and Community Care

*Family Care/Respite Care*

Around 59 percent of aging adults at some point rely on unpaid care at home, generally from friends or family members. More than 65 million Americans—29 percent of the population—care for chronically ill, disabled or aged family members each year, spending an average of 20 hours a week delivering this care.

While this type of care is considered to be "free," the value is estimated to be $375 billion a year, according to a study by the National Alliance for Caregiving and Evercare. Family care is often paired with some form of part-time or temporary paid care, known as "respite care," in order to allow primary caregivers to manage other responsibilities. This is particularly important since caregivers are often adult children who are also caring for their own children.

*Home Health Aides/Homemaker Services*

In-home paid care can take two basic forms. Home health aides offer skilled services, including nursing and physical therapy, generally under the supervision of a doctor, a nurse, or a physical, respiratory, speech or occupational therapist. Other aides can provide homemaker services involving non-medical tasks such as meal preparation.

### Therapeutic Devices/Home Modification

In some cases, specialized equipment, such as stair lifts, ramps and grab bars, can allow individuals to meet more of their own needs, providing greater independence and reducing the need for other care.

### Adult Day Care

Adult day-care services provide part-time, out-of-the-home care for individuals who continue to live independently or with family caretakers. Some adult day-care centers offer health services, while others are focused more on social needs.

## Facility-Based Care

### Assisted Living Facilities

Assisted living facilities—also referred to as Residential Care Facilities—offer many of the same services as home health aides and homemakers, but in a community setting. Residents generally have their own rooms or apartments, but receive services such as housekeeping, meals, assistance with personal care, and help with medications. Assisted living facilities generally also offer onsite staff to deal with emergencies.

### Nursing Homes

Nursing homes—also called skilled nursing facilities—provide 24-hour residential supervision for those who need help with basic Activities of Daily Living. Nursing homes can be used for relatively short periods of recovery or rehabilitation after illnesses and medical procedures. They can also be used for longer periods, especially in cases involving dementia, which can require years of around-the-clock care for an otherwise healthy person.

### Continuing Care Centers

Continuing Care Centers—also known as Continuing Care Retirement Communities—offer a variety of living arrangements, from independent housing to nursing home care, in the same location. This allows residents to stay in the same center as their needs change.

*Hospice Facilities*

Hospice facilities provide care specifically for individuals with terminal illnesses who are seeking comfort and pain management but not recovery.

## Cost By Type of Care

Costs depend on how much care is required and on how individualized it is. Whether home and community care or facility-based care is more cost-effective can change based on how much care is needed and the availability of friends and family members to replace or supplement paid care at home.

Generally, as you age, your long-term care needs will change. Because of this, people often use a variety of types of services at different times over the course of their lives. On average, people spend more time receiving care at home than in facilities.

### Care Costs (2010 National Averages)

| Type of Care | Per Hour | Per Day | Per Month |
|---|---|---|---|
| Home Health Aide | $21 | | |
| Homemaker Services | $19 | | |
| Adult Day Care | | $67 | $2,037 (if used every day) |
| Assisted Living Facility (One-Bedroom Unit) | | $108 | $3,293 |
| Nursing Home (Semi-Private Room) | | $205 | $6,235 |
| Nursing Home (Private Room) | | $229 | $6,965 |

Source: Department of Health and Human Services, National Clearinghouse for Long Term Care Information

Chart 2

## Regional Differences in Costs

As with many expenses, when it comes to long-term care costs, location matters. Local economic factors can have a huge effect on the cost of care. For those with a choice of where to retire, long-term care costs may be an important factor, to be weighed against the proximity of family members who might be able to replace or supplement paid care. Based on real estate costs and average wages, some areas may be cheaper for facility-based care, but more expensive for home care, or vice versa. While rural areas often have lower costs, this is not necessarily true in highly remote locations, such as Alaska, where care costs may be higher. Kansas has some of the lowest costs, while New Hampshire has some of the highest, according to a 2010 study by the insurer MetLife.

## Care Usage

| Care | Average number of years used | Percent of people used by |
|------|------------------------------|---------------------------|
| Unpaid Home Care | 1 year | 59% |
| Paid Home Care | Less than 1 year | 42% |
| Any Home Care | 2 years | 65% |
| Assisted Living Facility | Less than 1 year | 13% |
| Nursing Home | 1 year | 35% |
| Any Facility-Based Care | 1 year | 37% |
| Any Services | 3 years | 69% |

Source: Department of Health and Human Services, National
Clearinghouse for Long Term Care Information

Chart 3

## Trajectory

It's difficult to anticipate exactly how long-term care costs will change in the future. Most likely, as the population ages, demand for long-term care services will increase, driving up costs. The aftereffects of the Baby Boom, combined with longer lifespans, will put an increasing amount of the population at risk of needing long-term care. Already, costs for assisted living facilities are rising nearly 6 percent a year, according to a survey conducted by long-term care insurance provider Genworth Financial, Inc.

## Care Costs (2010 Regional)

| Region | Avg. Daily Nursing Home Rate: Private | Avg. Daily Nursing Home Rate: Semi-Private | Avg. Monthly Cost in Assisted Living Facility | Home Health Aide Average Hourly Rate | Homemaker Services Average Hourly Rate | Adult Day Care Daily Rate |
|---|---|---|---|---|---|---|
| Kansas State Average | $158 | $144 | $3,214 | $19 | $18 | $75 |
| New Hampshire State Average | $293 | $265 | $4,068 | $24 | $21 | $62 |
| Atlanta | $194 | $173 | $3,028 | $17 | $17 | $53 |
| Georgia State Average | $177 | $164 | $3,116 | $18 | $17 | $62 |
| Miami | $302 | $271 | $2,912 | $16 | $15 | $53 |
| Florida State Average | $242 | $218 | $2,996 | $18 | $17 | $58 |
| New York City | $381 | $361 | $4,503 | $19 | $18 | $124 |
| New York State Average | $350 | $336 | $3,701 | $21 | $19 | $99 |
| Los Angeles | $238 | $198 | $2,533 | $19 | $18 | $78 |
| California State Average | $287 | $227 | $3,601 | $21 | $21 | $75 |

Source: 2010 MetLife Market Survey of Long-Term Care Costs, cited by Department of Health and Human Services, National Clearinghouse for Long Term Care Information

Chart 4

## Care Costs Increases

| Care | 2011 to 2012 Increase | 5-Year Annual Growth (2007 - 2012) |
|---|---|---|
| Home Health Aide | 0.00% | 1.09% |
| Homemaker Services | 0.00% | 1.15% |
| Adult Day Care | 1.67% | N/A |
| Assisted Living Facility (Single Occupancy Unit) | 1.19% | 5.71% |
| Nursing Home (Semi-Private Room) | 3.63% | 4.50% |
| Nursing Home (Private Room) | 4.23% | 4.28% |

Source: Genworth 2012 Costs of Care Survey

Chart 5

## What about Medicare?

While Medicare does, in certain situations, pay for some of the types of care discussed here, it generally does so only when care is needed for short-term recovery from an illness or injury, not when care is needed indefinitely due to permanent loss of the ability to perform Activities of Daily Living. Care in an institutional skilled nursing facility is only covered by Medicare if it begins within 30 days after a hospital stay of three days or more. Even then, Medicare pays 100 percent of the cost only for the first 20 days. For the next 80 days, individuals must make a set co-payment ($152 per day in 2014), after which Medicare covers the rest of the cost.

Medicare does not pay any costs beyond the first 100 days.

Medicare also provides some coverage for home health services, but, again, care is covered only following a hospital stay, and is limited to 100 visits. Another important limitation is that home health services are covered only when the need for skilled nursing services is "intermittent," not full-time, as determined by a physician. Home health services must be provided by a Medicare-certified home health agency to be covered.

## What about Medicaid?

Medicaid, the government safety net for health care, pays for more than 40 percent of overall long-term care costs, according to the SCAN Foundation, a non-profit organization dedicated to improving the quality and affordability of long-term care. However, it requires individuals to use virtually all of their assets before becoming eligible for coverage. Eligibility requirements vary by state. In most states, individuals or couples must have incomes below the poverty line and assets of no more than $2,000 for individuals, or $3,000 for couples. For couples, if only one spouse requires institutional care, the spouse who does not require care is generally allowed to retain a higher set dollar amount, up to $117,240 in 2014, without affecting the institutionalized spouse's eligibility.

There are certain exceptions to what assets count for the purposes of Medicaid eligibility, including a primary residence.

Medicaid eligibility can also be affected by gifts made during a five-year "look-back" period prior to application. The amount of any gifts made during that period is divided by the average monthly cost of care in the region, and benefits are delayed that many months.

Essentially, this means that benefits do not start until the individual would have used up whatever money was given as gifts on care costs. States also have the ability to seek repayment, after a Medicaid recipient's death, from any assets remaining in his or her estate, including assets not counted for the purposes of the eligibility requirements. An exception to this is made if the Medicaid recipient's spouse is still living, in which case the repayment is sought after the spouse's death. Medicaid recipients' heirs are also able to apply for hardship waivers, protecting them from the repayment requirement. Because of these restrictions, while Medicaid can serve as a payment method of last resort, it usually should not be a part of a primary long-term care financing strategy.

## Long-Term Care Insurance and How It Works

The bottom line is that there are three important facts about long-term care: Most people are likely to need it, it is likely to be expensive and the bulk of it will not be covered by Medicare or Medicaid. For many people, it's a quick leap from these facts to the decision to get long-term care insurance. More than 7 million Americans have long-term care insurance, according to the insurance industry-backed research group LIMRA International. For reasons that I will discuss later in this chapter, I think this is, in most cases, a mistake.

### Quick Facts:
### The Bottom Line on Long-Term Care

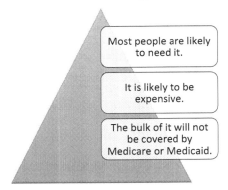

Most people are likely to need it.

It is likely to be expensive.

The bulk of it will not be covered by Medicare or Medicaid.

Before examining the utility of long-term care insurance, however, it's important to have a clear understanding of what it is and how it operates.

Long-term care insurance works essentially like other forms of insurance, such as car or homeowner's insurance; policyholders pay regular premiums, and then, if certain triggers occur, the insurer pays to cover costs. For long-term care policies, the most important trigger is the loss of the ability to perform a certain number of the Activities of Daily Living discussed earlier in this chapter. Cognitive impairments, as well as physical ones, can create the need for long-term care and trigger coverage from a long-term care insurance policy. Policies differ, however, in exactly how they define ADLs and in how many of the ADLs a person must be incapable of performing in order to qualify for coverage. Generally, more expensive policies allow policyholders to begin receiving coverage based on the need for assistance with a smaller number of ADLs. Policies also differ in terms of when tests or physician certification are required as proof of the need for care.

## Daily Limit vs. Lifetime Cap Policies

Once coverage is triggered, there are two main possibilities for how policies pay costs: based on a daily limit and based on a lifetime pool.

Policies that pay on a per day basis offer a set amount of coverage per day. Some policies will pay up to the daily limit each day that coverage is used, based on the actual costs, and others simply pay the daily limit every day coverage is used, even if the actual costs are lower than the limit. In either case, the number of days the policy will pay for may be capped. Some policies will continue to pay for the entirety of the policyholder's life, as long as coverage is needed, but these are generally more expensive.

The daily limit a policy will pay is another key variable. This limit should be high enough to cover expected daily costs, with annual increases for inflation, which will be discussed later. It is important to note, however, that many policies will pay only a fraction of the daily limit if services are provided at home, rather than in an institutional setting. In addition to a daily cap, policies may also have an annual or lifetime benefit cap.

A less common type of policy provides a pool of assets used to cover the cost of care over one's lifetime, with no restrictions on how this is distributed over time. These policies will pay however much is needed each day, but stop paying altogether once the lifetime cap is reached.

Each of the two types has potential disadvantages. With a daily limit policy, there may be high out-of-pocket costs and a minimal overall payout from the policy if the need for care is brief but acute, with costs concentrated over a small number of days. Lifetime maximum policies, meanwhile, work well in this sort of situation. But if, instead, the need for care is extended, policyholders with lifetime caps might end up running through their entire lifetime maximum in the first few years and then be left with no coverage at all.

### Why Long-Term Care Insurance Doesn't Usually Work

As I mentioned at the start of the last section, the reason many people buy long-term care insurance is that the risk of needing care is so high, making insurance seem like a good bet. Unfortunately, for exactly the same reason, long-term care insurance itself is unlikely to make it to old age.

Insurance works by pooling risks over a large group of people. Insurers can charge relatively small premiums for each individual because they only need to pay out money to the few who end up filing claims. Individuals gladly replace a large potential loss with a small certain loss: the premium. Meanwhile, insurers make a profit on the spread between what individuals are willing to pay to avoid risk and the actual cost of covering claims. Insurance, therefore, is a good solution in situations where the risk of something happening is low, but its potential costs are catastrophic. In this sort of situation, individuals have a strong motivation to seek coverage, because of the high potential costs, but insurers can set premiums fairly low, since the portion of policyholders who end up having claims is small.

If the potential costs of an unlikely event are minimal, rather than high, individuals have little motivation to seek coverage, and the spread between what policyholders are willing to pay in premiums and what it costs the insurer to cover claims shrinks. Eventually, this spread becomes small enough that it is insufficient to cover the insurer's administrative costs, making the business of providing insurance a losing proposition. This is why there is no insurance for having your dollar bill eaten by a vending machine or breaking a wine glass.

Insurance can also become impractical if the loss being insured against is suffered by too many policyholders. In this case, in order for the insurer to pay out all of the claims, it must charge nearly as much in premiums as policyholders would pay to cover the costs themselves. An insurer attempting to provide coverage for an event that is absolutely certain would, in fact, need to charge premiums higher than the actual cost of the event—or develop an alternate revenue stream—in order to cover its administrative costs. As discussed in Chapter 9, this is actually what happens with whole life insurance, which "insures" against the certain event of eventual death by combining insurance against the rare event of early death with an investment plan designed to eventually accumulate the funds needed to pay out the benefit. The special circumstances of estate planning make this a reasonable option for many people. In most cases, however, people have no reason to pay for a certain or near-certain expense through insurance premiums if they can instead pay for it directly at the same or lower cost. The case against insurance is particularly strong for likely, but not certain, expenses, since, by paying directly, you always have a chance of not paying at all, whereas, by paying through insurance, it is guaranteed that you will have to pay.

Long-term care falls under the category of a likely, but not certain, expense. As the likelihood of needing care approaches certainty, in order to cover claims, insurers need to charge premiums that, when earnings on the premiums (also known as the "time value of money") are considered, are nearly as high as the full costs of care. However, there are still some people who will never need long-term care and could avoid costs altogether by planning to pay themselves.

There are three possible ways for insurers to address the problem of attempting to insure against likely events: try to reduce the rate of claims, raise premium prices, or get out of the business altogether. Long-term care insurers have tried all three approaches. None of these approaches, except the final one, has the potential to resolve the problems faced by the industry, and I expect that, in the end, long-term care insurance will be considered a brief and unsuccessful experiment. A small number of people who bought policies early on and whose insurers have managed to keep premiums stable may benefit from the product. Many more people, however, will likely end up caught in cycles of rising premiums or be forced to deal with the consequences of their insurer's failure or other exit from the business.

## Anna's Advice

### Could long-term care insurance be for you?

As a rule, the math of long-term care insurance does not bode well for the success of these products or of the customers who buy them. But as with most rules, there are possible exceptions.

If you are at particular risk of needing long-term care, especially at an early age, you might consider these policies if insurers do not charge you substantially more than the usual rate for someone your age. People with family histories of early onset Alzheimer's, or who engaged in contact sports that may have led to repeated concussions, are prone to dementia at earlier ages. If your health risks are significant or your ability to save money for future needs is especially low, you might consider LTC coverage despite its costs and limitations.

-AP

## Evaluating Existing Long-Term Care Insurance

There are very few, if any, situations in which it would make sense to purchase a new long-term care policy now. But if you have a policy already, don't assume that you should immediately cancel it. There are a few important questions to consider in deciding whether or not to maintain your existing policy.

*Does your coverage meet your needs?*

Regardless of the economics of the long-term care insurance market, it makes sense to keep a policy only if it will provide the care you actually expect to want or need. You should look closely at the daily (or lifetime) benefit cap, the waiting period, and the types of care that are included and excluded.

*Is your insurer likely to still be in the long-term care business when you need care?*

The most dramatic example of an insurer's exit from the market thus far came in 2008 when Conseco Inc., now CNO Financial Group Inc., not only stopped writing new policies, but also stepped away from more than 140,000 existing policies. The policies were placed into a nonprofit trust, endowed with $175 million to be used to pay claims, and were put under the oversight of the state of Pennsylvania. When it set up the trust, Conseco had already plowed more than $900 million into the policies and estimated that it would have to collect an average of $2,083 in additional premiums from policyholders over a five-year period to stay afloat. While the trust has the advantage of not having to consider future viability, allowing it to use up its initial capital, there is still a strong chance that it will not be able to meet claims. If that happens, the Pennsylvania Life & Health Insurance Guaranty Association may eventually be required to step in. The Guaranty Association, however, only covers policies up to $300,000, meaning that some policyholders may never receive their full benefits.

More recently, MetLife Inc., once one of the biggest players in the long-term care insurance market, with around 600,000 policyholders, stopped writing new policies at the end of 2010. MetLife has said that, unlike Conseco, it will continue to serve existing customers.

As more insurers exit the market, it's important to consider how likely it is that your insurer will continue to service your policy. This depends partially on the financial strength of the insurer and partially on your age. If you are still relatively young, there is probably a longer time left before you will need care, during which your insurer might decide to walk away from its policies, as Conseco did.

*Are your premiums likely to increase?*

Again, this depends partially on your insurer and partially on your age.

If your premiums have historically been steady, and you are relatively close to the time when you expect to potentially need care, premium increases are likely a less important concern. If, on the other hand, your insurer has a history of increasing premiums and there is still a long time before you are likely to need care, you should consider whether the policy would still be worth keeping if your premiums increased 20 or 30 percent. If you know that you would abandon your policy if premiums went up, and you expect that they will, then, assuming that your policy does not include a non-forfeiture provision, you may do better to cancel the policy sooner, rather than later to avoid putting more money into something you most likely will not use.

*How likely are you to need coverage?*

This is the question that, in the aggregate, spurs adverse selection, but it is a reasonable one to ask as an individual. If, based on your personal or family health history, you think you are especially likely to need long-term care, you may do well to keep your policy. This is particularly true if your reason for thinking you are likely to need care is based on something, such as recent health problems, that neither you nor your insurer could have anticipated when your premiums were initially set.

*What are your other options?*

As discussed in the next section, when it comes to paying for long-term care, there are a wide variety of alternatives to long-term care insurance. Whether one of these other options might fit your needs better will depend on your reason for having insurance, your age and your financial situation.

## Alternatives to Long-Term Care Insurance

While insurance may not be the best way for you to fund long-term care needs, that doesn't mean that you don't need to plan in advance. The three basic facts about long-term care that prompt many people to get insurance—that you will probably need it, that it is expensive and that government assistance will not fully cover it—are still true.

In planning for long-term care costs, most people have two connected, but distinct, concerns. The first is financial access to necessary care. The second is having assets left, after care costs, to leave to heirs, or to support a spouse with his or her own long-term care needs.

Long-term care insurance can be appealing because it addresses both of these concerns by making sure that care costs are paid in a way that doesn't diminish the policyholder's assets. In considering other alternatives, however, it can be useful to separate these two concerns. Forgoing insurance and paying for long-term care out-of-pocket may mean spending down assets, but there are other, more direct ways of providing for a spouse or heirs, including through annuities and life insurance. Considering the need to meet care costs and the need to provide for heirs separately also has the important advantage that it protects not only against depleting assets through long-term care costs, but also against any other expenses that might be incurred during retirement. Relying on long-term care insurance, on the other hand, ensures only that you won't spend your assets on long-term care, not that you will actually be able to leave any particular amount to your heirs.

## Paying for Long-Term Care Without Long-Term Care Insurance

There are two main ways of paying for long-term care, aside from with long-term care insurance: strictly out-of-pocket, or self-insurance, and with another sort of insurance mechanism. Which of these is best for you will likely depend on your risk tolerance and the rest of your retirement and estate plans. In either case, however, it is important to plan in advance, since, the longer you wait, the less time you will have to accumulate assets to pay out-of-pocket and the more expensive premiums on insurance products will be.

## Out-of-Pocket

### Savings/Self-Insurance

The most basic, and arguably best, way of paying for long-term care is simply to treat it like any other potential retirement expense and save accordingly. This allows you to invest the money you might need for long-term care until you need it, using the tools and techniques discussed in Chapters 12, 15 and 16, and to use it for other purposes if you don't need care. Saving for and potentially paying for the cost of long-term care yourself benefits either you or your heirs, instead of the insurance company.

**Quick Tip:**
Consider these alternatives to long-term care
insurance:

**1. Paying Out-of-Pocket**

- Savings / Self-Insurance
- Reverse Mortages
- Life Insurance Viatication

**2. Using Other Insurance Mechanisms**

- Long-Term Care Annuities
- Life Insurance Living Benefits Riders
- Continuing Care Centers

In determining how much to set aside, you should consider your personal and family health history. The more likely it is that you will need care, the more money you should set aside for the cost of your future care. You should also consider the type of care and providers you prefer. Unlike with buying an off-the-shelf policy, when you use "self-insurance" you can tailor the benefits to precisely what you want. It's important to consider not just what the care you expect to want costs now, but also what the cost will likely be in the future. You will want to make sure that your assets are invested in such a way that they can keep pace with the rising costs of care. Since you may need care suddenly, for example as the result of a stroke, it's also important to ensure that you have enough liquidity so that you can access resources when you need them.

As you get older, you may need to adjust and fine-tune your assumptions both about your possible needs and about the cost of care. A financial plan, however, gives you the flexibility to do precisely that. Consulting a financial adviser and developing a cash flow plan for long-term care and other retirement expenses might be a good choice if you find the details and necessary assumptions overwhelming. Such an investment in professional help can have outstanding returns, including your peace of mind.

In the event that you spend through all, or nearly all, of your assets on long-term care, you can use Medicaid to pay for care, as discussed earlier in this chapter. This program is intended to be a safety net and can function as such if necessary.

*Reverse Mortgages*

For individuals who aren't able to accumulate enough liquid assets to meet care costs, and who have homes they own and want to stay in, but ultimately don't need to leave to heirs, reverse mortgages can provide an additional source of funding. A reverse mortgage, like a second mortgage or home equity loan, allows individuals to take out loans using their homes as collateral. The loans can generally be structured as lump sums, monthly payments or credit lines. Unlike other mortgages, with reverse mortgages payments are deferred until the homeowner moves or dies, and the amount due is guaranteed to never exceed the value of home. When the homeowner moves or dies, the home is generally sold, with the principal and interest paid back as equity, subtracted from the sale price. Reverse mortgages are generally available only to those 62 years old or older.

Reverse mortgages typically require upfront fees, in addition to interest payments, meaning that borrowers get less than they would by simply selling their homes. However, they can be beneficial to those who need immediate income, for example to pay for in-home long-term care, but want to live in their homes for the remainder of their lives. Most reverse mortgages are Home Equity Conversion Mortgages (HECM), which are insured by the federal government. These tend to be less expensive, usually offer the largest loan amounts, offer more payout options, can be used for any purpose, and have the same loan caps and interest rates in every state. Distributions from HECM loans are also tax-free.

*Life Insurance Viatication*

Another means of accessing additional funds to pay for care is through life insurance viatication. Viatication is when a terminally ill person sells a life insurance policy on his or her life, generally for 50 to 80 percent of face value, to an investor who will collect the benefit. Viatication can be useful as a last-ditch way of paying for end-of-life care, but it requires selling one of the most important tools for inheritance protection.

**Insurance Alternatives**

*Long-Term Care Annuities*

Long-term care annuities may be useful for those who are reluctant to forgo insurance altogether but are concerned about the possibility of paying escalating premiums for something they may never need. Long-term care annuities work by combining an investment and an insurance policy. Like other annuities, they usually can be funded with either a lump sum deposit or structured deposits made over time. Once the annuity is funded, the beneficiary can either take regular distributions for a set period of time or simply allow the money to accumulate interest. What makes long-term care annuities unique is that part of the interest earned is used to fund an insurance policy, allowing the beneficiary to receive an additional monthly benefit if he or she needs long-term care. Generally, the insurance portion of a long-term care annuity will pay out up to two or three times the face value of the annuity, with monthly payments set as a percentage of the total available insurance amount. Because of this insurance element, long-term care annuities suffer from some of the same problems as long-term care insurance. As the likelihood of needing care increases, annuity providers will have to devote an ever larger portion of interest earnings to funding the products' insurance component. However, unlike traditional insurance, an annuity does still provide some benefit to those who never need care. Long-term care annuities also carry a tax benefit, if care is needed, since distributions taken to pay for long-term care, within certain limits, are not subject to income tax.

### Life Insurance Living Benefits Riders

A similar hybrid strategy involves pairing long-term care insurance with life insurance. Living benefits riders, added to life insurance policies, allow policyholders to use part or all of a policy's death benefit to pay for certain expenses while they are still alive. Generally, the living benefits element of the policy can be triggered by a catastrophic or terminal illness at any age or by the need for custodial or nursing home care later in life. The benefits are usually paid on a monthly basis and are treated as a loan, with interest, made out of the death benefit. Like long-term care annuities, life insurance living benefits riders have the advantage that some benefit is received even if care isn't needed. As with life insurance viatication, however, using a living benefits rider involves giving up a means of ensuring money for one's heirs.

### Continuing Care Centers

For individuals who are interesting in moving to a community setting before they need care, Continuing Care Centers can provide an alternative to insurance as a means of guaranteeing costs. Most Continuing Care Centers allow new residents to sign a lifelong contract, guaranteeing a fixed monthly rate regardless of whether they are living in the independent living, assisted living or skilled nursing portion of the facility. Generally, in addition to the monthly fees, these contracts require an entrance fee, which, depending on the facility, might range from $20,000 to $400,000. As with insurance, Continuing Care Centers assess how likely particular individuals are to need skilled care, based on age and health, and adjust rates accordingly. As with long-term care annuities and life insurance living benefits riders, however, Continuing Care Centers provide a benefit—housing suited to one's needs—regardless of whether residents ever need skilled care.

## Inheritance Protection Without Long-Term Care Insurance

As discussed earlier, for many people, the primary concern in financing long-term care is not actually paying for care, but ensuring that enough will be left over after care costs to pass on to heirs. The main advantage of the alternatives to long-term care insurance discussed here—with the exception of Continuing Care Centers—is that they don't deplete assets that could otherwise be passed on to heirs unless care is actually needed. But if care is needed, these methods all work by providing access to assets or insurance proceeds that would otherwise be available to heirs. For some people, whose heirs will not be dependent on the inheritance for support, this may not be an issue. Others, however, may want or need to guarantee that a certain amount will be left to their heirs. If you fall into the second category, it's important to set up strategies for inheritance protection that are not part of your plan for paying for long-term care.

### Life Insurance

With a living benefits rider, life insurance can provide a flexible way of either meeting long-term care costs or passing assets on to heirs. Without the rider, it can be a means of guaranteeing a meaningful inheritance for your heirs. As explained in Chapter 9, a life insurance policy intended as a means of transferring assets to heirs should be set up in an Irrevocable Life Insurance Trust to avoid the possibility of estate tax or Medicaid recapture. Note that life insurance will provide an inheritance even if you spend down your assets on expenses not related to long-term care.

### Annuities

Like a life insurance policy, an annuity can provide for a loved one even if you spend down your assets on expenses unrelated to long-term care. Annuities provide an income stream that can be used for any retirement costs including long-term care, especially if the annuity has a long-term care rider. Couples also have the option of a joint life policy, which pays until the second of two people dies.

## Long-Term Planning for Long-Term Care

Ultimately, the goal of a long-term care financing plan should be to make sure your financial position will be as strong as possible, whether you are part of the 69 percent of people who need long-term care at some point after the age of 65 or part of the 31 percent of people who don't. Your long-term care financing strategy should ensure that you can pay for necessary care, can access assets for other expenses if you don't need care, and are able to leave enough to support your spouse, children or other heirs, whether or not you need care. Unfortunately the likelihood of needing long-term care and the probable costs of that care are both likely to only increase with time. But if you plan in advance, you can be prepared for the long term, whether that includes long-term care or not.

# 11

## SOCIAL SECURITY AND MEDICARE
### Laurie Samay

---

*"People always live for ever when there is an annuity to be paid them."*
*– JANE AUSTEN, SENSE AND SENSIBILITY*

*"You can be young without money, but you can't be old without it."*
*– TENNESSEE WILLIAMS, CAT ON A HOT TIN ROOF*

Social Security is often a retirement plan's first pillar. In truth, it should be less of a pillar and more of a safety net. It is important to understand how Social Security works and how it fits into your overall financial plan, especially because the program faces a gap in its finances, with long-term benefit obligations that are considerably larger than its projected resources. Most people should plan to rely on other sources of income to support themselves in retirement.

## What Is Social Security?

Social Security is a means by which the government aims to support individuals and families, protect the elderly, keep families together and give children the opportunity to grow up healthy and secure. States, towns and individual families once shouldered these responsibilities. However, the Great Depression created overwhelming short-term needs along with great unease about the future. This prompted Congress to pass the Social Security Act of 1935. With this law, the federal government took primary responsibility for these societal needs.

Social Security provides Americans a way to earn retirement, survivors and disability insurance and hospital and medical insurance benefits as they work toward retirement. Social Security also offers programs for prescription drug benefits, extra help with Medicare prescription drug costs, supplemental security income, special veterans benefits, unemployment insurance and public assistance and welfare services.

Survivors and disability insurance benefits are beyond the scope of this chapter. You can visit the Social Security Administration's website at www.ssa.gov for more information on these benefits.

## What Is Medicare?

Although technically a separate program, Medicare is often considered part of Social Security. Medicare aims to provide high quality affordable health care and other related benefits to participants and can be categorized into four distinct parts:

1. Medicare Part A (Hospital Insurance): helps cover inpatient care, skilled nursing facility care, hospice care and home health care.

2. Medicare Part B (Medical Insurance): helps cover services from doctors and other healthcare providers, outpatient care, home health care, durable medical equipment and some preventive services.

3. Medicare Part C (Medicare Advantage): run by Medicare-approved private insurance companies and covers all benefits and services under Part A and B. Often, it also offers all benefits and services under Part D, along with extra benefits and services for an additional cost.

4. Medicare Part D (Medicare Prescription Drug Coverage): run by Medicare-approved private insurance companies and subsidizes the cost of prescription drugs.

## How Are They Funded?

Social Security and Medicare are largely funded by working Americans. The federal government collects taxes from most employers, employees and self-employed individuals in order to fund retirement, survivors, disability insurance and hospital insurance benefits. Beginning in 2013, the Affordable Care Act expanded Medicare taxes to apply to non-wage income from high earners.

Many workers mistakenly believe that the money withheld from their paychecks for Social Security will be waiting for them when they reach retirement. In reality, Social Security's old-age trust fund does not work that way. Current wage earners actually fund the benefits of current retirees under the assumption that they, in turn, will receive benefits paid for by the next generation of contributors.

Other benefits are funded from different sources. For instance, the U.S. government and certain states fund Social Security's supplemental security income, while the U.S. government, certain states and beneficiaries (via monthly premiums) fund Medicare's prescription drug benefits.

## Eligibility

You become eligible for Social Security after serving 10 years in the workforce. This is the minimum amount of time it takes to earn 40 credits, which you accrue for every $1,200 you earn each year, for up to four credits per year. Regardless of when you become eligible, you must wait until you are at least 62 years old to begin receiving benefits. You must also be fully insured to do so.

Meanwhile, you become eligible for Medicare at age 65. However, people under 65 with certain disabilities are also eligible, as well as anyone suffering from end-stage renal disease.

Retirees are able to receive both Social Security and Medicare benefits, as well as prescription drug benefits.

## Retirement Age

Full retirement age, also known as normal retirement age, is the age at which you become eligible to receive full Social Security benefits. It varies based on your year of birth:

## Retirement Age (By Birth)

| Year of Birth | Full Retirement Age |
| --- | --- |
| 1937 or earlier | 65 |
| 1938 | 65 and 2 months |
| 1939 | 65 and 4 months |
| 1940 | 65 and 6 months |
| 1941 | 65 and 8 months |
| 1942 | 65 and 10 months |
| 1943-1954 | 66 |
| 1955 | 66 and 2 months |
| 1956 | 66 and 4 months |
| 1957 | 66 and 6 months |
| 1958 | 66 and 8 months |
| 1959 | 66 and 10 months |
| 1960 or later | 67 |

Source: Adapted from the Social Security Administration

Chart 1

## When to Start Taking Benefits

You can elect to take your Social Security benefits early, or at your full retirement age, or even later. Your decision should be based on your life expectancy, cash needs, spouse, working status and potential deductions. Deferring the benefit start date beyond your full retirement age increases your benefits, up until age 70.

Note that it is never optimal to postpone benefits past age 70, as this is the age in which you can begin receiving your largest gross benefit.

### Life Expectancy

In theory, you should expect to receive the same total Social Security benefits over your lifetime regardless of which option you choose, provided you have an average life expectancy.

If you expect to live longer than the average life expectancy due to family history or other reasons, you are probably better off postponing collecting Social Security retirement benefits (but not beyond age 70) if you can afford to wait. However, if illness or family history indicates you may have a shorter life expectancy than average, it may be in your best interest to begin collecting retirement benefits even before you reach full retirement age.

The Social Security Administration offers calculators you can use to estimate your expected benefits. Some third-party services allow you to calculate your break-even age—the minimum age you need to live to have made waiting a given number of years worthwhile. These estimates are not precisely accurate, as they require you to make certain assumptions about taxes and the income you might have generated from foregone benefits while you wait. However, they are a good starting point to help you with your decision.

**Continued Earned Income**

If you retire early, the monthly benefit amounts will be subject to a penalty should you earn income (through work alone, not investments) in excess of the annual earnings limit. For example, in 2014 the annual earnings limit was $15,480 for those who had not attained normal retirement age. A limit of $41,400 applied to beneficiaries who reached the normal retirement age (66) during the year, but the limit only applied in the months before the beneficiary turned 66. Individuals who were 66 or older during all of 2014 had no earnings limit. Beneficiaries who earned more than the applicable limit saw their benefits reduced. The full benefit rate is reduced by a certain percentage for each month you were under retirement age when the benefit began. That said, you will receive benefits for a longer period of time. If you retire late, the monthly benefit amounts will be larger, but received over a shorter period of time.

**Cash Needs**

If you cannot afford to sustain yourself on a reduced Social Security benefit, it is unwise to retire before reaching full retirement age. On the other hand, if you have sufficient resources to supplement a reduced Social Security benefit via investments, retirement accounts and other sources of income, you have the luxury of retiring earlier should you desire to do so.

**Your Spouse**

When considering when to take your Social Security benefits, you also must factor in your spouse's age, health and income. This is because lower-earning spouses are eligible to take the greater of their own earned benefits or 50 percent of the higher-earning spouse's benefits, either of which are subject to the early-benefit reduction should the lower-earning spouse retire before reaching full retirement age.

There are some strategies available to take advantage of spousal income discrepancies. The first is known as the 62/70 split. With the split, the lower-earning spouse files for Social Security benefits at age 62 and receives benefits based on his or her own earnings records less the early election reduction. The higher earner then files at his or her full retirement age, but suspends his or her benefits until age 70. This action increases the lower-earning spouse's benefit to 50 percent of the higher earner's benefits less the early election reduction, but still allows the higher-earning spouse to continue to accrue delayed retirement credits.

Another strategy focuses on hedging for survivor benefits. With this strategy, the higher-earning spouse claims his or her benefits at full retirement age based on the lower-earning spouse's earnings record. At age 70, that person then switches to his or her own higher benefit. In doing so, the lower-earning spouse's survivor benefit, which is equal to 100 percent of the deceased spouse's benefit, will be higher if the higher-earning spouse dies first, and the higher-earning spouse can continue to generate income until age 70. If the higher-earning spouse does not die before age 70, the lower earner can still switch to a spousal benefit, which would be equal to the higher earner's benefit at full retirement age less the early retirement reduction.

## How to Start Receiving Benefits

To begin receiving benefits, you must apply online, by phone or by visiting your local Social Security office. You must be at least 61 years and 9 months old to apply, and you should apply no more than four months before you would like to begin receiving benefits. Benefits are paid the month after they are due.

With your application, you will likely need to submit the following documents, unless they have already been submitted for an earlier Medicare or Social Security claim (such as for disability or Supplemental Security Income):

- Your Social Security card (or a record of your number)

- Your original birth certificate or other proof of birth date

- Proof of U.S. citizenship or lawful alien status

- A copy of your U.S. military service paper(s) if you served before 1968

- A copy of your W-2 form(s) and any self-employment tax returns for the previous year.

Note that while the last two documents can be photocopies, the first two documents should be original versions. The Social Security Administration will return all original documentation after processing your application.

If you would like your benefits to be directly deposited in your bank account, you will also need to supply your bank information.

If you have not started to receive Social Security benefits and have no plans to retire but would like to receive Medicare benefits, you should still submit a Medicare application three months before your 65th birthday.

## International Issues for Social Security

Obtaining benefits while living abroad, while more complex, is still possible under Social Security. "Abroad" for Social Security purposes is defined as any region other than the 50 states, the District of Columbia and any U.S. territories, which include Puerto Rico, the U.S. Virgin Islands, Guam, the Northern Mariana Islands and American Samoa. "Living" for Social Security purposes is defined as being outside of the aforementioned regions for at least 30 consecutive days, or not having returned to the aforementioned regions for at least 30 consecutive days.

### U.S. Citizens

U.S. citizens are generally able to receive payments outside the United States if eligible for them. However, there are certain restrictions; Social Security is restricted from sending payments to Azerbaijan, Belarus, Georgia, Kazakhstan, Kyrgyzstan, Moldova, Tajikistan, Turkmenistan, Ukraine, Uzbekistan and Vietnam. An exception can be made if the U.S. citizen agrees to conditions of payment, including appearing at the U.S. Embassy each month to receive benefits. The U.S. Treasury further prohibits payments to those in Cuba or North Korea. Regardless, unpaid benefits for U.S. citizens who do not qualify for an exception are payable once the U.S. citizen leaves the restricted country.

### Non-U.S. Citizens

Citizens of the following countries will continue to receive payments if eligible for them, regardless of time spent outside the United States: Austria, Belgium, Canada, Chile, the Czech Republic, Finland, France, Germany, Greece, Ireland, Israel, Italy, Japan, South Korea, Luxembourg, the Netherlands, Norway, Poland, Portugal, Spain, Sweden, Switzerland and the United Kingdom.

## Quick Notes:

Citizens of the following countries will continue to receive payments if eligible for them, regardless of time spent outside the United States.

**Asia**
- Japan, South Korea

**Middle East, North Africa and Greater Arabia**
- Israel

**Europe**
- Austria, Belgium, the Czech Republic, Finland, France, Germany, Greece, Ireland, Italy, Luxembourg, the Netherlands, Norway, Portugal, Spain, Sweden, Switzerland, the United Kingdom

**North America**
- Canada

**Central America and the Caribbean**
- **None**

**South America**
- Chile

**Sub-Saharan Africa**
- **None**

**Australia and Oceania**
- **None**

Citizens of the following countries are able to receive payments if eligible for them, regardless of time spent outside the United States, excluding dependent and survivor benefits: Albania, Antigua and Barbuda, Argentina, the Bahamas, Barbados, Belize, Bolivia, Bosnia-Herzegovina, Bulgaria, Brazil, Burkina Faso, Colombia, Costa Rica, Ivory Coast, Croatia, Cyprus, Dominica, the Dominican Republic, Ecuador, El Salvador, Gabon, Grenada, Guatemala, Guyana, Hungary, Iceland, Jamaica, Jordan, Latvia, Liechtenstein, Lithuania, Macedonia, Malta, the Marshall Islands, Mexico, the Federal States of Micronesia, Monaco, Montenegro, Nicaragua, Palau, Panama, Peru, the Philippines, Romania, St. Kitts and Nevis, St. Lucia, St. Vincent and the Grenadines, Samoa, Slovenia, San Marino, Serbia, Slovakia, Trinidad-Tobago, Turkey, Uruguay and Venezuela.

**Quick Notes:**
Citizens of the following countries will continue to receive payments if eligible for them, regardless of time spent outside the United States, excluding dependent and suvivor benefits.

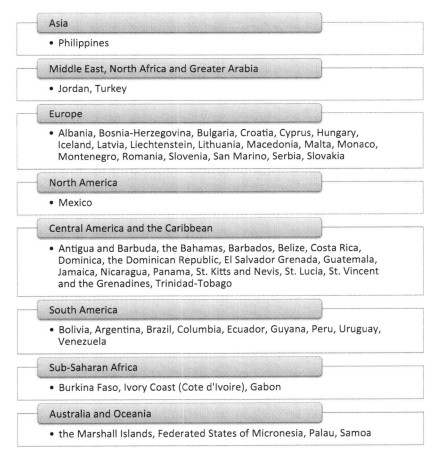

**Asia**

- Philippines

**Middle East, North Africa and Greater Arabia**

- Jordan, Turkey

**Europe**

- Albania, Bosnia-Herzegovina, Bulgaria, Croatia, Cyprus, Hungary, Iceland, Latvia, Liechtenstein, Lithuania, Macedonia, Malta, Monaco, Montenegro, Romania, Slovenia, San Marino, Serbia, Slovakia

**North America**

- Mexico

**Central America and the Caribbean**

- Antigua and Barbuda, the Bahamas, Barbados, Belize, Costa Rica, Dominica, the Dominican Republic, El Salvador Grenada, Guatemala, Jamaica, Nicaragua, Panama, St. Kitts and Nevis, St. Lucia, St. Vincent and the Grenadines, Trinidad-Tobago

**South America**

- Bolivia, Argentina, Brazil, Columbia, Ecuador, Guyana, Peru, Uruguay, Venezuela

**Sub-Saharan Africa**

- Burkina Faso, Ivory Coast (Cote d'Ivoire), Gabon

**Australia and Oceania**

- the Marshall Islands, Federated States of Micronesia, Palau, Samoa

In order for dependent and survivor beneficiaries from these countries to receive payments while abroad, they must have lived in the United States for at least five years, and, during those five years, the family relationship on which the benefits are based must have existed. Children who are beneficiaries can meet this residency requirement on their own or if the worker and other parent (if any) meets it, with the exception of children who have been adopted outside the United States. The residency requirement does not apply to dependent and survivor beneficiaries if they were eligible for benefits before January 1, 1985, were entitled on the record of a worker who died while in the U.S. military service or as a result of a service-related disease or injury or are residents of a country with which the United States has a social security agreement. These countries include: Australia, Austria, Belgium, Canada, Chile, the Czech Republic, Denmark, Finland, France, Germany, Greece, Ireland, Italy, Japan, South Korea, Luxembourg, the Netherlands, Norway, Poland, Portugal, Spain, Sweden, Switzerland and the United Kingdom.

Non-U.S. citizens are ineligible to receive payments due during their time spent in Cuba and North Korea.

Payments to citizens of countries that have not yet appeared in this chapter will stop after the beneficiary has been outside the United States for six full months, with the following exceptions:

• You were eligible for monthly Social Security benefits for December 1956 or are in the active military or naval service of the United States;

• The worker on whose record your benefits are based had railroad work treated as covered employment by the Social Security program or died while in the U.S. military service or as a result of a service-related disability and was not dishonorably charged;

• You are a resident of a country with which the United States has a social security agreement. Note that dependent and survivor beneficiaries are able to receive benefits while residing in Austria, Belgium, Germany, Sweden or Switzerland if:
  » The worker is (or was at the time of death) a U.S. citizen or citizen of your country of residence; or
  » You are a citizen of one of the following countries, and the worker on whose record your benefits are based lived in the United States for at least 10 years and earned at least 40 credits under the U.S. Social Security system: Afghanistan, Australia, Bangladesh, Bhutan, Botswana, Burma, Burundi, Cameroon, Cape Verde, Central African Republic, Chad, China, the Republic of Congo, Ethiopia, Fiji, Gambia, Ghana, Haiti, Honduras, India, Indonesia, Kenya, Laos, Lebanon, Lesotho, Liberia, Madagascar, Malawi, Malaysia, Mali, Mauritania, Mauritius, Morocco, Nepal, Nigeria, Pakistan, Senegal, Sierra Leone, Singapore, the Solomon Islands, Somalia, South Africa, Sri Lanka, Sudan, Swaziland, Taiwan, Tanzania, Thailand, Togo, Tonga, Tunisia, Uganda and Yemen.

As previously mentioned, payments will resume after you return to the United States for a whole calendar month.

Note that the lists of countries in this chapter may have changed since publication. You can receive the latest information by visiting the Social Security Administration's website or by contacting your nearest Social Security office, U.S. Embassy or consulate.

## How to Protect Your Benefits

To keep track of beneficiaries living abroad and their eligibility for the program, the Social Security Administration will periodically send out a questionnaire. To best protect your rights, fill out and return the questionnaire as soon as possible. In addition, it is important to notify the Social Security Administration of any changes that could affect your payments in the interim, such as a change of address, working status outside of the United States, a return to the work force, improvement in your disability, marriage, divorce or annulment, adoption of a child, end of a child's dependency, a child nearing age 18 becoming full-time student or disabled, death, inability to manage funds, deportation or removal from the United States, changes in parental circumstances and eligibility for a pension from work not covered by Social Security. Failure to do so could result in loss of payments, or even fines or imprisonment. When contacting your local office, include your name, the subject of the report, the date that the subject matter occurred and your claim number.

## Direct Deposit

Residents of the United States were required to enroll in electronic payments of Social Security benefits by March 1, 2013. If they did not, the U.S. Department of Treasury began automatically sending your benefits via the Direct Express® card program, which provides a debit card with access to your benefits. One of the incidental benefits of this requirement is that it allows citizens to avoid check cashing and currency conversion fees while living abroad.

Direct deposit is available in the following countries: Anguilla, Antigua and Barbuda, Australia, Austria, the Bahamas, Barbados, Belgium, the British Virgin Islands, Canada, the Cayman Islands, Cyprus, Denmark, the Dominican Republic, Estonia, Finland, France, Germany, Greece, Grenada, Haiti, Hong Kong, Hungary, India, Ireland, Israel, Italy, Jamaica, Japan, Malta, Mexico, the Netherlands, Netherlands Antilles, New Zealand, Norway, Panama, Poland, Portugal, St. Kitts and Nevis, St. Lucia, St. Vincent and the Grenadines, South Africa, Spain, Sweden, Switzerland, Trinidad-Tobago and the United Kingdom.

## Lost or Stolen Checks

For those who are living abroad, but are not enrolled in direct deposit, payments are sent in check form. You should expect your checks to take longer to arrive than in the United States, and for delivery time to vary from country to country and even from month to month. If you have waited a reasonable amount of time and have not yet received your check, it may be lost or stolen. In this case, you should write to the Social Security Administration or contact the nearest U.S. Embassy or consulate. They will replace your check as soon as possible.

## Taxation

Up to 85 percent of U.S. citizen and resident Social Security benefits is subject to federal income tax and is reportable on Form 1040.

For non-U.S. citizens and residents, federal income tax of 30 percent will be withheld from 85 percent of the benefit amount, unless they reside in countries that have tax treaties with the United States that do not allow the taxation of U.S. Social Security benefits. These countries include Canada, Egypt, Germany, Ireland, Israel, Italy, Japan, Romania and the United Kingdom. In addition, Switzerland residents (who are not U.S. citizens) are taxed at a lower rate of 15 percent. Finally, nationals and residents of India are entirely exempt from this tax to the extent that their benefits are based on U.S. federal, state or local employment.

Some foreign governments may tax U.S. Social Security benefits as well. U.S. residents planning to live abroad can contact that country's embassy in Washington, D.C. for more information.

Note that Social Security benefits are calculated in U.S. dollars, and that no adjustments are made for international exchange rates.

## Medicare

In general, Medicare does not cover health services provided outside the United States. The hospital insurance portion of Medicare is available to you if you return to the United States. Unlike for medical insurance, no monthly premium is withheld from your benefits for this protection.

If you plan on living abroad for an extended period of time, you should consider canceling your medical insurance with Medicare if you have already signed up or delaying enrollment until you return to the United States to avoid paying premiums while abroad. This decision is not without consequence. If you cancel your coverage, you will continue to receive one more month of insurance (and associated premiums). If you delay signing up, your premiums will be 10 percent higher for every year you could have been enrolled, but were not.

## The Future of Social Security and Medicare

Now that you understand how Social Security and Medicare work, it is important to consider the future of the programs, and how best to incorporate them into your retirement plans.

First, consider the nature of Social Security. How sure can you be of receiving your full benefits? While the program is sometimes referred to as a sure thing, a closer look suggests otherwise.

---

## Laurie's Advice

**What steps should I take to reduce my future dependence on Social Security?**

For starters, you can ramp up your savings, especially in tax-advantaged retirement accounts like IRAs and 401(k)s. At age 55, you are able to contribute an extra $1,000 a year to an IRA and an extra $5,500 a year to a 401(k). Also, you can consider delaying your planned retirement date. The delay allows you to postpone withdrawals from your retirement accounts while giving your savings more time to grow. Finally, you can reduce your expenses by downsizing and rethinking your standard of living in retirement.

-LS

---

There are political differences of opinions over the program's nature. Most Democrats see Social Security as a social contract in which each generation assumes the responsibility of supporting the generation that preceded them. Republicans tend to see the program as a Ponzi scheme – an empty promise to most seniors and an obligation to younger generations that has become increasingly unfair. This division springs, in part, from the program's past.

Social Security was never intended to fund a full retirement for workers seeking to maintain their standard of living. Instead, it was designed as a safety net, keeping those who either earned too little to save effectively for retirement or whose savings were lost due to misfortune of one kind or another, and who did not have family willing or able to support them, from poverty in retirement. The whole idea of retirement as we know it is a fairly modern concept. In most countries, it was unknown prior to the late 19th or early 20th centuries.

Nor did the original program anticipate medical advances that would increase the number of Americans living past age 65. When the Social Security Act was passed in the mid-1930s, life expectancy was only 58 years for men and 62 years for women, though these numbers skew low due to the high infant mortality rate at the time. According to the Social Security Administration, over the 20th century, the percentage of the population surviving from age 21 to 65 has risen about 20 percent. Adults today who reach age 65 have a life expectancy, on average, five years greater than that of a 65 year old when the program began.

The baby boomers, rapidly approaching retirement, will soon be supported by a younger generation of workers, not their own past contributions. The theory is that today's young workers will support the boomers through their retirement and, in turn, will be supported by the generations that follow. Demographically, there are simply fewer of these younger workers, and Social Security's Board of Trustees has reported growing program costs over the last few years. If Congress takes no action, the Board projects that the total Social Security retirement trust fund reserves will be depleted by 2033, leaving 23 percent of scheduled benefits unfunded. This represents the shortest period to trust fund "exhaustion" since 1983, when Congress was forced to cut benefits, raise taxes and provide an estimated $168 billion in order to sustain the program. In addition, today's younger workers are having children later, and having fewer of them, meaning the problem will only grow more acute over time.

Medicare is in worse fiscal shape than Social Security. The Medicare Hospital Insurance Trust Fund is projected to be depleted in 2030. It is likely that the Affordable Care Act will impact Medicare's long-term fiscal health, but in ways that have yet to be seen. Medicare, however, offers a greater number of policy options to legislators if they choose to take action, which gives it a small advantage over Social Security.

Complicating matters is the rising cost of health insurance and medical care. Many expect that, contrary to its name, the Affordable Care Act will actually drive prices higher over the next few years; consequently, Medicare may pay for fewer procedures or a lower standard of care. Many retirees choose to obtain supplemental insurance, which can dovetail with Medicare to cover out-of-pocket expenses not covered by Medicare.

It is certainly possible that Congress will take action to reform or restructure Social Security and Medicare before their reserves are completely spent. Former President George W. Bush wanted to allow workers to divert part of their Social Security taxes into private accounts, allowing them some measure of control over their own future benefits. During his first term, President Barack Obama cut workers' payroll taxes in order to stimulate the economy without cutting benefits, illustrating the program's "pay-as-you-go" nature while aggravating its funding problems. Given that guaranteed pensions are steadily disappearing in the private sector and face a funding crisis in the public sector, politicians will eventually be forced to grapple with an aging population with few other options.

For now, however, we cannot know what Congress will do or when. This is not to say you will not get your full Social Security benefit, or any benefit at all. It is, however, prudent to be aware of the program's limitations and challenges going forward. The less you must rely on Social Security for retirement planning, the better.

# 12

## RETIREMENT PLANS
### Paul Jacobs, CFP®, EA

---

We all look forward to retirement. Whether you choose to spend your retirement traveling, learning new things, enjoying time with family or all of the above, it is truly a great opportunity to do all of the things that you didn't have time to do during your working life. But while most people have plans for what they'd like to do when they have retired, they do not all have retirement plans.

The purpose of this chapter is to cover issues worth considering when putting together a retirement plan. While not every piece of information in this chapter may apply to you, there are so many options and ways to save for retirement that it's likely something here can help improve your individual retirement plan.

The first question that anyone planning their retirement should ask is how much they need to save. The calculations involved with your retirement plan should not be something you worked out on the back of a napkin; they can be quite complicated. If you are not sure how to proceed, you may want to meet with a financial adviser who can ask you the right questions and help you come up with a solid long-term plan. Broadly speaking, a rule of thumb is that you should be able to maintain your lifestyle in retirement on about 60 to 80 percent of your annual preretirement income. Of course, rules of thumb do not apply to everyone equally. Some retirees find that their spending actually increases in retirement, while others may find their spending drops dramatically. If you start saving at age 25, you should save at least 10 percent of your gross (pre-tax) income to achieve the necessary level of savings. If you start saving later in life, the percentage of income you'll need to save increases dramatically.

## Types of Plans

Not all methods of saving are the same, of course. We are long past the time where any but the most irresponsible saver would stash his savings in his mattress and call it a day. Many employers offer their employees benefits in the form of tax-favored retirement accounts, and employees can choose how they use these plans. Given the many vehicles available for retirement saving, one of the first and most important steps in planning for retirement is to consider the different options available to you in conjunction with your own needs and goals.

### Qualified and Nonqualified Plans

Qualified plans receive income tax benefits that are not available to nonqualified plans. For example, employees typically aren't taxed on any contributions their employer makes in the current year, and earnings on plan investments are not immediately taxable, either. Funds are generally taxed only when they are withdrawn as distributions. Some plans permit loans, which are not considered distributions for tax purposes. Qualified plans are also protected from creditors by federal law. In exchange for favorable tax treatment, qualified plans must meet a variety of federal requirements.

Tax deferral is not always a good thing. If you expect your tax rate to be higher in the future, it may not be advantageous for you. Also, because qualified plans may require employers to deal with complex compliance issues, some employers choose not to offer them.

Nonqualified plans can supplement qualified plans or substitute for them. In many cases, they still allow you to defer taxes to some degree. They can also be attractive to top-level executives, since, unlike most qualified plans, such plans do not necessarily have to be offered company-wide.

### Defined Benefit and Defined Contribution Plans

A helpful way to differentiate between plans is by whether the plan has a defined benefit or defined contribution. In defined benefit plans, such as traditional pensions, the plan provides a specified benefit to the employee. The annual funding amount will vary, and is greater for older employees in order for the plan to be fully funded by the time the worker retires.

Defined benefit plans are often attractive to employees because they guarantee money at retirement. A defined benefit plan also removes the stress of making the wrong investment decision, because plan participants do not direct their own accounts. These plans are attractive to professionals and closely-held business owners, among others, who may be the elder employees in the plan. A defined benefit plan allows a significant benefit to be funded in a relatively short space of time.

Defined benefit plans feature commingled accounts, a clearly-identified benefit for which the employer is responsible, and a benefit limit. The investment risk is entirely borne by the employer.

However, defined benefit plans may be unattractive if you expect to be in a higher tax bracket when you retire. You also may prefer to direct your own investments. For savvy investors, these plans can mean foregoing the opportunity for greater returns. It is also difficult or impossible to access your retirement funds prior to a defined retirement age.

In today's world, defined benefit plans are becoming a relic from a time when people stayed with the same employer for many years. Employees who leave before retiring may receive relatively little benefit. Many employers also tend to shy away from these sorts of plans today, because it is the employer who bears the market risk, as well as the expense of annual actuarial work.

In contrast, with a defined contribution plan the employer establishes and maintains individual accounts for each plan participant. There is no guarantee of how much the participant will ultimately receive – only what contribution the employer will make. In this way, the employee bears the investment risk, rather than the employer. There is generally a contribution limit, for both employees and employers, and "in-service" withdrawals, meaning withdrawals while the employee still works for the employer, are allowed if the plan document permits them.

401(k)s are the most common defined contribution plan, and offer employees several benefits. Employees have more investment options and more control than they would have in a defined benefit plan. With careful choices, this can lead to better returns over time. The funds in the plan are often portable and easy to transfer to an IRA or other retirement account should the participant change jobs or face altered life circumstances. And, if needed, many 401(k)s allow you to make early withdrawals or to borrow funds. While not ideal, because there may be fees or penalties involved, such withdrawals can allow flexibility that a defined benefit plan cannot.

It's important to keep an eye on fees, which can eat up contributions and returns if left unchecked. Not all 401(k)s are created equal; many do not offer a wide selection of investing options, which can make diversification more difficult. Employers can also choose to reduce the size of their matching contributions, which means employees rely more and more on their own contributions to keep their retirements on track. And, of course, unlike defined benefit plans, defined contribution plans such as 401(k)s do not guarantee money at retirement. Since only the contributions are guaranteed, troubled market conditions or poor investment choices can lead to dramatic loss of value in a 401(k).

Two other common defined contribution plans are money purchase plans and profit-sharing plans. Money purchase plans require the employer to adhere to a fixed contribution requirement each year, regardless of the company's profits, while profit-sharing plans allow employers to decide how much to contribute each year or even skip annual contributions entirely. Contributions are calculated as a percentage of compensation. With these plans, an employer can choose to have contributions vest over a period of time, which can encourage employee retention. There are rules specific to how vesting can be handled, depending on whether the vesting is graded or happens all at once. Maintaining these plans can be complex, including requirements such as an annual tax filing.

SEP IRAs, like profit-sharing plans, allow employers to contribute a different amount each year, but unlike profit-sharing plans, they vest immediately. They are simpler for an employer to maintain (no tax filing is required), but are not as supportive of employee retention because contributions vest right away.

Other defined contribution plans include: stock bonus plans and ESOPs, both of which involve employees receiving company stock instead of cash; savings/thrift plans, which are similar to 401(k)s for U.S. government employees; 403(b) plans, which are similar to 401(k) plans but are adopted only by certain tax-exempt organizations and public schools; and 457 plans, which are similar to 401(k) plans but are adopted by state and local public employers and certain nonprofits.

## Employer Deferred Compensation

In employer deferred compensation plans, employees can voluntarily reduce their taxable wages by making payroll deductions, in order to invest a percentage of their gross pay in the plan. This sort of plan can be either qualified or nonqualified.

The important concept to understand with these plans is that they avoid "constructive receipt." Taxes are deferred on contributions because the plan participant is not considered to have ever received any funds. As long as your contributions remain in the plan, they may remain at risk in the event your company experiences financial difficulties. For example, if you contribute to a nonqualified deferred compensation plan and your employer goes bankrupt, your money could be completely gone. You should make sure you are very comfortable with the financial position of your employer before entering one of these plans.

## Traditional and Roth IRAs

Traditional Individual Retirement Accounts (IRAs) can be attractive because they allow you to deduct your contributions from your current taxable income. Similar to the defined contribution plans discussed above, assets held in a traditional IRA are not subject to federal income tax until they are withdrawn. Besides the tax benefits, IRAs are also useful because they allow those who are 50 or older to make additional "catch-up" contributions.

However, unless you have a pressing need, such as medical expenses or higher education expenses, withdrawing funds before you reach age 59½ from a traditional IRA triggers a 10 percent penalty. Also, individuals over age 70½ cannot establish or contribute to a traditional IRA. Once an individual reaches that age, annual withdrawals are required, starting April 1 of the year following the year the saver turns 70½. Failure to take an annual required distribution can lead to a 50% penalty tax on the required distribution amount.

While anyone under age 70½ who has earned income or received alimony can make a traditional IRA contribution, the contribution may not be deductible if the saver's income exceeds a certain limit and his or her employer offered a workplace retirement plan. Nondeductible traditional IRA contributions can help in certain situations, but are generally more trouble than they are worth. Don't make nondeductible contributions unless you are sure there is a good reason to do so.

Roth IRAs share certain characteristics with traditional IRAs. However, they are distinct in ways that make it smart to maximize your contributions to them, especially if you are a younger investor.

First, while Roth IRA contributions are nondeductible, a distribution from a Roth IRA is generally not includable in the Roth IRA owner's gross income. This allows your money to grow tax-free, as opposed to traditional IRAs, which grow tax-deferred. The minimum annual distribution rules do not apply to Roth IRAs as long as the owner is alive. Contributions can be made after age 70½ as well, as long as the owner earns compensation or receives alimony.

Also, contributions (though not earnings) can be withdrawn tax-free and penalty-free at any time. Investment earnings can only be withdrawn after the Roth IRA has existed for at least five years, and one of the following conditions is met: the owner has reached age 59½; the owner is disabled; the owner has died; or the owner is withdrawing up to $10,000 in order to purchase his or her first home.

Funds in a traditional IRA can be converted to a Roth IRA, regardless of how high your income is. If you choose to convert, you must pay taxes at the time the rollover occurs, much as if you took a distribution from your traditional IRA.

Why is conversion attractive? Mainly for the same reasons a Roth IRA is useful in the first place. If you can convert and pay tax now at a lower rate than you expect to face in the future, that's a winning proposition. Even if you expect your tax rate to stay the same, a conversion can still be beneficial, because it reduces the government's cut on your investment gains going forward.

## Quick Notes:
## A few characteristics of traditional and Roth IRA accounts you should know about

| Traditional IRA | Roth IRA |
|---|---|
| • Allows you to deduct your contributions from your current taxable income.<br><br>• Assets held are not subject to federal income tax until they are withdrawn.<br><br>• Unless you have a pressing need, such as medical expenses or higher education expenses, withdrawing funds before you reach age 59½ from a traditional IRA triggers a 10 percent penalty. | • Contributions are nondeductible, however a distribution from a Roth IRA is generally not includable in the Roth IRA owner's gross income.<br><br>• Minimum annual distribution rules do not apply to Roth IRAs as long as the owner is alive.<br><br>• Contributions (though not earnings) can be withdrawn tax-free and penalty-free at any time. |

If you are interested in converting, it's also important to know that conversions are much more attractive if you have funds outside of your IRA that you can use to pay the associated tax. Also, if a conversion pushes you into a higher tax bracket than usual, you may be better off converting your IRA over a period of years.

The best part of conversion is that you have the ability to reverse the switch until the tax deadline for the year of conversion. For example, if you converted $100,000, and your investments declined in value to $90,000, you could "recharacterize" the conversion and then re-convert the assets the following year. So instead of paying tax on $100,000 in year 1, you could pay tax on $90,000 in year 2. Because of this, we view converting as a "heads I win, tails I break even" proposition.

## Plan Rules and Regulations

Since your retirement plan is unique, the outline above is designed to give you a broad overview of the variety of plans available. What, then, are particular rules you should consider when understanding your specific plan?

### Rules for Qualified Plans and IRAs

Qualified plans, by their nature, are subject to stricter federal regulation than nonqualified plans. There are several fundamental concepts plan participants should make sure they remember when dealing with qualified plans or IRAs.

For these plans, one of the first things you will want to understand are the rules regarding required minimum distributions (RMDs). The IRS defines an RMD as the minimum amount that a retirement plan account owner must withdraw annually, starting the year he or she turns 70½ years old or the year he or she retires, whichever is later. (Note that, in the case of IRAs, it must be the former, regardless of whether the account owner has retired.) If the owner fails to take the proper RMDs, stiff penalties can result.

The amount that comprises an RMD is calculated using tables published by the IRS. If you only have multiple traditional IRAs, you can take just one distribution for the total RMD if you prefer; the same holds true if you have multiple 403(b)s. However, RMDs cannot be combined for other accounts, such as 401(k)s. If you have different types of accounts (such as a 401(k) and a traditional IRA), you must take separate RMDs for each. RMDs may not be rolled over into another tax deferred account.

The rules regarding RMDs apply to all employer-sponsored plans, including profit-sharing plans and 401(k) plans. The rules also apply to traditional IRAs, but not to Roth IRAs as long as the account owner is living.

Another term you will want to understand is the required beginning date. Qualified plans cannot require more than one year of service for eligibility, and any employee who is 21 years old or older must be allowed to enter the plan once he or she has met the plan's required waiting period. (This is known as the "21-and-1 Rule.") The waiting period may be increased to two years if the plan provides immediate and total vesting of employer contributions, unless the plan is a 401(k). Also, an employer cannot make an employee wait more than six months to enter the plan once the employee is eligible, which means qualified plans must have at least two entrance dates annually.

It is also important to understand the rules regarding premature distributions. In qualified plans, the law imposes a 10 percent tax penalty on funds withdrawn before age 59½, except under specific circumstances. These circumstances include the following:

- Distributions made to your beneficiary or estate after your death.

- Distributions made because you are totally and permanently disabled.

- Distributions made as part of a series of substantially equal periodic payments over your life expectancy, or the life expectancies of you and your designated beneficiary. If these distributions are from a qualified plan other than an IRA, you must separate from service with the employer in question before the payments begin.

- Distributions up to the amount of your deductible medical expenses, regardless of whether you claim itemized deductions.

- Distributions made due to an IRS levy of the plan under Internal Revenue Code Section 6331.

- Distributions to qualified reservists.

For qualified plans, but not for IRAs, the following premature distributions can also be taken without triggering the penalty tax:

- Distributions made to you after you separate from service with your employer if the separation occurs in or after the year you reach age 55, or distributions made from a qualified governmental defined benefit plan if you are a qualified public safety employee (at the state or local government level) who separated from service on or after you reached age 50.

- Distributions made to an alternate payee under a qualified domestic relations order.

- Distributions of dividends from employee stock ownership plans.

Note, however, that some plans will not let participants withdraw funds early at all.

Plan participants 50 years old and over may make "catch-up" contributions to certain qualified plans, including 401(k)s and 403(b)s. The IRS sets a dollar limit on such contributions. Participants may also make catch-up contributions to an IRA, though the IRS sets a separate contribution limit for these.

## Distribution Options

When you retire, some plans give you options as to how you want to receive your distributions. The available options will mainly depend on the sort of plan and whether the employer has narrowed the plan participants' choices.

It's important to be aware of the tax rules that broadly affect tax-free and early withdrawals. Tax-free withdrawals are generally withdrawals of money that has already been taxed at the time you or you or your employer contributed it. For example, Roth IRA contributions are not taxed again when you withdraw them – unless you withdraw earnings early, which can often trigger a tax penalty (except under circumstances described previously in this chapter).

Also, defined benefit plans can make in-service distributions to participants age 62 or older who have not yet retired or otherwise left the employer. Such plans must also provide spousal benefits. For unmarried participants, the automatic form of benefit is usually a single-life annuity. Money purchase plans, target benefit plans, and 403(b) plans are treated like pensions as far as annuity rules are concerned, despite being defined contribution plans.

So what are some of the distribution options you may encounter?

A lump sum distribution is more or less what it sounds like. The retiree receives the entire contents of a retirement account at once, or in the course of a single calendar year, allowing purchase of a home, further investment, or the start of a post-retirement business. Though the law permits many plans to provide lump sum distributions, employers often preclude it. Some retirees may find this option, if offered, attractive because it facilitates big-ticket purchases and major life changes. It also provides protection from an employer who may not meet its financial obligation in the future. Some retirees simply want the freedom to invest their funds in whatever way they see fit.

However, keep in mind that your retirement fund's tax shelter ends if you withdraw the entirety of your funds. If there is no pressing reason to sever ties with a former employer, foregoing the lump sum, even when it is available, can often be the smarter choice in the long term.

Another common distribution option is to take an annuity. The annuity is the standard distribution method for many defined benefit plans, such as a pension. It is, on the other hand, very unusual in most defined contribution plans, though not unheard of. A single life annuity starts at retirement and continues during the retiree's lifetime. A fixed-term annuity is less common; the annuity continues for a certain amount of time, regardless of the retiree's continued life, benefiting designated survivors if it outlasts the annuity holder. A joint and survivor annuity starts at retirement and continues for the combined life of the retiree and another person (usually a spouse).

Qualified plans are obligated to offer two forms of survivorship benefits for spouses (with the exception of certain profit-sharing plans). These are the qualified preretirement survivor annuity and the qualified joint and survivor annuity. The former is a provision that ensures once a plan participant's retirement assets have vested, the participant's spouse has the right to an annuity in the event of the participant's death before retirement. The qualified joint and survivor annuity, mentioned above, is a post-retirement death benefit for the participant's spouse. Waiving either of these annuities requires the spouse's consent in writing; such a waiver is irrevocable. A joint and survivor annuity must give the surviving spouse at least 50 percent of the amount the retiree received during his or her life.

Another option is to roll over the distribution. A rollover is simply a transfer of funds directly from one plan to another, whether this means rolling funds from one company's 401(k) plan to another company's 401(k), from a profit-sharing plan to an IRA, or a variety of other transfers. Rolling the funds over directly allows you to avoid the tax you would pay if you received the money as a lump sum and then re-invested the funds yourself. This can allow you to preserve a tax shelter while postponing retirement distributions. For plans where it's allowed, you can also choose to roll over certain assets in-kind, rather than liquidating them and rolling over the resulting cash. Direct rollovers are typically allowed for qualified plans, IRAs, 403(b) plans and some 457 plans.

If you choose to transfer the distribution yourself (known as an indirect rollover), it is important to be aware that the new custodian must receive the distribution within 60 days in order to continue deferring the tax. Further, eligible distributions from qualified plans may be subject to mandatory withholding. If you wish to do an indirect rollover that involves tax withholding, you must make up for the mandatory withholding using other funds.

There are some reasons to be cautious with rollovers, either direct or indirect. A spouse has no inherent right to his or her partner's IRA, which means rolling the funds over can strip your spouse of survivorship rights he or she might have otherwise expected. Rolling assets over into an IRA can also expose your assets to creditors when they might have otherwise been out of legal reach.

## Paul's Advice

### Can I borrow from my IRA?

While some qualified plans allow you to repay loans from your account over several years, Traditional and Roth IRAs do not provide the same flexibility. You can take a short-term, tax-free loan from your IRA, as long as you repay the full amount into the same or a different IRA within 60 days. This strategy can only be used once every 12 months. If you are not able to repay the entire amount within 60 days, any unpaid amount will be treated as a distribution subject to tax.

-PJ

Retirees with highly appreciated employer stock might also do well to consider an in-kind distribution. This allows the participant to pay ordinary income tax on the stock's original cost basis. The difference between the cost basis and the current fair market value, called net unrealized appreciation (NUA), remains tax-deferred until the securities are sold. The appreciation is then taxed at capital gain rates, rather than as ordinary income.

### State Tax Rules

As with all state laws and regulations, tax rules on retirement accounts vary, so it's best to check with your particular state. For example, some states exempt certain types of pension income from their income tax, while other states exempt all pension income.(This is discussed in more detail in Chapter 14.) Research your state's rules or consult your financial adviser so you can know what to expect.

### Withholding and Estimated Taxes

If you have a pension or annuity, usually federal tax is withheld from distributions unless you specifically choose otherwise. Once you begin taking distributions, instead of a Form W-2 for wages or salary, you may receive a Form 1099-R for pension income.

Depending on your income tax situation, you can choose to increase or decrease the amount withheld from your pension or annuity income in order to avoid a large refund or underpayment penalty. If you do not fill out a withholding certificate, tax will be withheld from distributions as if you were married and claiming three withholding allowances. You may also ask for tax to be withheld by your plan administrator, even in cases where withholding is not required by law.

If you choose not to have tax withheld, you may have to pay estimated tax. Generally, you must pay a percentage of your prior year's tax or the current year's tax through withholdings or estimated tax, or face underpayment penalties.

## Conclusion

I have never worked with a client who had to deal with all of the types of retirement accounts and strategies mentioned above, and chances are you won't have to deal with all of them either, but my goal is to provide enough helpful information to point you in the right direction with your retirement planning. Of course, this chapter could be a book by itself. It did not and could not comprehensively address all of the rules (and exceptions to the rules). If anything about your own situation is unclear, make sure you have covered all your bases by doing more research or consulting a professional before taking any action. Once you have the financial details buttoned up, you can spend more time planning how you'll spend your retirement, and less time on your retirement plan.

# 13

## FEDERAL INCOME TAX
### Benjamin C. Sullivan, CFP®, EA

---

*"Over and over again courts have said that there is nothing sinister in so arranging one's affairs as to keep taxes as low as possible. Everybody does so, rich or poor; and all do right, for nobody owes any public duty to pay more than the law demands: taxes are enforced exactions, not voluntary contributions."*
*– JUDGE LEARNED HAND*

Income tax is often considered a dry subject, best left to accountants. However, tax profoundly shapes all aspects of personal financial planning. In a world without tax consequences, the appropriate financial choices regarding where to live, how to save for college or retirement, and how to manage your investments would be totally different. Whether you are an individual approaching retirement, an attorney or an investment manager, being well-informed about the tax system can help you make better financial decisions and understand whether your advisers are also making tax-aware recommendations.

While few people enjoy paying taxes, the first rule of tax planning is to do no harm. Do not jeopardize your long-term financial well-being in trying to minimize your tax bills. When you consider tax planning strategies, keep in mind scenarios in which you may need access to your money sooner than you expected or require more money than you had planned.

The second rule of tax planning is to play by the rules. Tax avoidance, or using legal means to minimize your taxes, is perfectly acceptable. On the other hand, tax evasion, by bending or breaking the rules or fudging the numbers, is illegal. Since U.S. citizens have the obligation to pay taxes on their worldwide income, even if they move assets offshore they still must report the associated income to the IRS and pay tax on it. Nonetheless, law-abiding taxpayers have a few principal methods of minimizing their taxes. These techniques can broadly be categorized as follows:

1. Reducing income

2. Controlling the nature of income

3. Optimizing the timing of income and deductions

4. Taking advantage of credits and incentives in the tax code

Before jumping to the specifics of how to minimize your tax burden through effective tax planning, it is helpful to understand some background on the federal tax system.

## Background

### The Language of Taxes

In addition to tax bills and the risk of missing a deadline, tax season also makes people uncomfortable because of its endless jargon. Besides arcane terms like adjustment, bracket, credit, deduction, exclusion, exemption and on and on, practitioners also love referring to specific forms and schedules. You better have all your W-2s, 1099s, 1098s, and your Schedule K-1 before you prepare your 1040. If not, file Form 4868 and finish your return by the extended due date. We need not concern ourselves with most of the technical shorthand, but it is helpful to distinguish among the various measures of income since I will refer to them throughout the following discussion.

The broadest category of income is gross income, which includes all income from any source. It may be received in cash or another form. However, some items that could be considered income are specifically excludable based on statutes. For instance, fringe benefits that an employee receives, such as health care or employee discounts, do not need to be included in income. Gifts, inheritances, life insurance proceeds, scholarships, workers compensation payments and damages awarded for physical injury are also excludable from income.

The next category of income is Adjusted Gross Income, or AGI, which serves as the basis for calculating a number of deductions. The difference between gross income and AGI, if any, results from what are commonly referred to as "above-the-line" deductions. The deduction for alimony paid to a former spouse is one example of an above-the-line deduction.

"Below-the-line" deductions, plus any personal exemptions, make up the difference between AGI and taxable income. Itemized deductions such as state income taxes, mortgage interest and charitable contributions are below-the-line deductions. Taxable income includes your salary, but also other profits such as stocks or real estate sales, gambling winnings, or even earnings as obscure as the implied income from a bond issued at a discount. Individuals' tax liabilities are calculated based on their taxable income and the applicable tax rates for that year.

## Tax Rates and Brackets

A history compiled by the Tax Foundation shows that the U.S. has had 27 top tax rates for married couples since the modern income tax was enacted in 1913. On average, a "permanent" tax rate lasts only a few years. Visit Tax Foundation's website to see how tax rates have changed over time.

Despite the uncertainty regarding exact tax rates and income thresholds or brackets to which the rates apply, taxpayers can still improve their understanding of the tax system by learning some key principles about how tax rates and brackets work.

The federal tax rate is progressive or graduated, which means that marginal income tax rates increase as income rises. The marginal rate refers to the amount of tax paid on incremental earnings, or the last dollar of income you receive. Taxpayers sometimes mistakenly believe that receiving additional income can result in all of their income being taxed in a higher tax bracket. However, only the income exceeding the tax bracket threshold is taxed at the higher rate. For example, a married taxpayer earning $500,000 of ordinary income would be in the highest tax bracket, which is 39.6 percent in 2014, but only the portion more than $457,600 would be taxed at 39.6 percent.

While your tax bracket is the rate you pay on the "last dollar" you earn, your effective tax rate, which can be determined by dividing your total tax liability by your taxable income, is generally lower. That same married taxpayer earning $500,000 has an effective tax rate of slightly less than 29 percent of taxable income despite incurring a marginal rate of 39.6 percent.

Since 2013, and as of this writing, there have been seven tax brackets for ordinary income (ranging from 10 percent to 39.6 percent) and four filing classifications: single, married filing jointly (or qualified widow or widower), married filing separately, and head of household. The following chart details the income tax brackets for 2014:

| Tax Rate | Single | Married Filing Jointly | Head of Household |
|---|---|---|---|
| 10% | Up to $9,075 | Up to $18,150 | Up to $12,950 |
| 15% | $9,076 to $36,900 | $18,151 to $73,800 | $12,951 to $49,400 |
| 25% | $36,901 to $89,350 | $73,801 to $148,850 | $49,401 to $127,550 |
| 28% | $89,351 to $186,350 | $148,851 to $226,850 | $127,551 to $206,600 |
| 33% | $186,351 to $405,100 | $226,851 to $405,100 | $206,601 to $405,100 |
| 35% | $405,101 to $406,750 | $405,101 to $457,600 | $405,101 to $432,200 |
| 39.6% | $406,751 or more | $457,601 or more | $432,201 or more |

Chart 1

## Alternative Minimum Tax

While many people understand the tax brackets described above, often their eyes glaze over when you bring up the Alternative Minimum Tax, or AMT.

The AMT is a separate tax regime that eliminates or reduces many exclusions and deductions. It is designed to ensure that individuals pay at least a minimum amount of tax. Each taxpayer is required to pay the higher of either the regular tax or the AMT.

The main ways that AMT differs from the regular tax system is that the AMT does not allow for personal exemptions or for deductions for income taxes, property taxes or miscellaneous itemized deductions (subject to the 2 percent floor). Exercising incentive stock options can also cause taxpayers to be subject to the AMT.

The AMT rates on ordinary income are set percentages: 26 percent on the first $182,500 of AMT taxable income in 2014, and 28 percent on the remainder of AMT taxable income. However, due to an idiosyncrasy in the calculation of the AMT, often a taxpayer's marginal rate will be the highest regular tax rate, even when they are subject to AMT. Unlike ordinary income, capital gains and qualified dividends are taxed at the same rates used for regular tax purposes.

After your return is prepared, the easiest way to determine if you are subject to the AMT is to check whether a number appears next to "Alternative minimum tax" on page 2 of your Form 1040. If so, this is the amount by which your AMT exceeded your regular tax liability.

Understanding whether you will be subject to AMT in a given year can help you determine appropriate tax planning strategies, which will be discussed in subsequent sections of this chapter. Additional information regarding the AMT is available from the IRS Instructions for Form 6251, which is on their website.

## Net Investment Income Tax

Beginning with the 2013 tax year, a new 3.8 percent Medicare surtax applies to taxpayers who have net investment income (NII) and whose modified adjusted gross income (MAGI) exceeds the following threshold amounts:

- Single, head of household (with qualifying person), or qualifying widow(er) with a dependent child: $200,000

- Married filing jointly: $250,000

- Married filing separately: $125,000

- Estates and trusts: based on the top tax bracket for the taxable year ($12,150 in 2014)

It is important to understand how the IRS defines net investment income because that is the key factor in calculating the tax. If you're married and earn $1 million from your job and have no net investment income, you're not subject to the tax. If you're married and have $251,000 of MAGI income, of which $1,000 is net investment income, you will owe $38 tax on the $1,000 of NII.

Net investment income includes:

1. Gross income from interest, dividends, annuities, royalties and rents (other than those derived in the ordinary course of business or those that are earned passively).

2. Passive activity income, as defined by the IRS.

3. Net capital gains derived from the disposition of property. However, net capital losses do not reduce other types of investment income.

4. Less: allowable deductions allocable to each category.

This new surtax essentially raises the marginal income tax rate for affected taxpayers and is entirely separate from the regular income tax and alternative minimum tax.

## When to Pay

Now that you understand how your tax is calculated, it's important to consider when to pay your taxes.

The April 15 due date for the U.S. Individual Income Tax Return is one of the most widely dreaded days of the year. Despite the hassle, stress, and confusion that people experience in gathering their tax information and completing their returns, for most Americans, the real tax pain is felt throughout the year.

The federal income tax is a pay-as-you-go system. Tax payments are due throughout the year as you earn income. Many taxpayers are employees whose employers withhold taxes from each paycheck. Others, such as self-employed individuals, partners, landlords, those with substantial portfolios, or anyone with significant income that is not subject to tax withholding, are required to make quarterly estimated tax payments throughout the year.

As you approach retirement, you should be aware that you may need to begin making these quarterly payments. You can face substantial underpayment penalties and interest if you do not pay at least 90 percent of your current year's tax liability or 100 percent of your previous year's liability (110 percent for high income taxpayers) through quarterly payments or withholding.

Since it is often hard to estimate your income before the end of the year, it is usually easier to pay estimated taxes based on your prior year's liability. However, this method is not terribly precise and may leave you with either a large payment due or a refund in April if your income varied from the previous year.

Sometimes it's still hard to determine your income and deductions even after the year is over. For this reason, the IRS allows you to automatically extend the due date of your return by six months by filing Form 4868. Despite the extension of time to file the return, you still need to pay your tax liability in full by the April deadline. Typically, we recommend that you prepare (but not file) your return to the fullest extent possible in April and make conservative assumptions about any unknown items to determine the amount you should pay.

Now that you know how your tax liability is calculated and when to pay it, we can discuss strategies to reduce your tax liability.

## Reducing Your Income

While it may sound facetious, the best way to reduce your tax is to reduce your income. Unless your only goal is to reduce your tax liability, simply earning less is seldom a good strategy. Nonetheless, steps can be taken to reduce your gross income, your adjusted gross income, or your taxable income, all of which can improve your family's overall financial position.

## Strategy 1: Decrease Your Earned Income

Besides looking to earn less money, you can also reduce your earned income by funding qualified retirement accounts such as a 401(k), as discussed in Chapter 12, or by electing to defer the constructive receipt of your income by participating in a non-qualified retirement plan. In addition, you can also take advantage of flexible spending accounts and commuter expense allowances to further reduce your current earned income. These methods would all apply before you report any of the income on your tax return.

## Strategy 2: Decrease Your AGI

AGI is the basis for calculating a number of deductions, and it is also the income that determines whether you qualify for many tax benefits, such as Roth IRA contributions. This makes above-the-line deductions more valuable than other deductions on your tax return, because lowering your AGI can open up or increase additional tax benefits.

One of the most widely available above-the-line deductions is for contributions to traditional IRAs. If you meet the income thresholds and other requirements to make a deductible IRA contribution, it is a nice way to reduce your tax liability. One of the best features of traditional IRA contributions is that the due date is the same as the unextended due date for your tax return. For instance, you can still make a 2014 IRA contribution, which would be deductible on your 2014 tax return, up until April 15, 2015. Self-employed individuals can also take above-the-line deductions for contributions to their qualified retirement plans or SEP IRAs, but the due dates for those contributions vary based on the type of account.

Self-employed taxpayers can also use their business expenses to directly reduce their income. In addition, they can take an above-the-line deduction for one-half of their self employment tax liability. Employees don't have this option, and so would need to treat any unreimbursed business expenses as below-the-line itemized deductions. However, job-related moving expenses may be treated as above-the-line deductions if the move meets the distance and time tests discussed in the instructions for Form 3903.

Other above-the-line deductions include alimony paid to a former spouse, contributions to health savings accounts, interest on loans for higher education up to $2,500 (subject to phaseouts based on your income), and educator expenses.

## Strategy 3: Decrease Your Portfolio Income

You can also reduce your AGI by decreasing your portfolio income, but just looking for investments with lower returns is probably not the best way to pursue this tax planning strategy. Funding the pre-tax retirement accounts discussed above reduces the amount of investments that you can add to taxable accounts, and therefore reduces your taxable portfolio income. Although the contributions won't reduce your AGI, contributing to a Roth IRA or Roth 401(k) will likewise reduce the size of your taxable portfolio and therefore its overall income.

Another way to reduce your portfolio income is to give it away. While you can't assign your income to a third party in a lower tax bracket, you can choose to make a gift to such an individual of a specific investment that pays a high amount of income. If you have ample assets, making gifts can not only reduce your future income taxes, it can also reduce your estate tax exposure, which is discussed further in Chapter 5. It is worth mentioning here that once you make the gift, you have to fully release control of the assets and cannot have any implied agreement that the recipient will return the income or assets to you. The earlier you make a gift, the more time the assets have to appreciate and pay income to the recipient.

An even more efficient means of reducing your family's income tax liability is to fund Section 529 Plan accounts for the future higher education expenses of your children or others that you wish to support. Because any withdrawals from these accounts that are used for qualified higher education expenses are not taxed, funding a 529 can fully eliminate the tax burden of the assets used to fund the plan. An added bonus of 529 Plan accounts is that you have some discretion about how the funds are invested, and you can change the intended beneficiary within certain restrictions.

If you're not in a position to fund retirement accounts or give away assets, you can still reduce your portfolio income by investing in tax-efficient mutual funds or exchange-traded funds. Funds that don't trade frequently and instead invest for the long term are more tax efficient than those that make many short-term moves. In addition, index funds are usually the most tax-efficient investment vehicles, though you should consider more than just tax consequences when selecting an investment.

If you've determined that you would like to invest in funds that either trade frequently, or pay out a high percentage of their income in dividends taxed at ordinary income rates – such as Real Estate Investment Trust or REIT funds – you should consider putting these less tax-efficient assets in your retirement accounts, where their current income won't be taxed.

You can also reduce your portfolio's taxable income by investing in tax-exempt bond funds. These investments, issued by states and municipalities, typically earn less income than taxable bonds of a similar risk level. However, since the income is not taxable, you may wind up in a better ending position by investing in such funds.

When managing your own asset allocation, you should also consider rebalancing your portfolio by adding new funds to underweight asset classes, rather than selling existing investments in overweight assets classes. In terms of tax consequences, you should try to minimize the amount of appreciated assets that you sell and, when possible, sell positions that have been held for more than one year to take advantage of the favorable long-term capital gains rates.

The ideas above are all great ways to reduce your portfolio's taxable income. Since portfolio income is included in your net investment income, these strategies reduce your exposure to the regular income tax, the alternative minimum tax and the net investment income tax. However, you should never let tax decisions alone drive your portfolio trades. More detailed information on managing your portfolio is discussed in Chapter 15.

**Strategy 4: Reduce Your Taxable Income**

Once you've done everything you can to lower your AGI, there are even more ways to reduce your tax liability. The following below-the-line deductions can also reduce your taxable income, but are often subject to certain minimum thresholds. The benefits of these deductions also may be limited or fully eliminated if you are subject to AMT.

*Standard and Itemized Deductions*

Taxable income is calculated by subtracting either the standard deduction or allowable itemized deductions from your adjusted gross income. The standard deduction works as a minimum amount by which taxpayers can reduce their AGI to calculate their taxable income. The amount varies based on filing status and changes from year to year depending on inflation. Below is a chart showing the 2014 standard deductions as an example.

## Standard Deduction Amounts for 2014

| Filing Status | Deduction |
|---|---|
| Single and Married Filing Separately | $6,200 |
| Head of Household | $9,100 |
| Married Filing Joint and Qualifying Widow/ Widower | $12,400 |
| Dependent | The greater of $1,000 or the individual's earned income for the year plus $350, up to a maximum of $6,200. |

Chart 2

It is much easier to take the standard deduction than to itemize deductions, but is usually not the best option. Taxpayers have a better chance of benefiting from the standard deduction if they don't own a home or if they do not work or live in a state with its own income tax. These factors typically lead to large deductions that make itemizing worthwhile.

If allowable itemized deductions are greater than the applicable standard deduction, taxpayers should itemize their deductions. Itemizing deductions involves preparing Schedule A, which reports the actual dollar amounts a taxpayer spent on deductible expenses during the tax year.

Itemized deductions, by definition, are not related to conducting a trade or business, and generally have little to do with the production of income. They are personal expenses which, for policy reasons of varying merit, the government has chosen to subsidize through the tax code. This encourages certain kinds of spending – such as purchasing bigger homes that require bigger mortgages, whose interest is subsidized – over other kinds of spending, such as funding a family vacation.

Major itemized deductions include: costs for medical care; state and local income taxes; real estate or property taxes; mortgage interest; certain mortgage insurance premiums; investment interest; and charitable deductions. Job expenses and certain miscellaneous expenses are also itemized deductions. These expenses include unreimbursed employee expenses, tax preparation fees, and other expenses that related to generating taxable income.

As previously mentioned, some below-the-line deductions are limited based on a percentage of your AGI. Charitable deductions are generally limited to 50 percent of AGI. Medical expenses are deductible to the extent they exceed 10 percent of AGI, but taxpayers over age 65 have a lower 7.5 percent of AGI threshold for 2014 through 2016. Casualty losses exceeding 10 percent of AGI and miscellaneous itemized deductions exceeding 2 percent of AGI can also be deducted. Taxpayers can also face limitations on their total itemized deductions if their AGI is above the following 2014 thresholds, which are inflation adjusted each year:

- Married filing jointly: $305,050

- Head of household: $279,650

- Single: $254,200

- Married filing separately: $152,525

Itemized deductions for most taxpayers affected by the limitation would be reduced by 3 percent of the excess of their AGI over the threshold amounts. The ultimate result of this calculation is that most taxpayers will receive a full benefit for their marginal itemized deductions such as charitable deductions and therefore have no added incentive to plan the timing of these deductions.

While some itemized deductions are self-explanatory, others are nuanced. For example, deductible medical care expenses include payments for the diagnosis, cure, mitigation, treatment, or prevention of disease, as well as payments for treatments affecting any structure or function of the body. Taxpayers can claim medical expenses for themselves, a spouse, and dependents as itemized deductions. Only the medical and dental expenses that were paid during a year can be included on tax returns, regardless of when the services were actually rendered. Deductible expenses also include any health insurance premiums that you paid with after-tax money and mileage to and from doctors' appointments. On the other hand, anything that isn't necessary to improve your health is not a deductible medical expense.

As discussed in Chapter 10, individuals who can't live independently due to a disability or a physical illness often need long-term care (LTC). You can treat the amounts you pay for qualified long-term care services and premiums for qualified long-term care insurance contracts as medical expenses. The cost of medical care in a nursing home, a home for the aged or a similar institution can also be treated as a medical cost. However, the cost associated with meals and lodging is not deductible unless a principal reason for being in the home is medical or nursing care.

When you consider deductions related to your home, remember that mortgage interest on up to $1.1 million of indebtedness is deductible. However, if the mortgage debt is used for something other than acquiring or improving a home, it is considered home equity debt. Only the interest attributable to the first $100,000 of home equity debt is deductible. In addition, mortgage interest is deductible on only your primary home plus one additional residence. However, this limit does not apply to rental homes. Real estate taxes are deductible on any number of homes or other property that you own, such as undeveloped land, as long as the taxes are based on the value of the property.

Finally, consider "super-charging" your charitable contributions. By donating appreciated securities that you have held for more than one year, you can get the charitable deduction for the market value of the security and also avoid paying the capital gain tax you would incur if you were to sell the asset. Additional tips regarding charitable giving are discussed in Chapter 18.

More information on deductible expenses is available in the instructions for Schedule A. IRS Publication 529 also includes a more complete discussion of miscellaneous itemized deduction. IRS Publication 502 contains more specific information on deductions for medical expenses.

## Controlling the Nature of Income

The IRS is able to influence taxpayers' behavior by offering a variety of ways to reduce one's taxable income, but it can also affect financial behavior by offering special treatment for different income types. If possible, consider earning more income that is taxed favorably, such as tax-exempt interest, qualified dividends and long-term capital gains, and less that is taxed as ordinary income. It is also important to understand how different classifications of income interact with one another.

### Capital Gains and Losses

The IRS taxes qualified dividends and long-term capital gains at a favorable rate compared to ordinary income, which makes earning these types of income more attractive. Whether they buy stocks, bonds, mutual funds or houses, investors typically expect some rate of return on their investment. This return is typically driven by fundamentals of the investment itself, but also by overall price inflation. When you sell an investment, the excess proceeds above the original cost basis are taxed at the capital gains rate, which is, as of this writing, 15 percent for most investments held more than one year. People in ordinary income tax brackets up to 15 percent pay no tax on qualified dividends and long-term capital gains, while the highest-income taxpayers subject to the 39.6 percent ordinary income tax rate are subject to a 20 percent long-term capital gains tax rate. These lower capital gain tax rates encourage capital investment and also offset the impact of taxing gains that result from inflation.

Capital gains are attractive for more than just their lower tax rate. When investments are sold for less than their original cost, the resulting capital losses can offset other realized capital gains on that year's tax return. To the extent realized capital losses exceed capital gains, you can then use up to $3,000 of those capital losses to reduce ordinary income. You can carry forward any capital losses in excess of the $3,000 limit indefinitely to offset future realized gains or ordinary income up to the annual limit.

Generating income through capital gains has other tax benefits as well. First, you don't pay capital gains tax until you sell an asset, and you can usually control when you want to make a sale. Because short-term capital gains are taxed at the same rates as ordinary income, you must own an asset for more than one year before selling it in order to receive the lower rate. Being able to time the sale of an asset also allows you to determine the year in which it will be taxed, which can be useful if you are trying to minimize AGI in a given year in order to lower the threshold for certain deductions.

## Benjamin's Advice

### Should I hold tax-favored investments such as municipal bonds in my IRA?

Income from municipal bonds is generally tax-free, so there is little benefit to holding them in an IRA. Doing so actually causes otherwise tax-free income to become taxable because distributions from traditional IRAs are taxed. The best use for an IRA is to hold investments that generate a lot of taxable income, such as real estate investment trusts or actively managed mutual funds. Putting these tax-inefficient investments in an IRA helps their growth to compound faster than in a taxable account.

-BCS

While it's not always apparent that you can choose between earning capital gains or ordinary income, you can exercise such control in a few instances. The easiest way to control whether you're earning capital gains or qualified dividends, as opposed to ordinary income, is to choose your investments carefully. Dividends from Master Limited Partnerships (MLPs), Limited Liability Companies (LLCs), or Real Estate Investment Trusts (REITs) are considered non-qualified, and are taxed at ordinary rates. Therefore, it is wise to keep these assets in retirement accounts, which prevents the income from being taxed as it is paid. It is also effective to focus your taxable portfolio on growth assets that will generate much of their income in the form of capital gains or qualified dividends. Conversely, putting assets that will have high capital gains in your 401(k) or traditional IRA prevents you from benefiting from the lower capital gains rates on these investments because distributions in excess of your basis in these accounts are taxed at ordinary income rates regardless of whether the gains in the account were originally capital or ordinary in nature.

Another way you can convert future income to capital gains is by asking your employer for compensation in the form of an interest in the company. While the granting of that interest may generate ordinary income at the time of compensation, any future appreciation would be capital gains. Similarly, if you already own appreciated employer stock in your 401(k), there is a way to distribute the shares at their cost, rather than the market value at the time of the distribution. So long as you meet certain requirements, the remainder of the distribution will be treated as a capital gain. This strategy is referred to as Net Unrealized Appreciation and should be something you consider before rolling over employer stock to an IRA.

## Passive vs. Non-Passive Income

Perhaps the only redeeming element of investment losses is the tax benefits that they can generate. However, these benefits are not unlimited. As mentioned previously, capital losses can only be used to reduce capital gains and up to an additional $3,000 of ordinary income per year. Other types of investment losses can run up against limits in a given year as well, and taxpayers can never deduct losses in excess of the amount they have invested or placed at risk in an investment.

The most common limitation taxpayers face applies to investments in passive entities, such a stake in a privately held company in which the investor does not materially participate or a rental real estate investment. If an investment is deemed a passive activity, any losses associated with that investment can be used only to offset income from other passive activities; the losses cannot be used to reduce ordinary income unless the taxpayer disposes of the activity giving rise to the losses during the tax year. Total passive activity losses that exceed passive activity income in a year will be suspended and will carry forward until either the activity is disposed or there is passive income to offset.

It is also important to note that, although traditional stock and bond investing may sound passive, interest, dividend and capital gain income is considered portfolio income. Passive activity losses cannot be used to offset portfolio income.

As with many tax rules, there are exceptions to those for passive activity. For instance, although rental activities are usually considered passive for individuals who are not real estate professionals, if a taxpayer's income is below $100,000 (as of this writing), he can deduct up to $25,000 of rental losses if he meets certain qualifications that characterize him as actively participating in the activity. This benefit is phased down to $0 of deductible losses once income reaches $150,000 or more. Most landlords are considered as actively participating if they make decisions such as approving new tenants or deciding on rental terms.

Another exception that would allow you to deduct otherwise passive losses against ordinary income is materially participating in the activity in question. In cases such as these, the activities are considered "non-passive," and there are far fewer restrictions on the deductibility of losses. In order to be treated as materially participating, an investor has to meet one of the following several tests:

- You participated in the activity for more than 500 hours during the year.

- Your participation in the activity for the tax year was substantially all of the participation in the activity of all individuals (including individuals who did not own any interest in the activity) for the year.

- You participated in the activity for more than 100 hours during the tax year, and you participated at least as much as any other individual (including individuals who did not own any interest in the activity) for the year.

- The activity is a significant participation activity for the tax year, and you participated in all significant participation activities during the year for more than 500 hours.
  » A significant participation activity is any trade or business activity in which you participated for more than 100 hours during the year and in which you did not materially participate under any of the material participation tests (other than this fourth test).

- You materially participated in the activity for any 5 (whether or not consecutive) of the 10 immediately preceding tax years.

- The activity is a personal service activity in which you materially participated for any 3 (whether or not consecutive) preceding tax years.
  » An activity is a personal service activity if it involves the performance of personal services in the fields of health, law, engineering, architecture, accounting, actuarial science, performing arts, consulting, or in any other trade or business in which capital is not a material income-producing factor.

- Based on all the facts and circumstances, you participated in the activity on a regular, continuous, and substantial basis during the tax year.

In addition to the above exceptions, the IRS has also indicated that an activity involving the trading of stocks and bonds is not a passive activity, regardless of whether the investor qualifies as materially participating based on any of the above tests. Investors in trading partnerships, such as hedge funds, often overlook this exception, which is supported by Reg. Section 1.469-1T(e)(6). As a result, taxpayers might carry such losses forward as if the investments were passive, when they should actually reduce their current year income instead.

The rules regarding passive activities are very complex, and the exceptions can be nuanced. If you participate in a number of passive activities, it's likely worthwhile to contact a tax professional. For additional information on passive activity rules, please see the instructions for Form 8582 on the IRS website.

## Hobby Losses

Chapter 19 of this book discusses starting a new venture in retirement to make money and keep occupied. The IRS doesn't want to support pensioners' non-business leisure activities by providing them with overly generous deductions, so there are certain rules in Section 183 of the Internal Revenue Code that limit deductions if an activity is determined to be a hobby and not a business.

If you're knitting sweaters as you watch TV and occasionally sell one to a neighbor, you probably shouldn't take advantage of the home office deduction or report a related loss on your tax return. If, on the other hand, you have an entire room devoted to knitting and routinely sell your sweaters online or to a local boutique, there's a good chance you're operating a small business while pursuing an activity you enjoy.

The deciding factor on whether an activity is a business or a hobby is whether there is a profit motive. Qualitative factors will determine whether a profit motive exists, but operating an activity like a business is the best way to prove its character. The owner should try to improve profitability on an ongoing basis, keep books, records and a separate bank account for the company, and have a reasonable expectation for profitability in the future. The IRS will not question whether an activity is a business if it turned a net profit in at least three of the last five tax years.

If the activity is deemed to be a hobby, deductions are only allowed as itemized deductions, rather than as above-the-line deductions against ordinary income. In addition, deductions related to the hobby cannot exceed the income. Therefore, taxpayers starting small businesses should be sure to follow common business practices and seek a profit if they want to benefit from losses when they occur.

## Income in Respect of a Decedent

The final type of income that you (and your future beneficiaries) should note is income in respect of a decedent (IRD). Income in Respect of a Decedent is income earned, but not received, by an individual who passes away. This income is taxed on the return of the person who inherits or receives the income - whether a spouse, a child, an estate, or some other assigned beneficiary.

IRD can result from unpaid wages, self-employment income, interest, dividends, rents and royalties, sales proceeds, deferred compensation, installment sale receipts, or income from a partnership or S corporation. IRD also includes traditional IRAs and other retirement plans with pre-tax assets. The income retains the same tax character it would have had in the hands of the decedent.

The major issue to keep in mind with IRD is that retirement accounts, such as 401(k)s and traditional IRAs, are typically pre-tax money and are taxed on the decedent's estate tax return at their market value on the decedent's date of death. However, because they are pre-tax assets, the beneficiary ultimately has to pay tax on the income before receiving it. In a simple example, if a decedent has a $1 million IRA that is being taxed on the estate tax return at 40 percent in 2014, the recipient would also need to pay additional tax on withdrawals from the IRA when he receives it. Assuming no growth in the assets and that the beneficiary is in the top income tax rate of 39.6 percent, the recipient would need to pay $396,000 income tax as a result of the bequest, and the estate would have also paid $400,000 of estate tax. This results in a tax of $796,000 from the $1 million of assets, instead of a $400,000 tax if the assets were in a taxable account. The assets in a taxable account would have their cost basis adjusted to the fair market value on the date of death, so the recipient typically would not have to pay much, if any, income tax to access the assets.

The additional tax is a bit overstated in the example above, because the estate tax paid on the IRD can be an itemized deduction that is not subject to the 2 percent floor. Nonetheless, it illustrates the point that it is better to minimize IRD and this double taxation if possible. It may make sense to take distributions from your own pre-tax accounts in certain situations, because paying the income tax during your life allows you to reduce your ultimate estate tax exposure. IRD is also an important consideration when ensuring that all beneficiaries are treated equally after accounting for taxes.

## Optimizing the Timing of Income and Deductions

In theory, a good way to manage your tax burden is to shift income toward years when you anticipate your marginal tax rate will be lower, and shift deductions to years when you anticipate your marginal tax rate will be higher. However, in reality, determining the optimal timing of income and deductions is a complicated endeavor involving many calculations specific to each taxpayer's situation. It is important to run multi-year projections of your tax returns, since tax planning requires the consideration of the current and upcoming years, and also of your exposure to the AMT. Tax planning moves that help an individual subject to the regular income tax may hurt a taxpayer subject to AMT.

Besides the complexity inherent in tax planning, the largest problem most taxpayers face is their relative lack of control over the timing of the majority of their income or deductions. The uncertainty of future tax rates further complicates planning.

The easiest way to control the timing of your income is by deciding when to sell your investments. You could also ask an employer to accelerate or postpone any year-end bonuses or commissions. You could also hold off on taking retirement plan distributions that aren't Required Minimum Distributions. If you are self-employed or a landlord, you also have some flexibility regarding when you bill clients or pay invoices.

If your marginal income rate won't change between one year and the next, it is generally best to accelerate deductions and postpone income, so that you will pay the tax later. Sometimes it's beneficial to bunch deductions subject to either the 2 percent or 10 percent of AGI floors. This may allow you to deduct items in one year; whereas, if you paid them over two years, they wouldn't be deductible at all.

Typically, if you have a high income year, you will also face higher state tax liabilities that year. If you were not subject to AMT at the time, you would want to accelerate tax payments to occur in the same year that your income spikes higher, because you are likely to get more of a benefit in that year. On the other hand, if you had a high-income year, you might not have enough medical expenses to reach the 10 percent of AGI threshold. In this scenario, you would want to postpone any medical expenses to the following year to have a better chance of getting a benefit.

The best planning moves are based on your specific facts and circumstances. Probably the most important takeaway from this section is that you should consider the tax consequences of timing your income and deductions when making decisions. Shifting some of these items may save you substantial tax.

## Taking Advantage of Credits and Incentives

The tax code is loaded with narrowly targeted benefits. In addition, the rules regarding some credits change almost annually. However, some of the most popular incentives that apply to broad groups are covered below.

### Exemptions for the Sale of Your Home

In addition to the help that the tax law gives homeowners through annual deductions for real estate taxes and mortgage interest, the law grants them one last tax benefit when they sell their homes. You can exclude up to $250,000 of the gain from the sale of your primary residence, or twice that amount for married couples filing joint returns, in most cases.

You are eligible for the home sale exclusion only if you have owned and lived in your home for a period totaling at least two years out of the five years prior to the sale. This does not apply to a vacation home or a property solely owned for investment purposes. There is no limit on the number of times you can use the home-sale exemption in your lifetime; however, you can claim this exclusion only once every two years. The home sale exclusion may be claimed on a limited basis if you didn't live in the home for two years, or if a portion of the gain is allocated to periods of nonqualified use. The IRS doesn't require the ownership and use periods to be overlapping or continuous. Surviving spouses are also allowed to use the $500,000 exclusion if they otherwise qualify and sell the home within two years after their spouse's death.

The home sale exclusion discussed above helps reduce any gain realized on the sale of a home. To figure out whether you have a gain or loss on the sale, you need to figure out your adjusted cost basis, which is what you originally paid for the home, plus the cost of capital improvements, less any depreciation deduction to which you have been entitled. Capital improvements are costs that have added value to your home, prolonged its useful life, or adapted it to a new use. Examples include a new roof, a swimming pool, new flooring or a remodeled kitchen. Capital improvements only increase the basis of your house if they remain as part of the home when it is sold. Therefore, if you installed carpeting in your home then replaced the carpeting 10 times while you lived there, you should only increase the home's basis by the cost of the final carpet. Routine expenses, such as painting, maintenance or repairs, do not increase the basis of your house.

## Foreign Tax Credit

The IRS lessens the burden of foreign income being taxed twice – first by a foreign government and then by the IRS – by allowing U.S. taxpayers to claim a credit on their return for income taxes paid to a foreign country. The credit is calculated by preparing Form 1116, and the rules are discussed in that form's instructions.

Many Americans might miss this benefit, because they don't realize they are paying foreign taxes in the first place. Most mutual funds that invest in non-U.S. companies pay foreign income tax. The mutual fund investors' pro-rata share of this tax is reported on their annual Form 1099. If you hold foreign investments in taxable accounts, you should be sure to report the foreign tax paid in addition to the income from these investments.

## Other Tax Credits

The specific rules for other popular tax credits often change and some typically apply to younger or lower income taxpayers, so I will only mention them briefly. The dependent care tax credit can provide a credit of up to 20 percent of qualified dependent care expenses up to $3,000 for one dependent or $6,000 for two or more qualifying dependents, resulting in a maximum credit of $1,200. This credit is calculated on Form 2441. It is important to remember that this credit may also be available for adult dependents who are physically or mentally incapable of self-care.

Education credits are available for qualifying higher education expenses by preparing Form 8863. Residential energy credits may be available to homeowners that have improved their home's energy efficiency or installed certain renewable energy generation devices. These credits are calculated on Form 5695.

It seems that the people to whom more obscure benefits apply have a way of becoming experts in the topic. Almost all the whaling captains recognized by the Alaska Eskimo Whaling Commission surely know that they may be able to deduct up to $10,000 of whaling expenses as charitable contributions. While tax rules may be nuanced, it's helpful to listen to what people who have similar circumstances as you say about taxes. However, when getting tax advice from lay people, you should always double check with a tax professional or the IRS to confirm the advice's accuracy. Your tax preparer will often have other clients in similar situations, and will be the best person to identify tax benefits that may apply to your return.

## Tax Benefits and "Penalties" for Older Taxpayers

While many older taxpayers are retirees who may not benefit greatly from the planning techniques they used in the past, they have other tax benefits to consider. On average, older Americans are more likely to benefit from home sale exclusions and deductions for medical expenses and long-term care insurance than their younger counterparts. In addition, they also have access to a few additional benefits that are not available to younger taxpayers.

Taxpayers age 65 or older who do not itemize their deductions are eligible for a higher standard deduction (an additional $1,550 for single taxpayers and $1,200 for married taxpayers in 2014). Those who do itemize their deductions should remember to include Medicare Part B, supplemental medical insurance, premiums and Medicare Part D, voluntary prescription drug insurance, and premiums as medical expense deductions, even if they were deducted from Social Security income.

Taxpayers with lower incomes (less than $25,000 for married couples and less than $17,500 for single individuals) may be eligible for the Credit for the Elderly by completing Schedule R with their individual income tax returns. However, most people who receive non-taxable Social Security income are not eligible for this benefit. Additional information is available in the instructions for Schedule R on the IRS website.

Depending on a taxpayer's adjusted gross income, up to 85 percent of Social Security income may be included in gross income. If a married couple's AGI, excluding Social Security, is less than $32,000, none of the income is taxable; however, if this amount exceeds $44,000, then 85 percent of the Social Security income is taxable. Additional information about Social Security planning is discussed in Chapter 11 of this book.

In addition to the federal tax benefits discussed above, many states offer benefits to older taxpayers such as excluding some retirement plan distributions from income and providing them with property tax relief. Additional information on state benefits is discussed in Chapter 14.

The IRS also has some "penalties" for older taxpayers. As discussed in more detail in Chapter 12, distributions must begin from certain retirement accounts, such as 401(k)s and traditional IRAs, by April 1 of the year following the year the owner reaches age 70 ½. Failing to take these required minimum distributions (RMDs) by that year will result in the shortfall being taxed at a 50 percent rate. Information on how to calculate RMDs is available in Publication 590, Individual Retirement Arrangements (IRAs). The fact that RMDs are not required for Roth IRAs is another of the Roth IRA's attractive features.

## Closing Thoughts

The information in this chapter should enable you to better plan your finances in order to legally minimize your tax burden. By shifting income to accounts with favorable tax treatment, to beneficiaries in a lower tax bracket, or to a year in which you have a lower income tax rate, you can increase the money available for your own needs and comfort.

Given the complexity and ever-changing nature of the tax rules, it is often worthwhile to seek professional help in planning and preparing your taxes. A good tax preparer can provide you with peace of mind, ensuring that your return is prepared in compliance with the rules and regulations. They may even help identify tax benefits that you can miss with do-it-yourself software.

# 14

## STATE INCOME TAXES
### ReKeithen Miller, CFP®, EA

Max and Ruth, a hypothetical couple, have recently retired. Their adult children live far from them and from one another. Ruth likes to travel, and Max has always dreamed of a vacation home at the beach.

Their discussion of whether to move their primary residence, buy a second home or both includes many considerations. Some of the discussions about these choices will be enjoyable, as Max and Ruth plan how much more time they can spend with their grandchildren or how much they might like a new climate. But Max and Ruth are practical, so they also carefully consider the financial consequences of their choices. Eventually, this will lead to a serious consideration of the effects of state-specific taxes.

If you have ever read an article or book about the "best places to retire," you undoubtedly know that income taxes are usually a major factor in such lists' rankings. Florida is not the only state with abundant sunshine and miles of sandy beaches, but the fact that the state has no personal income tax gives retirees an added reason to set down new roots there.

State income tax laws are diverse and sometimes complicated. There are 43 different codes to consider (because seven states do not levy personal income tax at all), and that number does not include the District of Columbia or the plethora of cities and municipalities that levy their own income taxes in addition to state laws. While detailing each state's requirements is beyond the scope of this chapter, taxpayers should keep in mind that each state is unique. While some state income tax laws do have similarities to one another, and to federal statutes, the primary financial planning issues at the state level arise from the differences.

Income tax is not the only piece of the tax puzzle that varies by state. It is also important to consider state laws regarding inheritance and gift taxes (see Chapter 6), tax breaks on retirement income and deferred compensation, sales tax and property tax. Nor should financial and tax considerations trump the many other factors you should evaluate when deciding where to retire, such as proximity to family, population demographics, climate, geography and a host of others. Such factors can, and often should, weigh more heavily than tax considerations in your decision.

That said, once you have decided where you will spend your golden years, it is important to understand your new home state's income tax law and to comply with it in a way that maximizes the law's benefit to you.

## Residency vs. Domicile

One of the most important principles to understand when determining to which state or states you owe income tax is the difference between residency and domicile. Your state of residency is generally a state where you physically live or where you maintain a permanent home. A person can have residency in multiple states.

On the other hand, an individual can only have one legal domicile. Black's Law Dictionary defines domicile as "that place in which a man has voluntarily fixed the habitation of himself and family, not for a mere special or temporary purpose, but with the present intention of making a permanent home, until some unexpected event shall occur to induce him to adopt some other permanent home." Domicile is the place you (or the courts) consider your true, permanent home – the place you intend to return after a trip or long absence.

For many people, their state of residency and their state of domicile are the same, and the distinction becomes irrelevant. However, the distinction is very important for individuals who spend time in multiple states or who have recently moved from one state to another, because a person's state of domicile typically levies income taxes on that person's worldwide income even if they are only present in the state for a relatively short time period (for example, 30 days) during a particular year. Most states have implemented safe harbor rules that will treat a domiciliary as a nonresident if they are away from the state for a specified number of days. In some instances, states require that the individual not maintain a permanent place of abode in the state during the year in order to qualify for safe harbor treatment. Additionally, when an individual is domiciled in a state that levies an income tax but resides in another state with an income tax, that individual could end up needing to pay taxes in both states. (Later in this chapter, I will discuss tax credits that states provide for taxes paid to nonresident states; in certain circumstances, these credits can mitigate the effect of double taxation.)

Some states have adopted "statutory residency" provisions, in which an individual is automatically considered a resident of the state if he or she spends a certain amount of time there during the year. The most common cutoff is 183 or more days spent in the state during the tax year. Two notable exceptions are New Mexico, which has a cutoff of 185 days, and Oregon, which requires taxpayers spend 200 days in the state and maintain an abode before they are automatically considered tax residents. Each state has its own nuances regarding the statutory language about residency, so it is always a good idea to check the rules if you plan to spend time in multiple states.

## Establishing a New Domicile

Say you have made the decision that you prefer enjoying the sunshine in Nevada to shoveling snow in North Dakota. What steps do you need to take to establish your new domicile once you move?

To establish a new domicile, you must be physically present in the new state, with the intention to remain permanently or to treat the new state as your permanent home. In addition, you must abandon your old domicile. Should there be a question regarding your domicile, the burden of proof usually falls on you, the taxpayer, to rebut the claims of the tax authorities. However, there are steps you can take to demonstrate that you have abandoned your old domicile and intend to remain permanently in your new state. These steps may include some or all of the following:

- Register to vote in the new state and vote when the opportunity arises

- Obtain a driver's license or state-issued photo ID in the new state

- Register your vehicle(s) in the new state

- Establish a permanent address in the new state

- Pay state-specific taxes in the new state, such as income or property tax

- Renounce any homestead exemption you claimed in old state and establish one in the new state, if applicable

- Notify your former state's tax authorities of your change in domicile

- Record your change of legal residence with your financial institutions

- Move items such as family heirlooms, photo albums and important legal documents to your new state

It is also wise to keep a record of the dates and total number of days that you were present in the state during a tax year. The more of the above steps you complete, the stronger your case for domicile will be if you face a challenge. The authorities tend to pay special attention to taxpayers who move from a high-tax state to a relatively low-tax state. If you move just prior to a large financial transaction, it could also increase the chances the authorities will question your change in domicile.

Maintaining your residence or leaving significant property in your original state will also raise questions about your intent to make your new state your permanent and primary home. This is because changing domicile is not just about completing a checklist; it is about the individual's intent. If you leave things like family portraits, jewelry, or personal documents such as wills and birth certificates in one home but claim domicile in another, the claim may not hold up under court challenge. States will also scrutinize a person's civic activities, their social and business connections, and their general behavior. The steps mentioned in the list above may not be enough to prove a change in domicile alone without further evidence.

How hard you need to work to prove a change in domicile will, to some extent, depend upon how aggressive your state of former domicile chooses to be in pursuing you. This can vary widely. For example, New York is notorious for holding on to its former residents to the greatest extent possible and for its broad definition of residency.

At my firm, I have seen first-hand some of the various domicile and residency issues that individuals 55 and older may experience, in New York and elsewhere. One such issue centered on moving a loved one for medical reasons and the subsequent impact on the patient's income tax situation. A case outlined in a 2006 advisory opinion issued by the New York State Department of Taxation and Finance closely mirrors our client's situation.

The opinion was issued to a taxpayer who sought advice on whether his wife, a patient with Alzheimer's disease, would be considered a statutory resident of New York due to her presence in a nursing home in the state. New York automatically considers someone who maintains a permanent place of abode and spends more than 183 days in the state a resident for income tax purposes. Before the taxpayer moved his wife to the facility in New York, she maintained her domicile in Florida. The advisory opinion concluded that the wife's time in the nursing home would not count towards New York's 183-day limitation, mainly because she lacked the intent to change her domicile. Though this opinion only directly affects domicile issues involving New York, it provides some insight on the thought processes of tax authorities regarding these issues.

As you approach retirement, you may consider changes such as purchasing a vacation home in another state, spending more time at a second home you already own, moving to be closer to family and friends, or making decisions about out-of-state care for a loved one. In any of these situations, you should be aware of how your choices can impact your residency and domicile for tax purposes.

## State Income Tax Systems

Except the seven states that charge no personal income tax at all — Alaska, Florida, Nevada, South Dakota, Texas, Washington and Wyoming — most states begin the computation of taxable income for state purposes by referring to the income calculated on a taxpayer's federal tax return. As with most generalizations in this chapter, however, there are exceptions. New Hampshire and Tennessee only tax interest and dividend income. Even then, these states provide certain exceptions. For example, Tennessee does not tax interest earned from savings accounts, checking accounts or money market accounts at banks, savings and loan institution or credit unions; however, dividends or interest from money market funds held in a brokerage accounts are taxable.

This is only one of the countless exceptions to common rules in the 43 state tax codes. In this section I will highlight some of the general themes found among different states' methods of determining taxable income. I will also point out some of the states that go off the beaten path.

**Graduated Tax Rate vs. Flat-Tax States**

## U.S. Tax Brackets - 2014

| Single Taxpayer | Rate |
| --- | --- |
| 0 to $9,075 | 10% |
| $9,076 to $36,900 | 15% |
| $36,901 to $89,350 | 25% |
| $89,351 to $186,350 | 28% |
| $186,351 to $405,100 | 33% |
| $405,101 to $406,750 | 35% |
| $406,751 or more | 39.6% |

Source: Internal Revenue Service

Chart 1

A graduated tax system is one in which the marginal income tax rate increases along with the taxpayer's taxable income. The most familiar example of such a system for most readers is our federal income tax system, which uses graduated rates. My colleague Benjamin Sullivan provides a detailed overview of federal income tax in Chapter 13. The idea behind graduated or progressive tax rates is that individuals who generate more income can afford to pay more in tax, allowing the state to reduce the rates for lower income taxpayers, who may not be able to afford the same level of tax payments. Currently, 33 states use a graduated tax rate system.

A flat-tax system, as its name suggests, is one in which everyone pays the same tax rate, regardless of income. The chart shows the 10 states that employ a flat-tax rate system and their tax rates as of this writing.

| State | Tax Rate |
| --- | --- |
| Colorado | 4.63% |
| Illinois | 5.00% |
| Indiana | 3.40% |
| Massachusetts | 5.20% |
| Michigan | 4.25% |
| New Hampshire* | 5.00% |
| North Carolina | 5.80% |
| Pennsylvania | 3.07% |
| Tennessee* | 6.00% |
| Utah | 5.00% |

*Only taxes interest and dividend income

Chart 2

There is ongoing debate regarding which of these tax systems is the best. The argument has raged for many years, and I will not attempt to resolve it here, as the side someone takes is often a matter of personal circumstances and philosophy. As I will discuss later in the chapter, there are also special exemptions for income, especially for retirees, that can make the rate discussion moot for many taxpayers over 55.

## Filing Status

Your tax filing status determines your tax rate and the way in which standard deductions apply to your return. If you are single, your status is relatively straightforward: If you have no dependents, you will file as single. Single filers with dependents may qualify to file as a head of household (or as a widow/widower with a dependent) in certain cases.

Married couples are the point at which filing status becomes more complex. Most states use a joint filing system, as does the federal government. In a joint filing system, both spouses' incomes are added together and taxed as a single amount, effectively treating the family as a single economic unit for tax purposes. In contrast, some states allow spouses to choose a combined tax system, in which each spouse's income is taxed separately and then added together. This option can be beneficial to two-income households because it allows a portion of each spouse's income to be taxed at the lower rates at the bottom of the income tax brackets. Virginia also offers a spouse tax adjustment, which ensures married couples do not pay more tax on their joint return than they would if they had filed separate returns. While most couples perceive joint filing as beneficial, the pros and cons of each option will vary given the laws of your state and your family's particular situation.

Further complicating the issue of filing status for state income taxes is the issue of same-sex marriage. As of this writing, 19 states and the District of Columbia allow same-sex couples to marry. Due to the Supreme Court's decision in United States v. Windsor, couples married in these states now receive federal recognition as well, meaning they do not need to file separately on the federal level in cases where they can file jointly at the state level. (Prior to Windsor, married same-sex couples needed to file separately at the federal level even if their state allowed them to file jointly.) If the couple lives in a state that recognizes their marriage, they have all the same options for tax filing status as opposite-sex couples. However, many unresolved questions remain surrounding the treatment of same-sex couples who were married in states where such marriages are legal but who reside, or who must file as nonresidents, in states where such marriages are still prohibited.

In addition, three states (at this writing) allow for civil unions and five offer domestic partnerships with varying degrees of legal recognition. Some of these states allow or require individuals in such unions or partnerships to file together, but some do not. As this issue continues to evolve, same-sex couples will need to navigate a messy income tax landscape, especially if more than one state is involved.

## What Sorts of Income Do States Tax?

Every state that charges income tax has its own rules. Generally, however, if you are considered a resident of a state, that state will tax all your income, with any exceptions allowed by statute. If you are a nonresident in a state, the state will tax only income considered to have a source in that state, such as income you earned while working there or income from real estate within the state's borders. This section outlines the most common types of income that individuals receive in retirement and how those types of income are generally treated for state income tax purposes. As you may have guessed by now, however, there are exceptions to every state tax rule. For more information on your own state's rules, speak with your financial adviser or look online.

### U.S. Government Obligations

Certain sorts of income are not taxable at the state level. One of these is income earned on U.S. government obligations: Treasury bills, notes, bonds and other debts issued by the federal government and its agencies. While this income is subject to federal taxation, the U.S. government prohibits states from taxing interest earned on direct interests in these obligations. The key distinction here is that the prohibition applies unequivocally only to direct interests. Like many investors, you may own mutual funds that invest in U.S. government securities; some states, including California, Connecticut and New York, require that the mutual fund invest a minimum percentage of its assets in U.S. government obligations in order for the fund's earnings to be exempt from taxation. In addition, capital gains from the sale of U.S. government obligations may be subject to state income tax.

### Municipal Bonds

Another class of income many states exempt from state income tax is income derived from municipal bonds. A municipal bond is a security issued by a state, county or municipality, usually used to finance capital expenditures. Municipal bonds are exempt from federal income tax, as a reciprocal rule to the prohibition on states taxing income from federal obligations. Municipal bond income is likely to be exempt from state income tax if the bond was issued by the state in question, or by a locality within that state. In addition, bonds issued by Puerto Rico and the U.S.

possessions such as Guam and the U.S. Virgin Islands are also exempt from federal and state taxation. While capital gains on municipal bond-based mutual funds are subject to capital gains tax on a federal level, some states do not tax gains on their own securities either.

## Social Security Benefits

At the federal level, up to 85 percent of Social Security income is subject to taxation, depending on taxpayer's income, but the rules at the state level vary widely. Currently, 27 states exempt Social Security benefits from taxation completely. The 14 states that tax all or a portion of benefits are Colorado, Connecticut, Iowa, Kansas, Minnesota, Missouri, Montana, North Dakota, Nebraska, New Mexico, Rhode Island, Utah, Vermont and West Virginia. The Social Security Administration has determined that 52 percent of married couples and 74 percent of single individuals among elderly beneficiaries receive more than 50 percent of their income from Social Security. The generous terms states offer for this sort of income can bolster a retiree's budget.

## Pension Income (Military, State, Out-of-State, Federal)

The taxation of pension income at the state level can depend on whether the pension is part of a federal, military, private, public in-state or public out-of-state plan. States tend to exempt the majority of pension income from in-state and public pension plans. Before the U.S. Supreme Court decisions in Davis v. Michigan (1989) and Barker v. Kansas (1992), states would often provide more favorable treatment to state pensions than they would to federal (Davis) and military (Barker) pensions. Now states must treat federal and military pension no worse than they would their own state pension plans. States can, and often do, still differentiate between the treatment of public and private pensions and of pensions from in or out of state.

Nine states exempt federal, military, and in-state pensions from state income tax entirely. California, Rhode Island, Vermont, and Nebraska fully tax pension income of all types; Connecticut taxes all types fully except for military pensions. Most states fall somewhere in between full exemption and no exemption at all.

## Deferred Compensation and Retirement Plan Distributions

Deferred compensation, which may come from an IRA, a 401(k) plan or another retirement account, is a class of income whose treatment varies widely from state to state. As the name implies, taxpayers with this sort of income defer compensation into a plan that allows them to postpone taxation on the money until it is distributed. In essence, an individual could earn income in a high-tax state like California or New York and then move to a state with no income taxes before receiving their compensation. The Californias and New Yorks of the world did not care for these arrangements, for obvious reasons, and historically they would often tax the retirement distributions of nonresident individuals who had earned the income in their state.

In 1996, President Clinton signed Public Law 104-95, which prohibits states from taxing the retirement income of an individual who is not a domiciliary or resident of that state. Below is a list of the major plans exempted under the ruling:

• Individual Retirement Account (IRA) distributions

• Pension income

• 401(k), 403(b), 457 profit-sharing and stock bonus plans

• Self-employed employee pension plans (for example, SEP-IRAs)

• Government retirement plans

• Annuity plans

The law brought added relief to individuals who planned to leave high-tax states and move to states whose tax rules were more favorable. However, the law does not completely protect nonqualified deferred compensation arrangements (NQDC). These are plans that companies establish to provide benefits to executives and key employees that do not comply with ERISA, which prohibits discrimination in favor of certain employees. Examples of these plan types are Supplemental Executive Retirement Plans (SERPs), Excess Benefit Plans, and Executive Bonus Plans.

Public Law 104-95 specified additional requirements needed in order for the distributions from a NQDC plan to be subject to the prohibition on states taxing their former residents. Distributions from the plan must be a part of a series of substantial, equal, periodic payments made at least annually that continue for:

1. The life or life expectancy of the recipient (or the joint lives or joint life expectancies of the recipient and the designated beneficiary of the recipient), or

2. A period of not less than 10 years, or

3. The plan must be maintained solely to provide benefits beyond those allowed under qualified plans. The so-called Excess Benefit Plan must meet requirements designated by government in order to qualify.

The rules surrounding "source taxation" of these plans can be complicated. You cannot rely on your employer to get it right, especially when dealing with various state laws regarding withholding and employees working across state lines. In some cases, a company may withhold taxes erroneously or take a conservative position to withhold taxes from payments in order to avoid employer penalties.

Certain qualified plans are exempt from taxation altogether, even without the federal stipulation. States may go further: Alabama, Hawaii and Illinois also exempt certain types of private pensions. Pennsylvania and Mississippi go so far as to exempt all retirement income, including IRA and 401(k) distributions.

## Other Income

Some states offer general income exclusions for additional income earned in retirement. Often the exclusion is based on a person's age and income. For example, Georgia offers an exclusion that, in addition to offsetting retirement income, can offset earned income, interest income, dividends, capital gains, rental and royalty income, and other items. The exclusion is up to $35,000 for residents age 62 to 64 or who are permanently disabled; it rises to $65,000 for residents over 65.

States tend to offer income tax benefits to their retirees across the board, with few exceptions. The differences come from the ways these benefits apply. Depending on the type of income you receive in retirement and where you receive it, you may not owe much in the way of taxes at all if your state offers a special exemption. However, if you will or currently receive favorable tax treatment for your income, you should research your options before moving to another state or deciding to roll over a government retirement plan to an IRA. You could find that your new state does not treat out-of-state pension income or retirement plans as favorably as your current state; or you may find that rolling your government retirement plan over to another account could cause you to lose favorable tax treatment. Looking before you leap can save you from unwelcome tax surprises.

# Nonresident and Part-Year Resident Tax Filings

While many people reside in only one state or split their time between two, some people find themselves spending significant time in many different places. This can be due to the nature of their work, a far-flung extended family, or a portable lifestyle and personal inclination. A retiree who lives out of a recreational vehicle may have no obvious fixed abode. A business consultant may spend many more days working with a client in a different state than at home. You may realize a gain on the sale of a vacation home. A variety of scenarios may lead you to need to report income (and possibly pay tax on it) in more than one state.

## ReKeithen's Advice

**Should I defer my pension or Social Security until I move to a low-tax state?**

Several states exclude pension and Social Security from tax entirely, or provide a partial exemption. Residents who qualify for exemptions have less reason to defer benefits. If benefits would be taxed at a higher rate in the current state than in the new state, postponement may be worthwhile. However, it is generally unwise to skip or postpone income solely to save on state taxes unless the benefits can be claimed retroactively, or unless you are compensated through increased future payments.

-RM

If you earn income in states other than your state of domicile, the state where you earn the income will generally still tax you, assuming it is a state with income tax. However, there is usually a difference in how a state treats nonresidents and part-year residents, and it is important to understand which category describes you before you file.

Part-year residents are those taxpayers who resided in the state when earning the income, but who have since moved. For example, if you live and work in Oregon, but moved to California in order to start a new job in July, you are a part-year resident of both Oregon and California, and will need to file forms for both states. Many states have a form specifically for part-year returns.

States often prorate part-year returns, depending on when in the year the taxpayer moved. Actual length of residency is generally irrelevant; what matters is the percentage of your total yearly income earned in the state. Your human resources or payroll department can help you keep track of wages earned throughout the year, but unearned income, such as interest income and capital gains, can require more work. You can use statements from your financial institution to help you determine when income was paid throughout the year. If you sold a stock following a move from one state to another, you would allocate the capital gain or loss to your new state of residency. Keeping track of this information is important to make sure you are allocating your income properly. Part-year residents must also prorate deductions and credits based on their income allocated to each state.

When the tax is calculated, each state will usually calculate its tax assuming 100 percent of your income was earned in that state. Then the states will allocate the tax based on the percentage of your total income earned in the state during the year. To continue our example, assume you earned $200,000 during the year: $150,000 in California and $50,000 in Oregon (that is to say, 75 percent in California and 25 percent in Oregon).

Assume your California and Oregon tax liabilities were $10,000 and $8,000, respectively, before they were prorated. Your tax liability for California would be $7,500 ($10,000 multiplied by 75 percent) and your Oregon tax liability would be $2,000 ($8,000 multiplied by 25 percent).

In contrast to a part-year resident, a nonresident is someone who earned income in a state but was not a resident of that state during any part of the tax year. Some states simply base the tax on the amount you earned within their borders, giving you the benefit of any graduated rates. Other states, such as California, have the nonresident taxpayer calculate the tax as if they were a resident taxpayer; the taxpayer then multiplies the tax by the percentage of total income earned in the state. In these states, high-income taxpayers pay more than they would if only their in-state income was considered. Whether you will be able to take any deductions or credits on a nonresident return varies by state.

If you are in a given state for enough days during the tax year, especially if you earn income there, you could end up with a fairly complicated tax situation. In these cases, seriously consider consulting a professional for advice in navigating the various statutes you will need to understand.

## Composite Tax Returns

Nonresident income taxes are not only for those who spend their time traveling. You may need to pay nonresident income taxes to a state without ever setting foot there, due to your investments or business interests. For example, investors in publicly traded partnerships (PTPs), master limited partnerships (MLPs), certain commodity-related exchange-trade products, hedge funds or private equity vehicles can end up needing to file in multiple states. So may professionals, such as lawyers and accountants, who practice at firms that have offices in multiple states. That is because these investments and businesses are often set up as partnerships. Partnerships "pass through" income and deductions to their partners, meaning partners are responsible for reporting income wherever the partnership does business. Multi-state filings may be a simple matter of having one additional return prepared, but sometimes it can be much more complicated.

If you participate in such entities, you may be asked whether you would like to be included in a composite return. Unless you have encountered one before, you are likely to have immediate questions. What is it? What are its advantages or disadvantages? Are you even eligible?

A composite return is a group filing by some or all nonresident members of a pass-through entity (PTE). In order to participate in a composite return, you must typically meet certain requirements. Your income from the electing PTE must be your only income from the state in question. You must not have been a resident of that state at any time during the year, and your personal tax year must be the same as the PTE's tax year. In addition, most states prohibit partners that are entities (corporations, partnerships, certain trusts) from participating in composite filings.

There are several advantages to filing a composite return if you are eligible. Composite returns can relieve the administrative burden of filing tax returns in multiple states and the need to make estimated tax payments or deal with notices or audits. You may also find that your tax preparation expenses are less than they otherwise would be since you don't have to file as many tax returns. That said, composite tax returns are not always the way to go.

Composite filings typically disregard personal exemptions and losses from other entities or itemized deductions, which could lower or eliminate taxable income. In addition, states typically charge the highest marginal tax rate applicable to individuals or corporations on composite returns. Though they can save some personal aggravation, it's a good idea to discuss the pros and cons with your personal tax adviser before making your decision.

## Credits for Taxes Paid to Nonresident States

Taxpayers who owe income tax to more than one state may also benefit from credits on their resident state income tax returns. Part-year residents are often eligible for tax credits for income taxed by another state during their period of residency. Nonresidents, however, are not eligible for credits in the state where they file a nonresident return. The purpose of the credit is to alleviate the effect of double taxation.

Note that if you live in a state that has higher income taxes than the state where you earned your income, it is likely you will not receive a credit that will completely offset the taxes you paid to your resident state, because the credit is limited to actual taxes paid to nonresident states. For example, if you earned $100 of income in a state with a tax rate of 5 percent and the state where you claim the resident tax credit has a tax rate of 8 percent, your credit will be limited to $5 even though you owe $8 in tax to your resident state. The situation works in reverse if you live in a state with a lower tax rate than the state where you paid the tax. The credit will be limited to the income taxes you pay in your home state. Using the above numbers, if you lived in the state that charged 5 percent but earned your $100 in the state that charged 8 percent, your nonresident credit would be limited to $5.

## Reciprocal Agreements

In reciprocal agreements, two or more states, usually geographic neighbors, arrange to exempt the earned income of residents of neighboring states from income taxes. For example, if you live in Evansville, Indiana, but work in nearby Louisville, Kentucky, you can file an exemption form with your Kentucky employer instructing the company not to withhold Kentucky taxes from your wages and request that they withhold Indiana taxes instead. Depending on your employer and the particular state's arrangement, you may have to pay estimated taxes instead. At the end of the year, you would only need to file a tax return with Indiana. These arrangements simplify tax compliance issues for residents of neighboring states, alleviating the need to file multiple tax returns. Reciprocal agreements generally only apply to wages, not other sorts of income.

## What Are the Rules for Business Owners?

You may want to consider launching a new business in retirement, which can introduce new state-level tax considerations. In the case of corporations, they are separate entities from their owners, so their domicile for income tax purposes will be the state where the business is incorporated. State rules for taxing a business' income vary, and are beyond the scope of this chapter to describe completely, but perhaps the most important related principle to understand is that of nexus.

Nexus is the level of contact that must exist between an entity and a state before the state has the legal authority to assess a tax. Several questions help to determine whether nexus exists:

1. Does the business derive sales within the state?

2. Does the business own or lease property within the state?

3. Does the business employ people in the state for activities other than solicitation?

The threshold for how much of each of these activities constitutes nexus varies from state to state. The determination used to be relatively straightforward, but the rise of e-commerce has rendered the question of nexus an uncommonly tricky one. States are pushing to expand the concept of nexus as it related to sales tax, and some online retailers are pushing back. The definition of nexus will probably continue to evolve. However, the right of a state to collect income taxes is less controversial, since states have not been as aggressive in asserting that out-of-state vendors owe income tax merely because they ship goods or otherwise make sales to a distant state.

Income tax liability is generally subject to traditional nexus rules, resulting in much less uncertainty for business owners, even when their businesses operate partially online. In broad terms, if your business can answer a firm yes to any of the three questions above, nexus is likely to exist. Once nexus is established, state income tax rules apply.

Beyond income tax, business owners should be aware that their business will owe use tax on items purchased from out-of-state vendors on which no sales tax was charged or if the tax was paid at a rate less than that of the state where the item was used in your business. Use tax is also charged on items purchased from a supplier for resale that are used in your business, but no tax was paid to the supplier. This can create significant tax exposure, and the business may need to file its own use tax return. Your business may also owe franchise tax and, in most states, will need to collect sales tax as well. See Chapter 18 for further information.

## State Tax Concerns: A Practical Example

It is easy to get caught up in technicalities involving state taxes. Let's return to Max and Ruth, the hypothetical couple from the beginning of this chapter. (Note that, while I give exact figures that were accurate as of this writing, state tax laws often change.)

Recent retirees Max and Ruth want to move their primary residence in order to be closer to either their son, who lives in Oregon, or their daughter, who lives in South Carolina. Though the states' different climates and cultures, as well as the different personalities and living situations of the couple's two children, will be major factors in their decision, Max and Ruth want to consider the tax impact of each choice as well.

Oregon scores a large attractiveness boon right away because it has no sales tax at all, compared to South Carolina's 6 percent – though prescription drugs and unprepared food items are exempt, and seniors over

85 years of age pay 5 percent instead. Income tax, however, is another matter. South Carolina residents pay between 3 and 7 percent on their income, while Oregonians pay between 5 and 11 percent and are divided into more brackets.

For Max and Ruth, however, the specific concern is tax on retirement income, since neither plan to earn wages in their new home state. While both states exempt Social Security benefits, in Oregon all other retirement income, including pensions, is taxed. Oregon does offer a retirement credit up to 9 percent of income, but the Max and Ruth do not qualify because of their income level. In South Carolina, the first $3,000 of pension income is exempt; after 65, you exempt $10,000. After 65, filers can also take a senior income tax deduction of up to $15,000, offset by the amount you take as a retirement income deduction. Both spouses are entitled to individual deductions and, should one spouse die, the other can continue to take a deduction on the deceased's behalf.

In addition to tax on income and deferred compensation, Max and Ruth want to purchase a small home or a condo in whichever state they choose. This means they should consider property taxes in each state. Property tax in South Carolina is very low, and its tax breaks for seniors are more attractive than those Oregon offers.

Max and Ruth plan to leave an inheritance for their children, so estate tax is an additional concern. In Oregon, if their estate exceeds $1 million at the time of the surviving spouse's death, the couple's heirs will owe Oregon estate tax up to a maximum rate of 16 percent. In South Carolina, no state estate tax would apply, regardless of the estate's size.

On balance, Max and Ruth find South Carolina the friendlier tax climate. They can use this information as one piece of the puzzle in deciding where to retire – or, if they ultimately plan to spend substantial time in both states, they can use the information to determine which state they should actively make their domicile and in which they should be careful to retain nonresident status to avoid higher taxes.

State tax planning can be a one-time consideration when deciding where to move, or it can be a long-term component of your financial planning strategy if you have homes in more than one state, invest in assets that require multiple state tax returns, or travel for long periods of the year. This chapter gave you an overview of some of the factors you should consider or discuss with your financial adviser when making such choices. State tax law should not be the sole factor in the decision of where to retire, reside or buy a second home, but understanding the differences between state tax codes can help you to make smart decisions, wherever you choose to live.

# 15

## INVESTMENT APPROACHES AND PHILOSOPHY
### Paul Jacobs, CFP®, EA
### Anthony D. Criscuolo, CFP®, EA

Investment is often described as both a science and an art. What science and art have in common is they take time, practice and commitment to do well, with maybe a little innate talent added to the mix.

Although there are certain guidelines and rules that most investment managers tend to follow, there is no one optimal way to invest. Each investor's needs are different and each investment adviser has different preferences on how to best satisfy these needs. That said, there are broad investment principles that have proven reliable over time. Understanding these principles, as well as your own situation, will give you a basic set of tools to work with, whether you are making investment decisions yourself or with the help of an adviser.

This chapter will introduce essential investment terminology that all prudent investors should know. It will also set forth some basic investment principles. After completing this chapter, you should have a general understanding of risk and volatility as they relate to investments and the importance of asset allocation and diversification in an investment portfolio.

Some of the information in this chapter will apply to any prudent investor. Some is more specific advice, based on Palisades Hudson's particular investment philosophy. Many books have been written about different investment approaches and their benefits and limitations. This chapter is only an introduction, meant as a springboard from which to perform your own research or to give you questions to ask a professional so that you can be confident that his or her philosophy aligns with your own. Even if you hire a professional investment adviser, we believe everyone should have, at the very least, a basic understanding of how their assets are invested. After all, it is your money.

## Establishing Your Goals and Risk Tolerance

Before investing, you need to establish and understand your goals and your risk tolerance. These will shape any sensible investment plan, no matter what philosophy you employ. Your goals are your destination; your risk tolerance dictates how much risk you're willing to take to get there.

For most investors, goals are the easier of the two to define, but many people don't bother to explicitly define them. Most people have a variety of goals, and those goals don't all have equal importance. Are you investing to meet an immediate need, such as purchasing property or managing debt? Do you want to grow your wealth to secure a comfortable retirement income for yourself, or a cushion to take care of any long-term care needs you may one day face? Or do you want to create enough wealth that you can leave a generous estate for your heirs or for charity? Whether your goal is one or more of these, knowing why you're investing will help you make better investment choices and keep you motivated to stick to your long-term investment plan when circumstances become difficult.

Pinpointing your risk tolerance is usually more difficult, but no less essential. Your risk tolerance refers to the amount of short-term uncertainty you are willing to accept in exchange for long-term gains. Risk tolerance goes hand-in-hand with your goals; investing to meet your short-term needs and investing to bequeath money to your heirs can involve different investment returns and time horizons, for example.

In general, there is a direct trade-off between risk and return. The higher the expected return, the more risk you will need to take to achieve it. It is also important to remember that no investment strategy is entirely risk-free. Nor will simply taking the maximum amount of risk assure the highest long-term return. Realistically assessing how you will deal with short-term volatility is essential in crafting an investment strategy that will work for you over the long haul.

Volatility is the most common measure of risk. Statistically speaking, volatility is a measure of the dispersion of returns for a given investment. It refers to the fluctuations of an asset's value over time. Although most assets will increase in value over time (that is the goal of all investments), the path to higher value is rarely steady. Your individual risk tolerance is determined by how well you handle the frequency and severity of the change in value of your investments—especially when the value declines. Some people will follow the market's daily moves and stress over every downswing, no matter how small. These people typically have a high aversion to risk and may seek steadier investments, even if it means trading off a higher long-term return. On the other hand, investors with a higher risk tolerance may be comfortable with larger and more frequent downswings as long as their investments rise over a long period of time.

## Fixed Income (Bonds) vs. Equity (Stocks)

A portfolio's risk is determined by the assets it holds. The two most basic and fundamental asset classes are fixed income and equities. In general, fixed income is safer than equities. The increased risk associated with equity leads to higher expected returns. Within these asset classes, fixed income generally refers to bonds whereas equity refers to stocks.

A bond, by definition, is a debt instrument in which an investor lends money to an entity for a defined period of time, and expects to be repaid with interest. When companies or governments need to raise money, they will issue bonds as debt obligations. How the investor is repaid depends on the type of bond.

Zero-coupon bonds will pay an investor a lump sum at the end of the bond's term, knows as its maturity, while coupon bonds will make regular interest payments at defined intervals and return the face value when the bond matures. A bond's face value is the amount originally lent to the company or government.

There are many different types of bonds and bond investment strategies; however, the general theme with bonds is that the investor is guaranteed a fixed payment over a defined period of time. This guarantee is only reliable to the extent that the bond issuer can make the scheduled payments. The less likely an issuer is to follow through on its obligation, the higher the interest rate it must pay investors. As with all other investments, the riskier it is, the greater the expected return will be.

On the opposite end of the spectrum from bonds is equity. Equity is generally a stock or any other security that represents an ownership interest. When an investor buys a share of a company's stock, he or she is actually becoming a part owner of the company. As owners, all shareholders have a right to the company's profits. Equity investors are paid in one of two ways: dividends or capital gains. When a company makes a profit, it must decide whether to reinvest that capital into the company or to pay it out as a dividend. When the company lacks attractive investment opportunities, it will choose to pay dividends, which are payments from a company to its shareholders. Companies use dividends to distribute profits to their owners. Not all companies pay dividends, however. Typically companies that are growing quickly will reinvest profits, while more mature companies will pay dividends.

The other way stocks reward shareholders is through capital gains. As a company grows and increases in value, its stock price will rise. An investor can realize this increased value by selling the stock at a higher price than that at which he or she purchased the shares. The difference is considered a capital gain. Capital gains are typically expected, but certainly not guaranteed. While many stocks will increase in value over time, some stocks will not, and a few may become completely worthless in the event of a business failure.

While fixed income and equity can be much more complex than discussed above, the main point you should take away is that fixed income is safer and offers lower returns than equity. As we will discuss in more detail later in this chapter, how you allocate your portfolio between these asset classes will largely determine your portfolio's expected return and risk.

## Inflation and Appreciating Assets

When choosing an investment approach, being overly aggressive has its obvious pitfalls. However, being overly conservative also has its drawbacks. Typically, the more conservative an investor is, the more fixed income he or she will hold. Some, however, will completely avoid the markets by holding only cash. Contrary to popular belief, even the most risk-averse long-term investors do not belong entirely in cash. This is mainly due to one factor: inflation.

Inflation is the rate at which the general level of prices for goods and services rises. As inflation increases, your money's purchasing power erodes. Over time, the prices of goods and services almost always increase. Historically, inflation has averaged about 3 percent annually since 1913 and 4 percent annually during the past 50 years. A product that cost $1,000 50 years ago would sell for more than $7,000 today. The only way to combat this process is to invest in appreciating assets.

Figure 1 displays the growth of wealth for a stock market benchmark (the S&P 500), a bond market benchmark (the Barclays US Aggregate Bond Index), and the U.S. Consumer Price Index – a measure of inflation – over the last 30 years. The figure depicts the future value of $1 based on the growth of each.

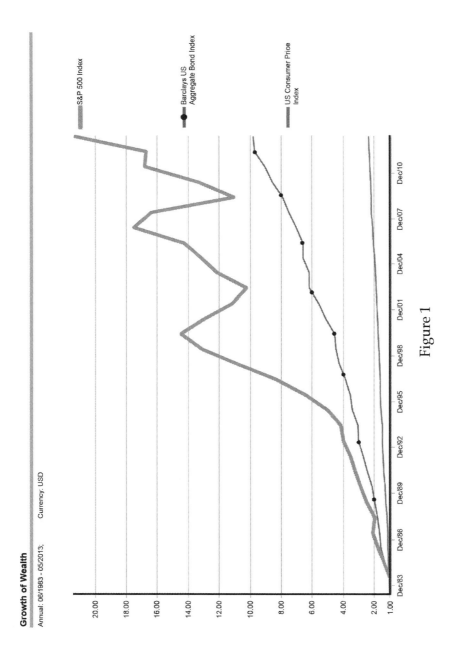

Figure 1

As Figure 1 illustrates, equity and fixed income have returned substantially more than inflation over this time period. Therefore, an individual invested in either of these asset classes, or a combination of them, would have outpaced inflation. On the other hand, an investor who solely held cash not only would have given up the opportunity for higher returns, but would have effectively lost spending power at the rate of inflation. Investing in appreciating assets is the only way to protect your wealth against inflation and the rising price of goods and services.

## Long-Term Time Horizon

The most important fundamental principle every investor should have is the idea of investing for the long haul. The central goal of investing is to increase value over time. While every worthwhile investment is expected to appreciate in the long run, short-term changes in value are often unpredictable. By their nature, riskier assets often generate higher long-term returns, but with greater short-term fluctuations. As we discussed, the magnitude of short-term fluctuations you are willing to accept in exchange for long-term returns will be determined by your risk tolerance. It's important to remember, however, that major short-term fluctuations in your portfolio's performance are possible, whatever your risk tolerance.

For example, even the most conservative portfolios can be severely affected by major financial events, such as the housing bubble and credit crisis in 2008. Although almost everyone was negatively affected by the ensuing recession, investors who pulled out of the market at the bottom, and thus missed the subsequent rebound, were hurt the most. Those who remained invested saw a steady recovery in asset prices after the market's bottom in early 2009, and within a few years had generally made up what they lost. This is why it is so important to cultivate a long-term mindset. Making emotionally driven decisions to abandon your investment plan during market downturns will always lead to poor investment results.

One of the worst things a long-term investor can do is unnecessarily respond to short-term events. The market tends to overreact, especially during crises, resulting in exaggerated market downswings. Countless investors have sustained substantial losses by selling after a major market decline, fearing the market would fall further, only to see the market rebound instead. Only by selling and completely exiting the markets do you sustain permanent loses. If you plan to buy back in once the markets have settled down, it is often too late. This can lead to a cycle of selling low and buying high, which will produce poor long-term results.

## Diversification

Besides a long-term outlook, the other fundamental principle to keep in mind is diversification. Diversification is a risk management technique that mixes a wide variety of investments within a portfolio. Buying and holding a diversified portfolio that includes various securities, asset classes, geographic regions, company sizes and investment styles can minimize exposure to any particular holding's risks.

There are two main types of investment risk: firm-specific risk and market risk. Firm-specific risk refers to risk factors that are unique only to the particular investment. One example of firm-specific risk is the sudden death of a CEO who is integral to the success of a company. Although this particular company is greatly affected, other companies are unaffected. On the other hand, market risk refers to factors and events that affect a wide range of securities. For example, during the recession of 2008-2009, nearly all stocks and many bonds lost value in unison.

Firm-specific risk can be eliminated or greatly reduced through diversification; however, market risk cannot. Take, for example, a company that declares bankruptcy. If your investment portfolio held stock in only that one company, the bankruptcy announcement would be disastrous for your portfolio. If, on the other hand, you invested in 500 companies, one of them going bankrupt is unlikely to have a major effect on your portfolio as a whole.

In a broader example, if you invest heavily in businesses located geographically near one another, a natural disaster such as an earthquake or a hurricane could create heavy losses for you. In a geographically diversified portfolio, losses caused by the same hurricane might be offset by gains in other regions. The more diversification you can build into your portfolio, the less specific risk you must bear. As a result, diversification leads to more consistent and often higher long-term returns.

## An In-Depth Analysis of Risk and Volatility

Often, investment advisers use the words "risk" and "volatility" interchangeably; however, a knowledgeable investor should recognize that these two terms are not identical. Risk can be broadly defined as the chance of an outcome being materially different from what is expected. In investment terms, risk is the chance that your returns will be different from what is expected, while volatility is a measure of risk. Risk is a broad term and there are many different forms of investment risk; not all of which are quantifiable.

One type of risk, which has already been touched upon, is systematic, or market risk. Beta is a measure of this risk and it tells an investor about the tendency of an investment's return to respond to swings in the overall market. Essentially, beta compares the movement in a security's returns to the movement of the market. A negative beta represents a security that moves opposite to that of the market. When the market rises, a negative beta security will fall and vice versa. On the other hand, a positive beta security will rise and fall as the market rises and falls respectively. The vast majority of securities have positive betas. This is intuitive considering the market is simply the aggregate of all securities and thus when the market rises, the majority of securities must also rise.

Another type of quantifiable risk, also touched upon earlier, is unsystematic or firm-specific risk. A measure of this type of risk tells an investor how much and how often a security changes in value separate from market movements. One measurement of firm-specific risk is a security's correlation coefficient relative to the market. Correlation is a statistical measure of how two securities move in relation to each other. Similar to beta, a positive correlation coefficient suggests that a security moves with the market, while a negative coefficient suggests a security moves opposite the market. A security's correlation coefficient ranges from -1 to 1 and the closer a security's correlation coefficient is to zero, the more random its price movements. Since price movements not explained by the market are usually due to firm-specific risk factors, the closer to zero a company's correlation coefficient is, the more firm-specific risk the company has.

In simple terms, volatility measures the chance that an investment's return will be something other than what is expected. It considers changes in a security's value that result both from broad market movements and from specific company events. Volatility can be measured using standard deviation, or dispersion of returns, over a given time period.

Figure 2 revisits the returns for the S&P 500 and the Barclays US Aggregate Bond Index over a 30-year period. As you can see, stocks tend to be much more volatile than fixed income. The more volatile a security is, the larger the dispersion of returns will be year to year.

These types of quantifiable risk are only part of the story. There are many types of risks that are not measurable. Two examples are management risk and political risk. Management risk is the risk associated with ineffective, destructive or underperforming management, which hurts shareholder value. Political risk is the chance that a change in government or its policies will affect a company. For example, an oppressive government can take control of a company by force to suit its political agenda. Such an action would negatively affect that company and its respective shareholders.

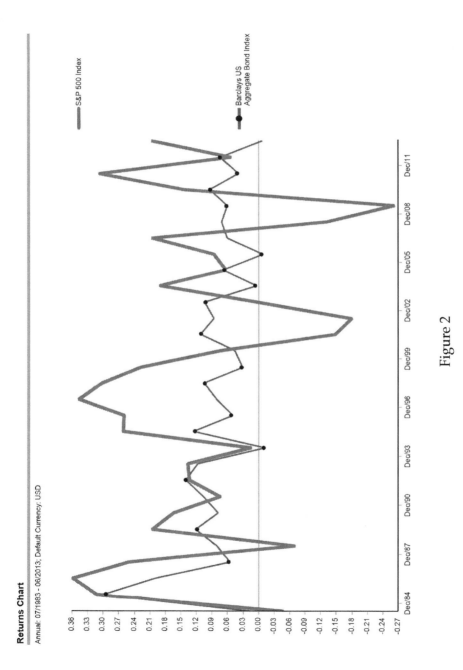

Figure 2

As you can see, no one measurement of risk is complete. Still, volatility is most often accepted as one of the best measures of risk because it considers both firm-specific and market risk, and because it is quantifiable. Generally, greater volatility equates to greater risk.

## Asset Allocation and Rebalancing

Once you understand your goals and risk tolerance, you should create a long-term plan and stick to it. An investment adviser can help you translate your needs and goals into a plan that will work for you, keeping in mind the principles of diversification and long-term perspective.

The first step in creating any diversified portfolio is to determine the optimal asset allocation that will satisfy your investment goals and risk tolerance. On its most fundamental level, asset allocation means the percentage of your portfolio devoted to different asset classes. Asset allocation is the most important determinant of overall portfolio performance, and the allocation you settle on will have a profound effect on your portfolio's returns over time.

Though asset allocation generally refers to the selected mix of stocks and bonds, it can also be classified into sub-asset classes. For example, fixed income can be further broken down into government bonds and corporate bonds, and also short-term bonds and long-term bonds. Equity can be broken down into common stocks and preferred stocks, and also by investment style, economic industry, firm size, geographic region, and so on.

One of the best ways to diversify is by geographic region, including a mixture of U.S. and foreign securities. The United States offers a huge variety of equities and investors often tend to feel an affinity for assets based in their home country (known as a "home-country bias"). Yet, it's important not to neglect non-U.S. companies. One of the most important reasons to diversify globally is protection against a prolonged economic downturn in the U.S. If the U.S. enters a recession, an investor holding only U.S. securities will suffer great losses. If, however, the investor is diversified globally, the losses should not be as severe. In fact, it's possible for one region of the world to grow rapidly, while another is in a major economic slump.

Another great way to diversify is by market capitalization, or market cap. A company's market cap is the total value of its outstanding shares and is a measure of a company's relative size. You should consider investing in equities that represent both large companies – sometimes called "large-cap" equities – and smaller or medium companies ("small-cap" or "mid-cap").

Small-cap stocks have more growth potential than larger capitalization stocks and thus provide a greater expected rate of return. They are appropriate additions to a long-term portfolio for someone who is financially secure. Based on data going back to 1926, the expected one-year total return for small-cap stocks is 16.55 percent, compared to 11.77 percent for the S&P 500. While the higher expected return of U.S. small-cap stocks is attractive, it comes with higher volatility.

Your equity allocation can – and often should – also include allocations to commercial real estate equities and natural resources equities. These can counteract general downward shifts in the broader stock and bond markets, and generally perform well during periods of high inflation. While buying pure commodities such as oil and precious metals will ensure direct exposure to inflation hedges, we generally forego direct exposure in favor of enterprises engaged in selling or extracting the underlying hard asset. These businesses can generate profit even if commodity prices decline by cutting costs or investing in research and development to find alternative products.

Asset allocation is not about picking one asset class over another, but rather developing the optimal balance of various asset classes to build a diversified portfolio that has an acceptable level of risk and potential return. A healthy portfolio shouldn't necessarily have everything in equal portions. That's where the "allocation" part comes in. How you allocate between safe and risky investments will determine your portfolio's overall return potential and risk level.

## Anthony's Advice

### Does a more diverse portfolio protect you from greater risk?

Diversification will help protect against many forms of risks, but not all risks. By definition holding a diverse portfolio of various types of assets means some will go up when others may go down. The goal of holding a diversified portfolio is not to ensure you will always have positive returns over every time period. Even a well-diversified portfolio will fluctuate, sometimes significantly. Rather, diversification protects against specific risk factors by not overly concentrating a portfolio in any single company, sector, or style. A portfolio that is not diversified may not perform as expected because company-specific risk factors can easily override asset class considerations.

-AC

This decision will boil down to your investment goals and risk tolerance. Once you have selected a reasonable asset allocation, it is essential to stay with it unless your financial objectives or situation materially change. This means you should always avoid attempting to time the markets. Do not try to predict which asset classes will perform the best or worst over some period of time and then shift your asset allocation in an attempt to profit from this prediction. Market timing often leads to emotionally driven decisions based on short-term market movements, which is a poor investment strategy.

The consequence of inaccurately timing the stock market can be significant. Consider the affect of missing the best single day in the market. Between 1970 and 2012, according to Standard and Poor's, the S&P 500 returned 9.94 percent on an annualized compounded rate. When you subtract the single best performance day, this return drops to 9.66 percent. Subtracting the best five days, the return drops even further to 8.84 percent. If you missed the best 25 days, your return would have been 6.33 percent, which is only about 1 percent greater than the one-month Treasury bill return over the same period of 5.30 percent. For reference, one-month T-bills are considered one of the safest investments and as such, offer a low expected return compared to equities. The lesson here is that you must remain in the market to succeed as a long-term investor. Attempting to time market upturns and downturns is not only near-impossible, but the consequence of timing incorrectly can be devastating to a portfolio's return.

Sticking with your asset allocation doesn't mean leaving your portfolio alone. In fact, it means the opposite. When rising markets lead to an over-concentration in one asset class, you should reduce your stake in it; conversely, when falling markets leave a segment of your allocation under-represented, increase your investments in that sector. This process is called rebalancing.

How frequently you should rebalance is a subjective question, and different advisers have different philosophies. Some use a calendar-based system, rebalancing a portfolio at some fixed interval, such as annually or quarterly. While this system is preferable to not rebalancing at all, it is generally too passive and arbitrary and a portfolio can wind up severely out of balance between rebalances. If you choose to rebalance on a calendar-based system, we typically recommend rebalancing semiannually, or twice a year. This frequency will ensure your portfolio does not go too far astray while avoiding higher trading costs associated with more frequent rebalances.

A better approach is to rebalance when your portfolio's asset allocation deviates outside an acceptable range. A banded approach ties rebalancing directly to a portfolio's changing asset allocation. In this method, a portfolio's asset allocation is banded within a certain threshold of the ideal balance (often within 5 and 15 percent). If an asset class rises above or drops below this range, this signals a rebalance is warranted. While frequent rebalancing can increase transaction costs and income tax liability, a methodical and disciplined approach to rebalancing will lead to superior long-term investment results.

## How to Implement a Diversified Portfolio

Up until now we have talked about how you can successfully manage your investments and stick to a long-term investment strategy. But how exactly do you enter in the markets? In general, you have two options. You can either hand pick individual securities, including stocks and bonds, or you can buy diversified vehicles such as mutual funds.

Although individual stock and bond picking is used by certain investors, at Palisades Hudson, we rely a great deal on mutual funds and exchange-traded funds (ETFs). A mutual fund pools capital from many investors and invests it in stocks, bonds, or other securities. Mutual funds issue shares to investors that are priced using the fund's net asset value (NAV) per share, which is the value of all of the fund's underlying holdings divided by the total number of shares outstanding. A mutual fund's NAV updates once per day after the market closes based on the change in value of all its holdings. Some mutual funds have a broad go-anywhere investment strategy, while others maintain a more focused investment mandate, such as investing only in U.S. small-cap stocks.

Mutual funds can be either passively or actively managed. A passively managed fund will typically try to replicate a benchmark index, such as the S&P 500. In an actively managed fund, the fund managers will pick individual securities they think will outperform the benchmark index. Actively managed funds will typically have higher costs in the form of fees and expenses.

Similar to passively managed mutual funds, ETFs also try to mimic a benchmark index. Unlike mutual funds, which only trade at the end of the day at their NAV, ETFs act more like stocks and can be traded throughout the day based on a market price. This market price changes throughout the day, just as a stock's price does.

Broadly, indexing is more appropriate for large-company stocks in efficient markets, such as the U.S. and western Europe. Active management (where fund managers have the opportunity to profit from market inefficiencies) is more appropriate in less efficient markets such as small companies in emerging markets such as Latin America or China. When selecting an actively managed fund, be sure to keep an eye on both the fund's long-term performance record and its fees, which can quickly eat away at your returns.

When it's appropriate, we also consider alternative investments, such as private equity, venture capital, and hedge funds. These investments can be especially risky because they are less diversified, and often rely on leverage strategies that may not ultimately pay off. They also tend to be illiquid, meaning it can be hard to retrieve invested capital. The reason we consider these investments is that they offer the potential for high returns. While alternative investments can be a worthwhile addition to a diversified portfolio, it is wise to limit your total commitment to these investments to a relatively small percentage of your overall wealth.

Investors who want to receive a stream of income often turn to annuities and income products. Annuities are financial instruments that provide a stream of payments for a predetermined number of years. While annuities can be useful, investors should be wary. Fixed annuities, which guarantee an income stream, are unappealing in a low interest rate environment, because you lock in a low interest rate. Variable annuities, which provide an income stream determined by an associated portfolio's performance, can provide higher returns, but generally carry steep fees and strict terms that make them unattractive.

## Measuring Investment Performance

Once you have a well-diversified portfolio and a system for rebalancing in place, the next question is how to determine whether your portfolio is performing as expected. This may seem self-evident; good portfolios are those that create satisfactory returns over time. But exactly what this means will depend on your goals and your investing strategy.

Many investors look for investments that generate income through bond interest payments and stock dividends. This form of investing, called income investing, is a traditional way to think about investing, but it is flawed. Investors only interested in income will ignore non-dividend paying stocks, which include many fast-growing companies, and this can be detrimental to a portfolio's overall long-term performance. In times of low interest rates, it can also lead to excessive risk-taking in a fixed-income portfolio in search of higher returns.

A more stable approach is to seek "total return" by investing for both income and capital appreciation. Instead of chasing high-yielding stocks and bonds, total return investors look for securities that will not only provide income in the short-term, but will also increase in value over time. Total return investors look for the best possible investment opportunities available, and typically have more diversified portfolios with higher returns than income-focused investors.

When evaluating your portfolio it is important to analyze relative performance and not simply absolute returns. For example, if your portfolio returns 8 percent over a given time period, you may conclude that your portfolio performed poorly. However, this performance must be compared to other benchmarks. If during the same time period, your benchmark returned 6 percent, your portfolio actually performed well. The opposite is true as well. If your portfolio returned 15%, but the benchmark returned 20%, your portfolio would have actually underperformed.

## Paul's Advice

### What benchmark should I use to evaluate my portfolio's performance?

We don't recommend simply comparing performance to one benchmark like the S&P 500 Index, which is made up of 500 large companies located in the U.S. Because a diversified portfolio will have exposure to uncorrelated investments such as international equities and fixed-income securities, we recommend comparing your portfolio's performance (and volatility) to benchmark indices for each major asset class in your portfolio. Your portfolio's performance will likely fall somewhere in between these indexes, depending on how much exposure you have to different asset classes.

-PJ

There are a number of different ways to measure a portfolio's actual performance. Different measures take into account different factors and thus have their strengths and weaknesses. The most common performance measure is the internal rate of return (IRR). This measurement is simply the ratio of money gained or lost relative to the amount of money invested.

Regardless of which statistic you use to measure performance, you must always keep in mind the performance of your total portfolio. Investors often have multiple accounts through which they invest, such as 401(k)s, IRAs, taxable brokerage accounts, and the like. It is the performance of all the accounts combined which make up your overall investment portfolio's rate of return. The performance or the level of risk in an individual account is not necessarily important.

A portfolio's performance over a given time period is important, but it is not the only issue to consider. It is essential to understand and conform to the investment strategy you select for the long-term. A portfolio's performance over some arbitrary time period can be misleading. For example, if you were to analyze your portfolio's performance between 2008 and 2009, you may be led to believe your investment strategy was flawed due to the negative returns. While any investment strategy can lose money in the short run, a good strategy will prevail in the long run. If you believe in your strategy for the long term and avoid allowing short-term performance to persuade you into changing your course, you should end up with positive results.

## Fees, Expenses, and Taxes

We have mentioned fees a few times in the discussion above, and at this point it's worth pausing to discuss expenses in a bit more detail. As you select investment products, it is important to be aware of the fees, commissions, and other costs that may be attached to a particular vehicle.

Some charges are intuitive and easy to understand, such as a fee for the fund manager or a commission when a certain fund is bought or sold. Other fees are less clear, and can require some digging to understand. For example, annuities usually set restrictions on when and how much money you can withdraw; if you have to withdraw your funds in a different way or at a different time, you may incur surrender charges. When evaluating how lucrative you expect a certain investment vehicle to be, it's important to factor in all the fees.

There is also the distinction between fee-only and commission-based investment advisers. Fee-only advisers are only paid by their clients, and their fee is usually based on a fixed percentage of a client's assets under management. Commission-based advisers charge a certain amount for every trade they execute or product they sell. Generally, fee-only advisers are preferable because their interests are completely aligned with their clients and they avoid any conflict of interest that is inherent with receiving commissions.

Taxes are equally important. The general rule is that any time income is received, taxes must be paid. This is not completely true when it comes to investing. Some accounts, such as 401(k)s, Traditional IRAs and Roth IRAs, are tax-free or tax-deferred. If you have multiple accounts through which you invest, you should consider the tax consequences of your investments.

You should also know the difference between short-term and long-term capital gains. Short-term capital gains, which are gains realized on the sale of an investment held for less than a year, are taxed at a higher rate (generally as ordinary income). Long-term gains often receive preferable tax treatment at a lower rate.

## Conclusion

Investment management is a complex and difficult task. It takes years to learn and even longer to truly understand and implement. The economic environment is constantly changing, but regardless of how the world has changed, certain investment principles such as diversification, asset allocation, and investing for the long term have proven reliable over time.

Regardless of the strategy you choose to implement, we encourage you to begin by thinking about your investment goals and risk tolerance. You must balance your desire for high returns with an understanding of how much short-term volatility is acceptable. These factors will help determine your asset allocation. And don't forget: there is no such thing as a free lunch, meaning higher returns come with higher risk.

# 16

## INVESTMENT PSYCHOLOGY
### Benjamin C. Sullivan, CFP®, EA

Most people know not to make life-changing decisions while riding a roller coaster. Adrenaline, euphoria and fear are not conducive to critical thinking. Although the highs and lows of the stock market tend to have the same effect on an investor's mindset as a high-speed amusement attraction, there are no safety harnesses to prevent ill-advised action in the rush of the moment. You may be approaching retirement, but there is still a long ride ahead of you. By making well-thought-out, logical decisions, you can ensure your finances stay on the right track.

One of the biggest risks to investors' long-term wealth is their own behavior. Investment professionals and laypeople alike are prone to fears and biases that lead them to make subpar financial decisions. Part of the problem is that what separates good investors from bad ones isn't simply education and experience. With time and effort, both can be improved. But human brains are wired to avoid predators, not to make optimal investment decisions. Subconscious patterns of behavior can trip up even experienced investors.

## The Cycle of Investor Emotions

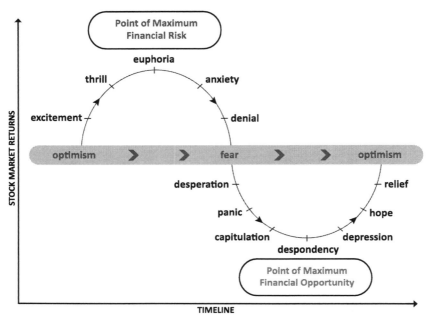

Source: Adapted from the Cycle of Market Emotions chart created by
Westcore Funds/Denver Investment Advisors, 1998.

Figure 1

We use mental shortcuts and emotional cues all the time in our day-to-day lives, but when it comes to investing, such habits can lead to trouble. That doesn't mean, however, that your brain is destined to hold your financial life hostage. You can improve your decisions by planning ahead and recognizing that emotion and spontaneity are your enemies, while data and planning are your friends.

Billy Beane, who became famous as the subject of the book *Moneyball* and the subsequent film of the same title, applied statistical data to the task of building a winning professional baseball team before such techniques were common. While others scoffed at such techniques, Beane accurately anticipated that using data instead of "gut instinct" could lead him to more consistent performance. The same reliance on data over emotion can protect investors from many common mistakes.

In this chapter, we will review some common errors that can lead to harmful investment decisions, as well as emotional traps that arise when investors suffer losses or face market volatility. With a better awareness of these common pitfalls, you can appreciate the need for a long-term investment plan to keep you calm when euphoria, panic or hype try to take control of your psyche.

## Fears and Biases

Experts in behavioral finance have identified some emotional shortcuts that investors use unconsciously as they make financial decisions. These shortcuts generally take the form of biases. Investors over- or under-value the information available to them in a variety of predictable ways. Some of these biases are cognitive, or logical, in nature. Cognitive biases include logical fallacies, errors in interpreting statistics and errors of memory. Other biases are emotional, springing from impulse or intuition rather than from conscious calculation. Both logical and emotional errors can have devastating impacts on a portfolio if given free rein.

It may be helpful to think of these biases as techniques your brain has evolved to save time and energy. If you had to fully and deeply process every decision you made, you would quickly become exhausted and unable to make any decisions at all. However, the cost of these shortcuts is that they can warp your perception of reality. In the context of finance, even small distortions in your perception can lead you to make costly mistakes. The following are common biases that you should anticipate when making financial decisions.

### Overconfidence

Most people believe they are better at many things than they actually are, from driving to investing. Compounding the problem, we don't notice this talent inflation, because people also generally tend to believe they are less overconfident than others. In many areas, self-confidence and optimism are boons; in finance, however, they can lead to taking risks that aren't worth the potential rewards.

Why are people prone to overestimate their own abilities? Generally, it is not a matter of conscious vanity, though temperament and socialization are factors. Rather, confidence springs from the story your brain has created regarding the task or activity you are about to perform. Since the brain prefers consistency to inconsistency, your confidence has much less to do with objective facts than with creating an internally consistent story.

To understand how a consistent internal narrative can lead to overconfidence, consider the example of stock picking. People ranging from bus boys to hedge fund managers are prone to think that they can beat the market by picking a few great stocks. Why? Because the internal narrative makes sense: They are generally smart people who are good at their jobs. They also have what they perceived to be useful information. They may get their ideas from friends, customers, Internet forums, research, the news or Jim Cramer. It is easy to believe that a hot tip or insightful article can give them an edge in the stock market, and it is consistent with their self-perception to think they should be better at evaluating such information than most. A smart investor plus good information should equal profit, in the simple but consistent story underpinning their actions. This is why stock picking is so alluring – and so dangerous.

The facts don't back up the story so neatly. More than 86 percent of professional mutual fund managers investing in large U.S. stocks underperformed the S&P 500 Index over the three years ending December 31, 2012. The results are similar over different time periods and in different markets. Although the jury may still be out on whether professional stock pickers can outperform index funds, the casual investor is sure to be at a disadvantage against the professionals. Financial analysts, who have access to sophisticated research and data, spend their entire careers trying to determine the appropriate value of certain stocks. Many of these well-trained analysts focus on only one sector — comparing the merits of investing in Chevron versus ExxonMobil, for example. And even so, these professionals still regularly underpeform the market. It is impossible for an individual to maintain a day job and also perform the appropriate due diligence to maintain a portfolio of individual stocks, especially one that is appropriately diverse. Overconfidence frequently leaves investors with eggs in far too few baskets and with those baskets dangerously close to one another.

Another manifestation of overconfidence is frequent trading, rather than long-term investing. Investing means buying something and holding it with the expectation that, over time, some combination of good management and societal progress will make the asset worth more than its original price. Diversified long-term investing is a game you can win.

Trading is something entirely different. Trading is buying something now on the expectation that you can sell it for more than you paid a few days, a few minutes or, these days, often just a few seconds later. Trading is not a game individuals can win. It's not even a game most businesses can win, even investment businesses such as mutual funds or pension plans. The only way to consistently win in trades against fellow traders is to have faster execution or better information than your rivals. In the modern world, this can come down to fractions of a second.

Yet, believing that they are above-average, investors come to think that they know more than the person on the other side of a trade. The truth is that it's nearly impossible for an individual to have faster execution or better information than institutional traders. While some individual traders do well due to pure luck, the typical trader is ultimately worse off after accounting for the taxes and trading costs incurred by frequent trades. Nonetheless, the draw of being the exception to the rule is often more than investors can resist.

Whether in picking stocks or frequent trading, overconfidence leaves investors focusing on games they can't win. Instead, investors would be better served by focusing on what they can control – their own behavior, including their overall asset allocation, and their spending and saving habits.

## Familiarity

Even the most confident investors know they are not omniscient. This insight may lead them to stick with what they know. Sticking with the familiar also feels good, because we tend to prefer things we know over the unknown. This is why people return to the same few restaurants again and again or read books by authors they already like. While these patterns may lead us to miss out on new experiences, there's nothing inherently harmful about them.

In investing, however, our bias toward the familiar is why many people invest most of their money in areas they feel they know best rather than in a properly diversified portfolio. The known feels safe; the unknown feels risky.

A bias in favor of the familiar can show up in a portfolio in several ways. A banker might create a "diversified" portfolio of five large bank stocks; a Ford assembly line employee might invest predominantly in company stock; a 401(k) investor might allocate his portfolio over a variety of funds that all focus on the U.S. market. Whether it means carrying too much of your employer's stock or investing too heavily in the geographic region where you live, familiarity is the enemy of well-balanced investing.

Sticking with one type of investment concentrates risk rather than reduces it. The market doesn't reward investors for risks that they can, and should, remove from their portfolios through proper diversification. Investors who give in to their bias toward the familiar can wind up creating portfolios with higher risk or lower expected rates of return than a properly diversified portfolio would offer.

## Endowment Effect

In addition to favoring familiar investments, we also tend to overvalue things we already own and undervalue things we don't own yet. This tendency can spring up in a variety of places for an investor. It can lead you to overestimate the resale value of your home or to hold an overly large position in a company because you inherited the shares from a relative. Although you might value the memories created in the home or the legacy that your family has with the company, the market does not.

Since it is generally easier for individuals to decide to buy something than to sell it, it's important to make an effort to think as rationally about sell decisions as you do about buy decisions. One trick is to stop and consider whether, if you didn't already own the asset, you would go to the trouble to acquire it again. If the answer is no, it is probably time to sell.

## Anchoring

While there are complex models that can help calculate the value of an investment, our brains usually want an easier answer. This desire leads many people to default to either the original cost of an investment or to some other benchmark, such as the value on last quarter's statement. Although both measures might provide a framework for determining value, the past is more often irrelevant to the current situation. This tendency to fixate on a point of reference may seem like an easy mistake to spot, but in practice, it can be hard to dislodge a perception that is anchored this way.

Some investors become overly focused on the dollar value of their account statements and may anchor to the amount they had at retirement. This becomes a problem because obsessively checking on your portfolio or investments can make you hyperaware of fluctuations, leading to greater (and unnecessary) anxiety. In addition, the desire for a balance that never declines does not allow for other factors that affect your account, such as the withdrawals you make to fund your living expenses.

Anchoring may also prevent a purchase that is objectively a good idea. If you knew a stock traded for $30 per share two months ago and it now trades for $60, you might think that the stock is overvalued. However, if the company's prospects are skyrocketing, the stock may still be relatively cheap, despite having doubled in price from its former cost.

Alternatively, an owner might also needlessly avoid selling an asset due to this effect. If an investor paid $1 million for his home during the peak of the frothy housing market in early 2007, he may insist that what he paid is the home's true value, despite the depressed market that investors faced in the Great Recession and beyond. Seeing comparable houses sell for hundreds of thousands of dollars less than their former values may not persuade him that his home is no longer worth $1 million. This inability to adjust to the new reality could disrupt the investor's life if, for example, he needed to sell the property in order to relocate for a better job.

## Loss Aversion

Not only do we tend to cling to what we know and anchor to historical prices that are clear in our minds, but we generally avoid facing the truth of a financial loss. An investor who makes a speculative trade that performs poorly will frequently continue to hold the investment, even if new developments have made the investment's prospects ever more dismal.

In Economics 101, students learn about "sunk costs" — costs that have already been incurred. Students also learn that they should typically ignore such costs in decisions about future actions, since no action can recover them. Only the potential future return on the investment, and the associated risk, should matter. Knowing this theory and applying it are two different things. Sunk costs can lead investors to hold on to losers too long to avoid acknowledging mistakes, hoping to recoup their original loss. On the other hand, investors can also get rid of winners too quickly in a rush to mark the investment down in the "win" column and avoid the potential of a future downturn.

In most cases, people who are averse to risk when it comes to gains are willing to take much larger risks to prevent possible losses. This is because most of us place different emotional weights on gains and losses of equivalent size – the pain of losing $10,000 is generally much larger than the happiness of winning $10,000. Unwillingness to accept this pain is what often leads investors to hold on to failing investments too long in the vain hope that they will somehow recover, rather than accept the loss in value.

## Benjamin's Advice

### Is there a right amount of risk to take when investing?

The "right" amount of risk varies for each investor, depending on cash flow needs and risk tolerance. The odds of a positive stock market return increase as your investment time horizon extends. Therefore, you should invest funds that you'll need to withdraw from your portfolio within the next several years in safer investments, such as cash or short-term bonds. Beyond this reserve, you should try to determine how much short-term volatility you can comfortably tolerate in the pursuit of the higher expected returns associated with stocks. Don't be overconfident. Over-investing in stocks often leads to costly mistakes.

-BCS

This tendency can not only lose investors money, but it can also cause investors to miss the opportunity to capture tax benefits by selling investments with losses. Realized losses on capital investments can offset first capital gains, and up to an additional $3,000 of ordinary income per year. By using capital losses to offset ordinary income or future capital gains, investors can reduce their tax liabilities. But first they have to admit that their losses are real.

Of course, being wary of loss is not always a problem. Some losses are too big to easily withstand, while the costs of avoiding them are tolerable. Buying fire insurance on your house is usually a sound choice; the cost of the insurance premium is relatively cheap, while a loss of the house could be financially devastating. The problem is not aversion to loss, but rather letting such wariness absolutely control your financial behavior.

As discussed in Chapter 15, it is important to understand your risk tolerance when creating an investment plan. A portfolio that is appropriate for someone else may be too risky for you. When deciding on an asset allocation, you should focus both on the expected return and also on the potential losses the portfolio could incur in a market downturn.

It's vital that you don't allow loss aversion to prevent you from taking appropriate risks, however. Investors take notice when the dollar values of their accounts fluctuate, but they often forget to allow for the erosion of a dollar's purchasing power over time due to inflation. While those who fear loss may think it is safer to sit on a checking or savings account with little risk, the total purchasing power of their assets will slide downward over time, even if their account balances stay numerically the same. Taking some risk is the only way to maintain the purchasing power of your money.

While losses are never pleasant, investors should not focus obsessively on avoiding them. Understanding the magnitude of potential losses in a particular investment or portfolio of investments may help you stick with your plan when markets drop.

## Recency

In the years that immediately followed the financial crisis of 2008-2009, many investors focused on defending themselves against another market freefall, rather than on seeking opportunities to profit from the recovery as conditions stabilized. This is a great example of the recency bias, which is the assumption that conditions created by a recent event will persist or recur far into the future.

We are prone to pay undue attention to recent news, either good or bad, and as a result we may underemphasize long-term averages or trends. It's an adage in financial planning that past performance is no guarantee of future results. Performance in the recent past is arguably the least useful information about an investment to consider in isolation. Yet recent performance data is easy to access and remember, so it exerts an outsize influence on many investors' decisions.

The human brain seeks to identify patterns. This tendency can be helpful in a variety of areas, but it also leads us to interpret events as if they are part of a pattern when, in fact, they are random. If you do not stop to consider the reasons behind the pattern you perceive, it can be easy to buy into an illusory meaning and subsequently make choices based on data that is ultimately irrelevant.

Seeking patterns can lead to chasing "hot" funds or stocks, which will actually tend to hurt returns as you trail behind the market. The returns that investors earn from mutual funds are typically lower than funds' overall returns. According to a study by DALBAR Inc., the average investor's annual returns on U.S. stock funds of 4.25 percent was about half that of the S&P 500 index's return of 8.21 percent per year for the 20 years through December 2012. The difference is not mainly due to fees, but rather to the timing of when investors allocate money to specific funds. Funds usually experience greater inflows of new investment following periods of good performance, and investors seldom stay put as long as they should. The tendency to chase performance can seriously harm an investor's portfolio.

We can see this effect on a much smaller scale with something like a coin flip. If a coin is flipped 100 times and always lands heads, most of us will be inclined to guess that it will land heads the 101st time. Or perhaps a few of us will guess tails because a tails flip is "due." We intellectually know that the chance of either outcome is still precisely 50-50, regardless of how many times the coin has been flipped before, but it's hard to feel that way in the moment. We make a choice, and then back it up with a reverse-engineered reason.

Similarly, if you remember hearing a recent news report about start-ups that made a lot of money, you may feel as if venture capital is a sure thing. In reality, how well other companies have done in the past is more or less irrelevant to a particular investment you might consider. Nor is a stock that's had a long losing streak bound to get better eventually, just because an upturn is "due." Here again, data can help you, while emotion will lead you astray.

## Herd Mentality

It's funny how investing can sound so easy in theory – don't chase the latest hot idea or protect against yesterday's disaster. Yet it is still hard not to get caught up in hype when the crucial moment arrives. It isn't that we consciously decide to follow an irrational trend. It's that a belief begins to seem plausible when so many other people buy into it. It is also easy to accept the theory that if many people are doing something, it must be a good idea. In the long term, though, this sort of thinking can burn investors.

A stock or asset class usually begins to appreciate based on some valid, fundamental reason, such as a promising new product or a technological advance. As the asset's price increases, more and more people hear about the idea and buy in, causing further appreciation. Finally, every news channel and website ends up proclaiming that gold, Apple stock, emerging markets, oil or the investment du jour is the place all smart investors should put their money. You don't want to miss out, so you take the plunge and buy.

Unfortunately, all streaks come to an end. The cycle of positive news takes a turn and transforms into a negative feedback loop. Yesterday's market darling becomes today's burst bubble. From the tech bubble of the 1990s to the real estate bubble of the 2000s, bubbles grow because the people who believe growth is not a bubble generally reap rewards in the short term.

By the time the bubble's inevitable pop arrives, fear of missing out has trumped self-control for many investors, leaving them to suffer the consequences. They may buy a security after the gains have already been earned or stay in too long and take the brunt of the downswing. Conversely, following the crowd can lead investors to wait too long to invest in a down market. Waiting until signs of recovery are already apparent can lead investors to buy at higher prices than they should; waiting for signs of trouble can mean investors miss opportunities to sell at the market's height.

To avoid getting caught up in hype, you should be sure to base your investment decisions on quantifiable data that you understand, not simply headlines or news reports. Basing your financial strategy on the emotions of a crowd is no wiser than basing it on your own emotions.

## Confirmation Bias

The conclusion you seek often determines the data that you find. We tend to hear what we want to hear – or, put another way, we tend to make a decision and then search for data to back it up, ignoring any evidence that doesn't support it. This tendency is aggravated by both herd mentality and overweighting recent information. Investors' optimism or pessimism can thus be amplified as the market responds to it with price increases or decreases. Investors see these shifts as evidence their original confidence or fear was justified, leading them to double down on their conclusions and encouraging others to follow suit.

On a smaller scale, if you are convinced that a certain sector is a sure bet, you will be inclined to find and remember news that suggests it is growing strong and ignore or write off as flukes reports that should trigger you to act more cautiously. Remember to research both sides of an issue equally and to honestly consider any potential bias inherent to the news source. On the Internet, you can find data supporting any conclusion.

This bias works in reverse too; we are inclined to view events as more predictable than they really were when viewing them in hindsight. It's easy to pick out the evidence suggesting an outcome once that outcome has already occurred, but that doesn't mean you could have – or should have – done so before the event. There will always be someone who accurately predicts the next hot investment or the next market crash. There will also always be people who guessed wrong. If someone makes a correct prediction and was in the minority in their opinion, they are likely to be hailed as a clairvoyant prognosticator. Investors will often be inclined to listen to them and act on their recommendations next time, regardless of how often they have been wrong in the past.

## Action Bias

Inaction is a powerful choice that is generally undervalued. It feels better to do something rather than nothing, especially when the market is in turmoil. This psychological effect holds even if the action taken is not particularly wise.

If you are losing money, you may find it easier to believe that you are doing something wrong than that the market is experiencing short-term volatility. It can be hard to accept our financial fate is partially beyond our control. Yet if you follow a long-term investment plan with a portfolio that is appropriate for your risk tolerance, the plan should already account for the possibility of down markets. At Palisades Hudson, we generally recommend that clients keep five years of expected portfolio withdrawals in safe investments that aren't subject to the stock market's fluctuations. This precaution can give people added comfort, and can help them to recognize that changing course during a volatile period is unnecessary.

Inaction can feel neglectful or foolish, especially if everyone else is furiously taking action. In reality, however, rash decisions can do active harm by locking in your portfolio's losses, especially if your original investment plan allowed for down markets. Choosing not to act is itself a choice. Sometimes it's the right one.

## Mental Accounting

How easy it is to stay the course in a crisis may depend, for some, on the source of the money in question. One of the most prevalent and illogical of our emotional biases is treating dollars differently depending on their origins and their destinations. This mental accounting can lead to decisions that seem very sound on the surface. Sometimes this is because they are: Setting aside money for retirement may prevent us from spending it too early, for example. Many people budget by either figuratively or literally putting money for different sorts of spending into different envelopes. This can be a useful tool.

This sort of division becomes a problem, though, when we categorize our funds without stepping back to look at the bigger picture. Money you earned through work is no different than money you inherited, as far as your portfolio is concerned. Yet many investors are much more willing to take risks with one category than the other. On the outgoing side, it is possible to become overly focused on one goal at the expense of another. Maintaining an easily accessible emergency fund can distract from retirement planning; you may be reluctant to spend money set aside for vacation on a major health expense. It's essential to take stock of your assets as a whole, both incoming and outgoing, and not allow your mental assignments to keep you from rearranging if necessary.

Another common differentiation is how investors think of the components of their portfolio's growth. Some retirees budget to spend only their portfolio's income – interest and dividends. As a result, they look for investments that maximize their current income of their portfolio. At Palisades Hudson, we find this to be a meaningless and potentially harmful way of thinking. Interest and dividends are taxable income, so a high-income portfolio can be an expensive way to manage a portfolio after accounting for taxes. We prefer to focus on a portfolio's total return – the capital appreciation and the current income. Capital appreciation is only taxed once an investment has been sold, so the taxes can be deferred. Focusing too much on income can also constrain returns when interest rates are low. The government's current interest rate policy and companies' dividend policies should not dictate a retiree's spending. There's no reason why you can't live off the proceeds of the sale of an appreciated asset.

## Overcoming Biases

These many fears and biases may make it seem like the deck is stacked against you when making investment decisions. It is true that such mental shortcuts can be hard to notice in yourself, even when you know what to look for. This is because many of them operate on a unconscious level. We can convince ourselves that, in the moment, we aren't biased at all. It's only if you try to evaluate the actions under the lens of the tendencies discussed in the previous section that you may begin to see the emotional or illogical forces driving your decisions. You will not see a bias as it influences your decisions, but you might notice it in retrospect.

Knowing your own tendencies is vital, but it doesn't mean you can expect to rewire yourself. You, like your family, friends and yes, even your financial adviser, are only human. Since these biases generally work on your unconscious mind, being aware of them may help, but it won't eliminate their influence. So how can you avoid falling into traps created by your own mental shortcuts?

The most effective tool for combating bad mental habits is creating a written investment plan and committing to stick to it. An investment policy statement puts forth a prudent philosophy for a given investor and describes the types of investments, investment management procedures and goals that will define the portfolio. The plan should be focused on long-term results, and should include plans for eventualities such as a market downturn or the failure of a major investment. By considering such problems in advance as hypothetical situations, you can avoid the temptation to react emotionally in the moment.

Further, creating a detailed plan will allow you, perhaps with a financial adviser's help, to set benchmarks for your portfolio, such as what an appropriate amount of spending looks like, how much of a loss to expect in a market downturn, or what conditions should trigger rebalancing your portfolio. Keeping your asset allocation in line with your risk tolerance will help you to weather turbulent markets much more effectively than trying to react as volatile situations arise.

The development of an investment policy, alone or with an adviser, should follow the basic approach underlying all financial planning. This includes six steps:

1. Assessing your current financial condition

2. Setting personalized goals

3. Developing a strategy to meet those goals

4. Implementing the strategy

5. Regularly reviewing the results

6. Adjusting as circumstances dictate in a way that reflects the predetermined plan

For many investors, combining an appropriate asset allocation for long-term goals with a reserve for short-term needs creates a buffer, which makes it easier to maintain patience and confidence in sticking to the investment plan. In essence, you will sign an "investment contract" with yourself, agreeing that you won't let market conditions or outside influences cause you to abandon your original plan.

By setting up an investment plan, you will remove the temptation to rely on yourself to remain unbiased and unemotional in any circumstances. For example, a classic piece of investing advice is to "buy when there's blood in the streets" – that is, when there is panic in financial markets. Panics are the time to make money, as long as you avoid emotional reactions and stick to your plan. The market is effectively on sale in a panic, and yet people are inclined to buy less, not more. A plan can help you avoid this tendency without forcing you to rewire your own natural responses. Similarly, sticking to an investment plan can prevent you from acting on overconfidence borne of a market boom. Your plan will allow you to avoid impulsive action and to recognize your own tendencies for irrationality.

Hiring a financial adviser can help mitigate emotional responses and make sticking to your plan easier. An adviser can also be useful for those without the time or skill to manage their own investments properly. A professional has the time and resources necessary to perform sufficient due diligence for your investments, replacing emotion and guesswork with data. The adviser can also provide moral support or coaching in rough times when you begin to doubt the wisdom of your own plan.

Remember: Risk isn't the enemy. Calculated risk is an investor's best friend, since it is the principal driver of returns. Because investors seek to protect their assets, they demand higher returns for higher risk investments. The possibility of loss lies along the path to greater rewards. You should take on risk with discipline and within limits, however. You may find it easier to cope with risk by dividing your portfolio into chunks, each of which can have a different risk threshold and a different time horizon. In this way, mental accounting can work for you rather than against you, even while you consider the health and diversification of your portfolio as a whole. The idea is to handle risk calmly, based on good information and sound long-term strategy.

## Resisting Sales Manipulation

Although we have focused on avoiding the impact of biases, it is also important to realize that people who want to sell you various financial products and services are aware of these biases and shortcuts too. While you try to resist your own mental traps, others will actively try to exploit them. Once you can recognize persuasion techniques, resisting them may be easier than fighting your own biases, but it will still take attention and practice.

Remember to think critically and question any information a salesman or a marketing campaign feeds you. They may be trying to take advantage of your recency bias, selling you protection against yesterday's problem rather than tomorrow's. While it may seem like today's conditions will last forever, whether low interest rates, low inflation or low stock returns, the next big risk may be something entirely different.

Marketers may try to get you moving with the herd by bombarding you with examples of other people's decisions. It is easiest to sell what everyone is buying. As an investor, however, you need to focus on what is in your own best long-term interest. Buying an out-of-favor investment when it's "on sale" can be more profitable than buying the thing that everyone else wants today.

Marketers are also quick to exploit our tendency to trust or agree with someone we can label "an expert." This is why doctors often appear in ads for medication. Their position immediately triggers an air of credibility for the ads' claims. Similarly, you might be more inclined to buy a product if you hear it praised by a well-known financial expert, publication or investment firm. While these endorsements can be useful, they are not enough alone to serve as the basis of a sound decision.

Similarly, a popular figure paired with a concept or product can encourage viewers to transfer their positive feelings about the person to the concept. This is the basis of celebrity endorsements, whether it's a sports figure on a Wheaties box or an actress as the face of a makeup campaign. Even someone with no expertise in the product they're endorsing can make an idea much more attractive simply by saying they like it; this, however, has little bearing on whether the product is right for the consumer.

There are also behaviors a marketer can display that can influence investors' attitudes toward a product or idea. For example, we often feel obliged to return favors, which is why companies give away promotional items or offer free introductory services. People are also inclined to continue granting requests from the same source once they have said yes once. Think of how companies often try to get you to answer yes to small requests, such as giving five minutes of your time or sharing your email address, in order to make larger requests later.

Sellers may also make outrageously large requests, which then make smaller requests look like concessions once the large requests are refused. We may be more likely to consider the request that looks like we've gained some ground, even if it is not objectively a good idea. Further, most people feel awkward going back on an agreement, even if the terms change or new terms come to light. For example, hidden charges or fees can make an investment that seemed like a good idea at first much less appealing. Yet, even with new information, many people feel uncomfortable changing their minds if they previously expressed interest or approval.

Sales manipulation relies on listeners not applying critical thinking to the message they hear. We tend to find longer messages more accurate or trustworthy than shorter ones, regardless of content. We also tend to believe a story that is presented in an attractive package or told by a good storyteller. One of the best ways to counter active persuasion techniques is to force yourself to pay more attention to the strength and quality of the message's content than to the means of its delivery. Critical thinking requires motivation and concentration, and can be harder when you are tired or upset. Since it is one of the strongest tools investors have for cutting through hype and avoiding the temptation to blindly follow the crowd, you should be sure to be at your best when making major investment decisions.

Investor biases are one form of the human brain's adaptations for dealing with a complex world through patterns and shortcuts. The inclinations to focus too much on a few factors or to answer an easy question rather than a hard one are quite natural. Such mental biases are part of us and can never be eliminated completely. Yet that doesn't mean investors are powerless. Though we cannot eliminate our biases, we can recognize them and respond in ways that help us avoid self-defeating behavior.

Planning and discipline are the keys. Think critically about your investment processes from start to finish, rather than letting your subconscious drive your actions. Make plans calmly over time, when you are well-rested and well-informed. Once you have a plan, be diligent in sticking to it. Adhering to a long-term investment plan will limit the extent to which fears and biases can influence your behavior as an investor. We all make mistakes, but a plan that accounts for such foreseeable temptations can help protect you from avoidable missteps.

# 17

## RETIRING ABROAD
### Shomari D. Hearn, CFP®, EA
### Melinda Kibler, CFP®

Retirement is an excellent opportunity to relocate. Without jobs holding them in place, many retirees consider moving to be closer to their children or grandchildren, to return to a former home, to seek out new climates or cultures, or to live more economically. Depending on circumstances, any of these motivations can move retirees to new cities, new states – or even to new countries.

No one knows precisely how many American retirees live overseas, given disagreements over whom to count as an 'American' and how to define retirement. Estimates of the figure range from 350,000 (the number of Americans who receive Social Security benefits outside the United States) to 1.4 million. Most people, however, agree that the number is rising.

There are many reasons that people find retiring abroad attractive. Some countries offer a lower cost of living than Americans can find at home. After the cost of moving is factored in, retiring overseas can still often stretch retirement funds further than they would otherwise go. In some situations, retirees can secure medical care that is less expensive but of comparable quality. Of course, some retirees simply wish to travel and explore new cultures once they have the flexibility to do so.

However, an international vacation is very different from moving to another country permanently. Before you make a choice of this magnitude, it is important to carefully consider all the factors involved – including financial concerns.

## Initial Considerations

Many of the factors to consider will be similar to those you would evaluate if you were planning a move from New York to California. You will need to decide whether to buy or rent your new home (and whether or not to sell your old one); consider travel expenses for your family to visit you or vice-versa; and work through the logistics of transporting your belongings, forwarding your mail and performing other routine moving tasks, made less routine with an international component.

One of the first financial considerations will be handling your banking and investment accounts. Depending on where you are relocating, opening a local bank account and funding it with U.S. dollars may be fairly simple or very complicated. In some countries, it may entail weeks of hassle and paperwork, including identification documents, letters of credit and references from your U.S. bank. If you don't plan to renounce your American citizenship, most advisers suggest you keep the bulk of your assets in U.S. accounts and transfer funds to your local foreign bank as needed. Staggering the transfers removes some of the risk of currency fluctuations over time, and also protects you if your new country has an economy less stable than that of the United States. It also makes returning to the States simpler, should you wish to do so in later years, or if you plan to split your time between your foreign country of residence and the U.S.A.

The Securities and Exchange Commission and the Financial Industry Regulatory Authority, or FINRA, have established rules for investment managers that restrict their trading on behalf of clients living outside the U.S. If you plan to move abroad, you will need to confirm your adviser's ability to handle your accounts while you are overseas. If your adviser has the ability and inclination to continue working with you, we recommend you keep your current adviser and your existing accounts.

If your investment account is not one that you can keep when you move abroad, or if your adviser requires you to change your domestic account to an offshore account, you are likely to find fees are higher and investment options are fewer. You should also exercise extreme caution in opening a foreign investment account. Extensive regulations govern foreign investment accounts held by U.S. citizens. We will touch on some of these rules later in this chapter.

Since cheaper medical care is a factor that may drive some retirees to consider moving abroad in the first place, it is important to understand how your medical options will work. Medicare and Medicaid generally will not pay for medical services for retirees outside the country and its territories. Medicaid pays for services only in the 50 states, the District of Columbia, and U.S. territories. Medicare additionally provides coverage in Canada and Mexico in cases when an emergency situation arises in the U.S. but the nearest hospital is over the border. Medicare also covers you if you are hurt or become ill while traveling through Canada if your destination is Alaska. But neither program pays for any health services, even in an emergency, in any other countries or situations.

These strict rules, by design, create a disincentive for any Americans on Medicare who might wish to move abroad specifically to pursue lower healthcare costs. Americans living abroad, even part time, who are eligible for Medicare must continue to pay Medicare premiums, but must pay for their own health care out-of-pocket while abroad or forgo U.S. government-based health care entirely. If they stop paying Medicare premiums, citizens are penalized upon their return to the U.S. when they re-enroll in the program.

This situation may eventually change. A non-partisan group called The Center for Medicare Portability (CMP) is working to alter the government's rules on Medicare for retirees living abroad. CMP wants to make it possible for Americans living overseas to have access to the Medicare benefits for which they have already paid. In the meantime, however, be aware that you currently forgo Medicare benefits by leaving the country for retirement.

If you do decide to retire abroad, consider international health coverage plans, which can travel with you. You should also investigate the health system in the country to which you intend to relocate. Many countries have national health systems, but eligibility requirements vary, as does the availability of services and the quality of care offered by the country's plan. Even if your new home country will cover your basic medical care, you may wish to consider health insurance to cover private medical and dental care, as well as medical evacuation to the U.S. for emergencies.

Unlike Medicare, Social Security benefits travel well. U.S. citizens who are eligible can continue to receive their Social Security benefits, even if they live abroad. However, there are some countries to which Social Security cannot send payments. These countries include Azerbaijan, Belarus, Georgia, Kazakhstan, Kyrgyzstan, Moldova, Tajikistan, Turkmenistan, Ukraine, Uzbekistan and Vietnam. If you move to any of these countries, you can apply for an exception, which will require you to agree to the conditions of payment. These usually include appearing in person each month to collect your payment at the U.S. embassy. Also, if you live in a foreign country, the Social Security office will occasionally send you a questionnaire in order to determine whether you continue to qualify for benefits. If you fail to fill out this questionnaire and return it promptly, your payments will stop.

## Taxation

The United States is exceptional in that it is the only major country that taxes its citizens and resident aliens regardless of where they live. American citizens or permanent residents living abroad are generally subject to the same rules for paying estimated tax and for filing U.S. income, estate and gift tax returns as citizens living at home. However, living in a foreign country makes these rules more complicated.

What do we mean by "permanent residents" as it applies to those living outside the U.S.? Permanent residents are foreign nationals who meet the substantial presence test and therefore may still be subject to U.S. tax law. To meet this test, you must be physically present in the U.S. on at least 31 days during the calendar year and a total of 183 days between the current calendar year and the two preceding years (the past three years, total). When calculating the 183 days, use the total number of physically present days in the current year, plus a third of the physically present days of the preceding year, plus a sixth of the total physically present days in the second preceding year. Even if you are a citizen of a non-U.S. country and consider that country your permanent home, you may still need to be aware of federal income tax rules if you spend significant time in the U.S.

If you are an American retiring abroad, you may consider working a part-time job for a variety of reasons, from increased cash flow to personal inclination. Citizens living abroad are still required to file a U.S. income tax return unless they expatriate (which we will discuss later in this chapter). Assuming you retain your American citizenship, you are taxed on your worldwide income. There is, however, a foreign earned income exclusion, allowing you to exclude up to a certain amount of foreign earnings ($99,200 in 2014). Earned income includes salary, wages, commissions, bonuses, professional fees and gratuities. It does not include Social Security benefits, pensions, annuities, interest, dividends, capital gains or alimony. In order to qualify to exclude foreign income, you must be either a U.S. citizen or a U.S. resident alien who is a citizen or national of a country with which the U.S. has a current income tax treaty. In addition, you must be a bona fide resident of one or more non-U.S. countries for a continuous period that includes the entire tax year, or you must be physically present in one or more non-U.S. countries for at least 330 full days during any period of 12 consecutive months.

In addition to the foreign income tax exclusion, qualified U.S. citizens and resident aliens abroad can exclude or deduct certain foreign housing amounts. However, you must have foreign earned income to do so, and the exclusion applies only to amounts considered paid for with amounts provided by your employer.

Americans abroad receive an automatic two-month extension to file their federal income tax returns. This extension should help in cases where gathering paperwork is complicated or postal systems are unreliable.

You will likely need to pay taxes to your country of residence as well. To avoid double taxation of foreign income, you can claim a tax credit or a deduction on your U.S. income taxes. While no one rule covers every situation, most taxpayers will realize a greater advantage from taking a credit for qualified foreign taxes. A credit reduces your U.S. income tax on a dollar for dollar basis, rather than only reducing your income subject to tax. In addition, you can choose to take the foreign tax credit even if you do not itemize deductions on your return, which would be a requirement if you claim a deduction for foreign taxes. However, you will want to consider both options to see which makes more sense given your circumstances each tax year.

You can claim the credit in the year in which you accrue qualified foreign tax or the year in which you pay it. If you use an accrual accounting method, you report your income when you earn it rather than when you receive it, and deduct your expenses when you incur them rather than when you pay them. If you take this approach, you can claim the tax credit only in the year in which you accrue the tax. In most cases, you accrue foreign taxes when all the events that fix the amount of the tax and your liability have taken place – often the last day of the foreign tax year. If, on the other hand, you use the cash method of accounting, you report income in the year you actually or constructively receive it and deduct expenses as you pay them. Under the cash method, you can choose to take the tax credit in either the year you pay the tax or the year you accrue it. Most individual taxpayers use the cash method rather than the accrual method.

Typically, U.S. citizens will want to take a tax credit for foreign earned income in the year the tax is accrued, rather than the year it is paid. Doing so helps to avoid a timing issue that could limit the credit and result in double taxation. For example, if you claim the foreign tax credit on a cash basis, you would claim the credit for the foreign taxes paid in year 2, for income earned in year 1. If you earned significant foreign income in year 1 but expect your foreign income will be much lower the following year, the credit in year 2 will be limited due to the lower foreign income and will result in an overall higher tax liability for year one as a consequence. Note that you cannot claim this credit for taxes on excluded income.

The U.S. has tax treaties with several countries that can affect your individual tax situation, whether you are a U.S. citizen or resident. Each treaty is unique, so you should check to see if such a treaty exists for the country you are considering and, if so, what effect the treaty's terms may have on your situation. Most treaties contain provisions to eliminate double taxation; if you cannot resolve a double taxation issue with the non-U.S. country's authorities, you can contact the Internal Revenue Service for assistance.

## Foreign Bank and Financial Accounts Reporting

U.S. citizens and residents, as well as businesses, trusts and estates, must file additional paperwork if they meet certain conditions related to foreign financial accounts. Those who qualify must file an annual Report of Foreign Bank and Financial Accounts, FinCEN Form 114 (formerly Form TD F 90-22.1), often referred to as an FBAR. You must file if you meet the following criteria:

- A person or entity with a financial interest in or signature authority over at least one financial account outside the U.S., and

- The aggregate value of foreign financial accounts (including bank accounts, investment accounts, trusts or other types of foreign financial accounts) exceeded the equivalent of $10,000 in U.S. dollars at any time during the calendar year.

Even if the account produces no taxable income, the person who holds that account may need to file a report. The reporting obligation is met by answering questions on the federal income tax return about foreign accounts (see Form 1040, Schedule B – Part III) and by filing an FBAR. There are exceptions to the FBAR requirement; among them are certain accounts jointly owned by spouses, IRA owners and beneficiaries, participants in and beneficiaries of tax-qualified retirement plans. Trust beneficiaries may not need to file if another U.S. person reports the account on an FBAR filed on the trust's behalf.

The FBAR is a calendar-year report and is due on or before June 30 of the following year. Extensions are generally not granted. Since the FBAR is not filed with the federal income tax return, income tax extensions do not extend the FBAR deadline. Failure to properly file can result in a civil penalty of up to $10,000. Purposely deciding not to comply may result in both a monetary penalty, equal to the greater of $100,000 or 50 percent of the account balance at the time the violation occurred, and criminal charges that can result in a prison sentence – certainly not how you would envision spending your golden years.

Taxpayers with specified foreign financial assets above certain thresholds must also report those assets to the Internal Revenue Service on Form 8938, Statement of Specified Foreign Financial Assets. Unlike the

FBAR, Form 8938 is filed with the federal income tax return. This requirement is in addition to the FBAR; it does not replace it. (See the comparison chart below.)

| | Form 8938, Statement of Specified Foreign Financial Assets | FinCEN Form 114, Report of Foreign Bank and Financial Accounts (FBAR) |
|---|---|---|
| Who Must File? | Specified individuals, which include U.S. citizens, resident aliens, and certain non-resident aliens that have an interest in specified foreign financial assets and meet the reporting threshold | U.S. persons, which include U.S. citizens, resident aliens, trusts, estates, and domestic entities that have an interest in foreign financial accounts and meet the reporting threshold |
| Reporting Threshold (Total Value of Assets) | $50,000 on the last day of the tax year or $75,000 at any time during the tax year (higher threshold amounts apply to married individuals filing jointly and individuals living abroad) | $10,000 at any time during the calendar year |
| What is reported? | Maximum value of specified foreign financial assets, which include financial accounts with foreign financial institutions and certain other foreign non-account investment assets | Maximum value of financial accounts maintained by a financial institution physically located in a foreign country |
| When is it due? | By due date, including extension, if any, for income tax return | Received by June 30 (no extensions of time granted) |
| Penalties? | Up to $10,000 for failure to disclose and an additional $10,000 for each 30 days of non-filing after IRS notice of a failure to disclose, for a potential maximum penalty of $60,000; criminal penalties may also apply | If non-willful, up to $10,000; if willful failure to comply, up to the greater of $100,000 or 50 percent of account balances; criminal penalties may also apply |

Source: Internal Revenue Service as of February 10, 2014
Chart 1

As you can see, reporting foreign accounts is complicated and is probably best done with the help of a qualified tax professional.

## Mortgage Interest and Property Taxes

You may deduct mortgage interest and property taxes on a foreign property, just as you would for a property in the U.S. You are allowed to deduct mortgage interest for a primary and a secondary residence. The IRS usually defines a taxpayer's principal residence as the home in which the person lives most of the time.

If you have more than one additional home, you may treat only one of them as the qualified second home during any year. However, you may change which home you designate from one year to the next. If you acquire a new home, it can be treated as a second home as of the day of purchase. Should your main home no longer qualify as your primary home, you can choose to treat it as your second home instead; if your second home becomes your primary home, you can choose a new second home the day you begin using it that way. In total, you may only deduct interest related to a maximum of $1 million of home acquisition debt, plus an additional $100,000 of home equity debt.

Real estate taxes are deductible at any level (state, local or national) if the tax is levied for the general public welfare, whether in the U.S. or abroad. Therefore, you may deduct foreign property taxes as well, but only if they are based on the real property's assessed value and charged uniformly against all property in the taxing authority's jurisdiction. Generally, taxes charged for local benefits and improvements that increase the property's value cannot be deducted. You cannot deduct itemized charges for services, such as trash collection, assessed against specific property or certain people, even if the tax authority is charging them.

## State Income Taxes While Living Abroad

Your state's definitions of domicile and residency will determine whether you owe state income taxes while living abroad. If you take the proper steps to terminate tax domicile and residency in your previous home state, you will often be able to eliminate your state tax burden. While some states make it relatively easy to terminate domicile, others require definite proof that you have abandoned the state and established new domicile elsewhere. Some go so far as to claim that your domicile does not change until you demonstrate that you have no intention to return to the state. (See Chapter 14, State Income Tax, for more details about the ways in which state tax laws vary.) In most cases, you should file a part-year state tax return for the year you move to signal the end of your residency, but know that you should be prepared to substantiate your change in residency status in case of an audit.

If you lack the ability or desire to terminate domicile, you will likely need to continue to pay state income taxes. There are a variety of reasons maintaining residency or domicile might make sense. For example, if you wish to keep your home in the U.S., your state could deem this proof that you intend to return. Some states may allow you to end your domicile and only require you to pay tax if you are physically present in the state for more than a certain number of days, meaning you would need to be mindful of when you choose to visit and how long you stay. Note that a houseboat or mobile home also may qualify as a permanent residence.

Some states will only allow you to move your domicile within the United States. Virginia, for example, holds that Americans living abroad who were formerly domiciled in the state retain their domicile, meaning they have to pay Virginia's income tax on worldwide income, until they establish residency in another state. If your state's rules are similar, it may make sense to consider shifting your domicile to a state that does not have a state income tax before moving abroad.

You can establish a new domicile in another state by demonstrating intent and creating a fact pattern to support it. This could include a variety of actions, including but not limited to: acquiring a driver's license or state ID in your new state; registering and voting in your new state; changing your mailing address; changing your passport address; filing income tax returns in the new state; changing your address on principal bank accounts; and changing your car's title and plates.

## Expatriation

The choice to renounce U.S. citizenship was once relatively rare, but that is changing. The IRS, which is required to post a list of citizens who voluntarily expatriate, reported in the Federal Registry that 2013 saw the highest rate of expatriates in the prior 15 years.

The choice to expatriate is a deeply personal one, and should not be made lightly. You should carefully weigh a variety of factors. Do you still have family in the U.S. whom you would like to visit or to whom you plan to bequeath an inheritance? If you should become ill, what is the level and cost of medical care that would be available to you in your new country? What would happen if you started to run out of money in retirement – would it be easy, hard or impossible to work in the new country if you needed to? Although getting citizenship back once renounced is not impossible, it is not easy.

If you choose to expatriate, the first step should be pursuing citizenship in your new country. Going through the naturalization process can be very difficult or relatively easy, depending on the country, but will likely take some time. It is imperative you be naturalized before you renounce your U.S. citizenship. Otherwise, you risk becoming stateless. Consult with the embassy of your new country, so you are sure you understand the process for naturalization there.

Once you have secured citizenship abroad, there are several ways to end your American citizenship. You can lose your citizenship through a conviction for treason, but obviously you should avoid this method; you also automatically lose your citizenship if you serve in certain military or government positions for another nation. Most people who expatriate do so by formally renouncing their American citizenship. This involves signing an oath of renunciation, which must be done in the presence of a diplomatic officer (generally at an embassy or a consulate). In addition, expatriates must file Form 8854, Initial and Annual Expatriate Statement, with the IRS. Revocation is final when the State Department issues a Certificate of Loss of Nationality.

## Melinda's Advice

### What are the most popular countries for Americans retiring abroad?

Based on the Social Security Administration's 2013 tally of claimants living abroad, the most popular countries for Americans retiring outside the U.S. are Canada, Japan, Mexico, Germany, the United Kingdom and Italy, in that order.

-MK

In some cases, you may owe an "exit tax" upon renouncing your citizenship. This tax was established by the Heroes Earnings Assistance and Relief Tax Act of 2008 (the HEART Act). It applies to "covered" expatriates, who (with limited exceptions) are defined as any of the following:

- Those whose average annual net income tax for the five years prior to the date of expatriation is more than a specified amount. (This amount, adjusted for inflation, is $157,000 in 2014.)

- Those with a net worth of $2 million or more as of their expatriation.

- Those who fail to certify on Form 8854 that they have complied with all U.S. federal tax obligations for the five years prior to expatriation.

Covered individuals owe exit tax on the unrealized gains on their property. The expatriate is deemed to have sold his or her worldwide assets for their fair market value as of the day before expatriation. Those hypothetical sales are subject to U.S. short- or long-term capital gains taxes, as appropriate. A portion of the gains, the amount of which is adjusted for inflation, can be excluded. (For 2014, the exclusion amount is $680,000.) Similarly, tax-deferred accounts such as IRAs and Section 529 plans are treated as though the account owner received a full distribution as of the day before expatriation. There is some leniency with the standard rules of those distributions. For example, if expatriates are under age 59½ at the time of distribution, they are not charged the 10 percent early withdrawal penalty tax. The total exit tax is due with the federal income return for the year in which U.S. citizenship was renounced.

Should you fail to file IRS Form 8854 upon expatriation, you could face a $10,000 penalty, whether or not you are a covered individual. Form 8854 and the exit tax were designed largely to keep Americans from renouncing their citizenship simply to avoid tax obligations.

The HEART Act also affects transfer taxes from a former citizen to a current U.S. citizen. American citizens or residents who receive gifts or bequests from expatriates over the annual gift tax exclusion ($14,000 in 2014) incur liability for the transfer tax at the highest applicable rate, unless the transfers are reported on a U.S. gift or estate tax filed by the expatriate. If the expatriate gives to a U.S. trust, the trust must pay the transfer tax. If the expatriate gives to a foreign trust, no tax is due unless there is a distribution to a U.S. citizen or resident.

Deferred compensation becomes more complicated due to expatriation as well. Regulations make a distinction between eligible and ineligible deferred compensation plans. Plans in which the payer is a U.S. person (or a non-U.S. person electing to be treated as a U.S. person) and the payee has notified the payer of his or her status as an expatriate and has irrevocably waived any right to claim a withholding reduction on taxable distributions are deemed to be eligible plans. For eligible plans, the payer must deduct and withhold a tax of 30 percent on any taxable payment. Any deferred compensation plans that do not qualify under the rules stated above are deemed ineligible. Ineligible deferred compensation items are taxed as though the payee received the current value of all accrued benefits on the day before expatriation. Additionally, Form W-8CE, Notice of Expatriation and Waiver of Treaty Benefits, must be filed with the ineligible plan payer. The plan payer then responds with a written statement that includes the current value of accrued benefits for documentation purposes.

Even if you expatriate, you may still be subject to tax on FDAP (Fixed, Determinable, Annual or Periodical) income. FDAP income is any type of U.S.-sourced income, with the exception of: income effectively connected with a U.S. trade or business; gains derived from the sale of personal or real property; and income typically excluded from gross income. A tax of 30 percent is applied to any FDAP income, except in cases where a tax treaty reduces this amount. You may not take any deductions against the FDAP income. Even Social Security income is subject to the FDAP rules, and up to 85 percent of your Social Security income may be taxed at the 30 percent rate. For a nonresident alien present in the U.S. for 183 days or more during the year, your capital gains will be taxed at the 30 percent rate (again, unless a treaty applies). When considering whether or not to renounce your citizenship, keep in mind that expatriates may still find it difficult to avoid the U.S. income tax system.

## Long-Term Concerns

Once you have established yourself in a new country, and have handled basic banking, medical, Social Security and tax matters, you can turn your attention to some financial planning issues with longer time horizons.

An essential step is to consider how foreign residency will affect your estate plan. Ideally, you should consult a knowledgeable estate planning attorney who has experience in international tax and estate planning. He or she can help you navigate through the particular concerns of structuring your estate when you live abroad. These may include specifying that U.S. law will govern the execution of the estate, which is important to protect your heirs' inheritances, and examining the structure of trusts to make sure they are not caught in a tax net by your country of residence.

For example, consider Jim and Rose, an American couple who permanently reside in London. Prior to their move to London, they set up a trust in the U.S. for the benefit of their daughter, who lives in New York. Jim and Rose are listed as the trustees. British law, however, considers the residence of the trustee, rather than the country in which the trust was established, when determining tax liability. If Jim and Rose both die while living in London, the trust could be subject to U.K. income and capital gains taxes before any assets are sold. Most notably, once the trustee is living in the U.K., the trustee cannot be changed without paying British capital gains tax on the unrealized gains of the trust's assets as though all the trust's assets were sold at that point in time. Therefore, Jim and Rose would have been better off liquidating the trust or appointing a U.S. resident trustee before they moved to London.

If Jim and Rose have even a modest estate, they should also be aware that British estate taxes are much higher than estate taxes in America. If their combined estates total less than $10.68 million (the federal exemption is $5.34 million per U.S. citizen in 2014), they will be exempt from federal estate tax in the U.S., but the threshold in the U.K. for a married couple is only £650,000 (as of this writing, approximately $1.05 million).

Estate planning concerns such as these are not insurmountable, but many of them are easier to handle if you deal with them prior to leaving the United States. Talk to your current estate planning professional, and do not hesitate to seek out additional assistance from someone with international tax and estate planning experience.

Once their affairs are in order and they have settled into their country, many retirees want to begin taking advantage of the lower cost of living. This, in conjunction with lower costs for domestic help, means that many Americans living abroad may find hiring household help attractive. Whether or not you are accustomed to selecting domestic employees, it is worth taking the time to be methodical about the process.

## Shomari's Advice

### Can I manage my stocks and mutual fund investments from abroad?

Managing investments from overseas is technically simple, and permitted by U.S. law. However, some financial services companies restrict Americans' ability to execute brokerage transactions while living abroad, for fear of violating foreign regulations. Restricted activities include buying new mutual funds, switching holdings from one fund to another, and redistributing assets among funds already held. A possible workaround is to place investments in a revocable trust and appoint a U.S. resident as trustee. The investor living abroad could then ask the trustee to place the desired trades.

-SH

The first step is to assess your needs. Before you start looking to hire, you should be clear on both what you require, and what would be nice to have if possible. Do you want someone mainly to take care of cleaning? Laundry? Cooking? Driving? Gardening or lawn work? Do you want live-in help, or part-time help?

Once you know what it is that you want, you may find it useful to go through an agency. Look for established agencies with at least three years of business experience. Be sure the staff of the agency speaks both your native language and the language of their employees, if different. Their offices should be organized and efficient, and the company should respond to inquiries promptly and pleasantly. When you talk to the agency, the staff should discuss your requirements and offer advice before the selection process begins. A good agency will also offer the following:

- Sufficient background information on workers

- Professional service arrangement documentation

- Thorough and on-location training

- Consultation after you hire workers

- Ongoing interest in the welfare of their employees

- A guaranteed turnaround time for a replacement worker if you are dissatisfied with your current help

If you prefer not to go through an agency, you should be certain you collect full information on the person you hire at the beginning of the arrangement, including a copy of their government-issued identification, letters of reference or contact information for references, and contact information for the most recent previous employer. A personal recommendation from someone you know, either for an agency or for a particular domestic worker, is always worth considering. You might also reach out to other expatriates in your area for suggestions.

Many problems between domestic workers and their employers spring from misconceptions and ignorance about cultural practices and social norms. Depending on the country to which you move, these may be similar to what you are used to or drastically different. Your workers' expected social behavior, etiquette, hygiene norms and dietary restrictions may surprise you due to cultural or religious differences. Educate yourself on local customs, and be aware of areas where your needs may conflict with theirs. Respect requests for holidays you may not celebrate yourself. Make sure your expectations are explicit and clear from the start, so any culture gaps can be dealt with head-on. Treat your employees as you would wish an employer to treat you, with fairness and honesty.

If you plan to hire domestic help, be sure to explore the wage and tax requirements in your country of residence. You may need to cover taxes or meet other obligations as an employer. For example, in the U.S., families paying a domestic worker more than $1,800 annually need to pay federal, and in some cases state, taxes including Medicare, Social Security and unemployment taxes. They are also responsible for withholding the employee's portion of federal and state income taxes from the domestic worker's wages. Requirements will vary, but be sure you understand them before hiring anyone.

Settling into a new country brings extra financial planning concerns, but ultimately the broad principles will remain the same as any other move. If you take the time to understand your situation, plan and articulate your financial strategy, you will ultimately be able to relax and enjoy your new home.

# 18

## PHILANTHROPY
### Eric Meermann, CFP®, CVA, EA

---

Financial planning is not simply about finding ways to accumulate wealth. Good planning is the art of using resources wisely to accomplish something important. Along with providing for yourself and your family, philanthropic goals often top the list.

Each person's charitable goals are unique. Some want to contribute to the community or to teach their children and grandchildren about the importance of stewardship and generosity. For others, philanthropy and estate planning are intrinsically linked. After your death, there are three places your assets can go: your heirs, charitable or nonprofit organizations or the government (through taxes). Few people wish to maximize the amount of money going to option three.

Creating a philanthropic plan for your family can be daunting, given all of the available structures and the complex tax and administrative rules governing charitable donations. This chapter will outline some of the most popular ways to maximize your gifts' effectiveness, as well as ways to combine your charitable intentions with other financial planning goals.

## First Steps

Before you decide how to give, you will need to make some decisions. Taking the time to articulate what you would like to give, to whom and how much, will prove invaluable when you later evaluate which method of giving is right for your situation.

The first step is to define your philanthropic objectives. Do you already have a particular nonprofit organization or charity in mind? If not, do you know what cause you want to support or do you have a particular problem in mind you want to help solve? Many of us give because the organization in question touched us in some way: a school we attended, a cure for a disease that affected a loved one, or an arts organization that has been important in our lives. Other donors approach selecting a cause methodically, applying a more businesslike approach to vetting organizations to which they may give.

Some combine their philanthropy with other financial planning objectives. If you face an abnormally high-income year due to capital gains, an inheritance, or another sale or windfall, timing your charitable giving wisely can reduce your income tax bill. Some donors intend to create a long-term legacy, lending their family's name to a cause or group of causes they find worthy. Still others want to involve their children to pass along shared values, or wish to create jobs (paid or unpaid) for family members. Giving can be appropriate in all these cases, but being honest and articulate about what you want out of your charitable gift will help shape your plan from the outset.

If you don't already have a charity in mind, you may want to take some time to select one or more organizations to which to give. At Palisades Hudson, we recommend looking mainly at three attributes when evaluating charitable organizations: efficiency, effectiveness, and innovation.

An organization's efficiency is how well it manages the donations it receives. Investigate the percentage of donations that go to administrative expenses, such as paying staff, funding organizational overhead, or engaging in fundraising efforts such as mass mailings or benefits. While these functions can be important, you should know before you donate how much of your gift is likely to go directly to the cause that is important to you. And if an organization outright mismanages its funds, you will want to know that too.

Effectiveness is not always quite as easy to measure as efficiency, but in essence, it translates into how well the organization addresses the cause that drew you in the first place. Can the organization show what difference its efforts have made to date? How reasonable do its projections for the future appear?

The third quality, innovation, may or may not matter to you as much as the first two. Does the charity tackle the problem in a novel way? Compared to other charities dealing with similar issues, does this organization simply do the same thing better or on a larger scale, or is there a qualitative difference? While many charities do good work without being particularly innovative, encouraging new thought can make charitable giving in general more productive. If you are trying to decide between two similar organizations, consider innovation as a useful tiebreaker.

Reputable charities tend to release a lot of data about their activities and their finances. However, comparing organizations effectively can be time-consuming and is not always simple. Sites such as GuideStar and Charity Navigator can help you with this process. There will always be a subjective element, and there is no one "best" charity for most causes. But taking the time to be thorough will help you steer clear of ineffective or mismanaged organizations, and will create confidence that your gift will make a real difference.

It is worth noting that small charities, which tend to have less name recognition, are often a good value for those looking to make a gift go as far as possible. Smaller organizations tend to rely more heavily on volunteer workers and service providers, and spend relatively less money on increasing their visibility or fundraising. Many of them are new and bring novel, creative approaches to achieving their goals. Even a modest gift may make a huge difference.

To see how the decision-making process works in action, consider the following example. Victoria knows she wants to support a charity somewhere in the health and wellness sector, but she does not know which one. She first has to decide whether she wants to address a problem that is relatively common or one that is rarer. A common problem means more people will receive benefit from the charity's work, but it also means numerous other organizations are probably tackling it as well. Victoria also needs to consider whether she wants to concentrate her resources on awareness, prevention, basic research for new treatments, getting treatment to those who need it, or a combination of these. While looking at her options may spark ideas, at this stage Victoria mainly needs to reflect on her own priorities and make some decisions.

After thoughtful reflection, Victoria decides she wants to find a charity that focuses on sickle cell disease. This is a narrow enough focus that she can begin to research organizations online. Charity Navigator allows for a keyword search, and sorts the results by rated and unrated charities. GuideStar offers one master list of results. Both sites return many results for this cause.

There are a number of ways Victoria can sort her results. She can narrow her focus geographically, by type of organization, or by how much information the organizations provide. She can also choose to narrow by the organization's focus. For example, if she decided on primarily promoting awareness, does she want to focus on organizations that provide educational support services and advocacy or organizations that provide genetic counseling and education to parents who may be carriers? Does she want a charity that focuses its efforts locally, nationally or abroad? More research may also trigger additional ideas about what she wishes to make her gift's focus.

Victoria creates a short list of charities that seem to align with her goals. She takes the time to research these charities in depth. This will allow her to determine which ones are efficient, effective, and likely to use her gift in a way that will do the sort of good she hopes.

Of course, many people give to more than one or two causes. Your process will vary depending on your goals. But the more specific you can be about what organizations you would like to support and why, the easier it will be to tackle the next step: deciding on how to give.

## Ways to Give

There are many ways to structure your charitable giving. Here are a few of the most common.

### Outright Gifts

Given the number and complexity of giving methods, many donors may overlook the option of an outright gift. However, depending on your situation, a complex charitable giving structure may be unnecessary – or worse, needlessly burdensome and expensive. If your primary goals are to support a particular organization (or organizations) and to reduce your tax bill, an outright gift may be best.

The federal government provides an incentive for charitable giving through the charitable income tax deduction. Generally, individuals can deduct cash gifts of up to 50 percent of their adjusted gross income (AGI) per tax year. For gifts of appreciated property, the limit is 30 percent of AGI. These rules apply to organizations that qualify as public charities under the Internal Revenue Code section 501(c)(3). Gifts to most private foundations are deductible at 30 percent of AGI for cash gifts and 20 percent of AGI for appreciated property. In all of the above cases, gifts exceeding the limits may carry forward for up to five years.

Giving appreciated securities directly also offers the additional benefit of allowing you to permanently avoid capital gains tax on the appreciation. It works like this: Assume you own $1 million of a stock with a long-term hold period and a cost basis of $100,000. If you were to sell the stock and give the cash proceeds to charity, you would get a $1 million charitable deduction, but you would also realize a $900,000 capital gain, resulting in $214,200 of capital gains tax, assuming the 23.8 percent federal capital gains rate that applied to top-bracket taxpayers in 2014. If you were to give the $1 million of stock directly to the charity, you would end up with the same $1 million charitable deduction, but realize no taxable gain. Since the charity is a tax-free entity, it can sell the stock without paying any tax on the gain, and the charity will therefore receive the entirety of your gift.

If you have a high-income year and know what causes you'd like to support, as long as the AGI limits do not come into play, giving a direct gift can do good, capture tax benefit and create very little in the way of cost or administrative burden. Gifts to qualifying charities do not count against your lifetime federal gift tax exemption.

## Donor-Advised Funds

Sometimes you may face an unusually high-income tax year without the benefit of knowing what particular charity you would like to support. In this instance, you may want to consider a donor-advised fund.

In this sort of gift, you make an irrevocable gift to the fund in question. (Palisades Hudson has often used the Fidelity Charitable Gift fund, but there are many options available.) While many funds set a minimum contribution, you can usually contribute many sorts of assets to the fund. The gift is immediately tax-deductible.

The fund allocates your contributions in an investment portfolio, though you can generally advise the team how to allocate your gift, and allows the funds to grow. In the future, you can recommend the fund pay out grants to qualified charitable organizations. Givers can make such recommendations at any time after their initial contribution. In this way, you can offset taxable income in the present while taking your time to make philanthropic decisions. If your gift remains invested long enough, it is also likely to grow, allowing you to give more to the cause or causes of your choice.

Before giving, it is important to note that recommendations regarding distributions are nonbinding, and since the gift is irrevocable, you cede a great deal of control to the fund. However, because the fund is the one making the gift, donor-advised funds also allow for anonymity that is often impossible with a direct gift. The overall administrative burden is also low, as the sponsoring institution handles compliance with the rules governing the fund, including tax returns.

## Charitable Remainder Trusts

For those wishing to make larger gifts, a more complex mechanism may make sense. A common choice is a charitable remainder trust (CRT). These trusts are popular because they provide an income stream back to the grantor (or to another individual designated by the grantor) over a set term or the remainder of his or her life. After the term expires, or after the income beneficiary's death, any remaining assets in the trust pass to one or more charities, which can be established when the trust is created or selected later.

There are two ways to set up a CRT: as a unitrust (called a CRUT) or as an annuity (called a CRAT). The difference is in the way the income stream is structured. In a CRAT, the trust pays the grantor a fixed annuity based on the value of assets at the time of contribution to the trust. A trust structured as a CRUT instead pays out a certain percentage of the assets in the trust as of the prior December 31.

Funding a charitable remainder trust allows you to take an immediate tax deduction, equal to the present value of the remainder interest projected to pass to charity when the trust dissolves. A CRT can also allow you to defer capital gains tax if you give appreciated assets directly to the trust. Since a CRT is a tax-exempt entity, gains are not taxed unless and until they are distributed. The character of distributions proceeds from worst to best taxation; the earliest distributions are drawn from the income taxed at the highest applicable rate, and does not proceed to income of a different character until the highest-rate income is exhausted. You have to pay income tax or capital gains tax on the distributions, but only on as much as you receive, rather than the entire capital gain of the appreciated asset.

Because of this feature, a CRT allows you to quickly diversify a concentrated stock position. If you give the position to the trust, the trust can sell the asset immediately without triggering a large, immediate capital gains tax. It can then reinvest in a more appropriately diversified selection of investments, and you pay the capital gains tax only when and if those gains are distributed. Any gains that end up going to the charity are not taxed at all.

Here is a typical example, using a CRUT. Bruce funds a trust with $1 million, and will annually receive an 8 percent payout of the prior year's December 31 ending value. The trust can be invested for a high rate of return in a diversified equity portfolio, which we will assume returns 10 percent a year. We further assume that Bruce receives his distribution at the end of the year. That means the trust grows to $1.1 million over 12 months, at which time Bruce receives his distribution, which is 8 percent of the prior year's ending value ($1 million), or $80,000. After this year-end payout, the trust is worth $1.02 million. The following year's unitrust payout will be $81,600, which is 8 percent of this new, higher figure. In years where the market declines, the payout will be lower. On Bruce's death, any remaining assets in the trust pass to charity.

What about the capital gains tax benefit? It works this way: Bruce funds the trust with $1 million worth of stock with a $100,000 cost basis.

This time, he structures the CRUT with a 10 percent annual payout. The CRUT immediately sells the stock, and retains the $900,000 of realized capital gain, which is not taxed that year. The CRUT's trustee reinvests the $1 million of proceeds in a diversified portfolio.

In the first year, the annuity payout to Bruce is 10 percent of the $1 million value from the prior year, or $100,000. This distribution is taxable as $100,000 of long-term capital gains. The trust retains $800,000 of taxable long-term gains embedded in it. The next year, the portfolio appreciates by 12 percent, and is worth $1,008,000. Bruce's next payout will be $100,800, on which he will pay tax, while the rest of the gain remains in the trust. This process continues until the trust terminates. Any of the gain that wasn't distributed to Bruce will go to charity, and no tax will be owed on that portion.

CRTs are governed by many complex rules and regulations, and can be costly to set up and administer. The income stream and the trust's tax advantages may make it attractive, but such trusts should be structured with the help of skilled counsel.

## Charitable Lead Trusts

For donors who are not concerned about their own income, but who may wish to use a charitable trust for estate planning purposes, a charitable lead trust may be a more attractive option. Charitable lead trusts, or CLTs, are the mirror image of charitable remainder trusts. In a CLT, the grantor funds the trust, which then pays an annuity (in a CLAT) or a percentage of the trust's assets (in a unitrust, or CLUT) to a charity over a term of years or a lifetime. At the end of the trust's term, any remaining assets either revert to the grantor or pass to designated beneficiaries – often the grantor's children.

How you structure a CLT determines its tax treatment. If the remainder is set to pass to heirs, rather than revert to you, the projected remainder may constitute a taxable gift under the transfer tax rules. You can avoid this outcome by setting the initial remainder interest at zero. This remainder is calculated using a hurdle rate, set by the IRS. If the assets outperform this rate, beneficiaries can still receive some assets at the trust's termination, even if the structure assumes they will not. In this instance, the transfer is still gift tax-free. (Note that, in the case of CLATs, the IRS sets a prescribed annuity rate that must be met.)

A CLT can result in a charitable deduction if the grantor chooses to pay the tax on the trust's income. In this instance, the deduction is equal to the net present value of the charitable annuity at the time of the trust's creation. Because of certain income tax benefits related to contributing appreciated securities to charity, low-cost-basis securities are ideal for funding CLTs. CLTs allow you to pass assets to heirs in a tax-beneficial way while also fulfilling your philanthropic goals.

Like CRTs, CLTs can be complex and costly to set up and administer. They should be structured with the assistance of skilled professionals.

## Quick Notes:
### A few features of charitable trusts you should know about

| Charitable Remainder Trust (CRT) | Charitable Lead Trust (CLT) |
|---|---|
| • Provides an income stream back to the grantor (or to another individual designated by the grantor) over a set term or the remainder of his or her life<br><br>• Can be set up as a unitrust (called a CRUT) or as an annuity (called a CRAT)<br><br>• Allows you to take an immediate tax deduction, equal to the present value of the remainder interest projected to pass to charity when the trust dissolves | • Pays an annuity (in a CLAT) or a percentage of the trust's assets (in a unitrust, or CLUT) to a charity over a term of years or a lifetime<br><br>• Remaining assets at the end of the trust's term either revert to the grantor or pass to designated beneficiaries – often the grantor's children<br><br>• Can result in a charitable deduction if the grantor chooses to pay the tax on the trust's income |

## Private Foundations

If one of your main motivations for philanthropy is to establish a legacy that will outlast you, a private foundation is a popular choice. Private foundations are nongovernmental, tax-exempt 501(c)(3) entities. They sponsor or aid charitable, educational, religious or other institutions that serve the public good. Foundations' primary function is usually to make grants to various nonprofit organizations.

As you might imagine, setting up and running a private foundation is substantially more complex than many of the other giving options in this chapter. A private foundation requires articles of incorporation and a board of directors. Those wishing to set up private foundations are subject to a variety of rules, including prohibitions against self-dealing and certain limitations on the foundation's investment activity. As such, professional help is nearly always necessary in order to properly establish and run a private foundation.

Considering the work and up-front cost involved in establishing a foundation, private foundations are best for large sums of money to be managed over an extended time frame. In addition to the high required start-up legal fees, foundations need to deal with ongoing meeting expenses, administrative fees and investment management fees. These expenses can add up, making foundations ultimately expensive to administer, even once they get off the ground.

However, in the right circumstances, private foundations can be excellent vehicles for creating long-lasting legacies, and offer the potential to do a lot of good in many areas. The largest private foundation in the world, and one of the best known, is the Bill & Melinda Gates Foundation. The foundation supports healthcare objectives, anti-poverty efforts, and those working to expand American educational opportunities and information technology access. Though the Gateses are not the sole sources of funding (Warren Buffett is also a prominent donor), the foundation serves as a longstanding legacy for the Gateses, allowing them to support causes they find worthwhile even beyond their own lifetimes.

A private foundation can also offer the chance to involve family members. Seinfeld fans will remember George Costanza's entanglement when his late fiancée's parents set up a foundation in her honor and appointed him to the board of directors. In real life, however, offering family members a seat on the board or another post in the foundation can be a boon. Such a position can create visibility and influence, and it can help involve younger generations in the philanthropic legacy you hope to establish.

Gifts to a foundation are immediately eligible for a charitable tax deduction, though the deduction is capped at a lower percentage of AGI than gifts to nonprofit organizations. Gifts of certain appreciated property are also limited to the asset's cost basis, which can defeat the purpose of giving appreciated assets rather than liquidating first. As with many other gifts, giving assets to a foundation can remove them from the reach of creditors in the case of personal bankruptcy. Many of these stricter rules do not apply to "private operating foundations," which are foundations that devote a large share of their resources to directly operating an exempt activity rather than merely making grants to other charities. Most private foundations, however, are classified as nonoperating foundations, because grantmaking is their main activity.

## Charitable Bequests

Bequests are, simply put, gifts made after death via will, charitable trust, or other estate planning techniques. There are four main types of charitable bequests. A specific bequest is an item of property that can be easily identified and distinguished from the other property in an estate. For example, a specific bequest might leave a Monet painting to a museum or donate a parcel of land to a conservation agency. The gift is specific, easily separated from the rest of the estate, and cannot be substituted with another item if the original gift does not exist or is no longer in the testator's possession.

A general bequest is a gift of property payable from the general assets of the deceased's estate. Most often, this is a stated sum of money, though it can also be a gift of securities or other appreciated assets. Occasionally, instead of a dollar amount, a bequest will be expressed as a percentage of the estate's value at the time of the testator's death.

A demonstrative bequest is a bequest that combines features of the general and specific bequests; generally, it is a gift of a certain amount of property from a specific source. For example, a gift of $10,000 to be paid out of the sale of a particular stock position would be a demonstrative bequest. Unlike a specific bequest, if the specified property is disposed of before the testator's death, the bequest is taken out of the estate's general assets.

The fourth main sort of bequest is a residuary bequest. As the name implies, the bequest is a gift of the remainder of an estate after all other bequests, taxes and administration expenses have been paid out.

If you wish to remember a nonprofit in your estate planning, you can also name such an organization as the beneficiary of a life insurance policy or as a recipient of your IRA or retirement fund. However you choose to give, many of the pros and cons of bequests are similar to those discussed earlier in this chapter regarding outright lifetime gifts. As for tax benefits, bequests to charity can help reduce estate taxes, should that be a concern. For more information on general estate planning concerns, see Chapter 5.

## Remainder Interests

A gift of remainder interest is often used as a structure for making donations of real estate, though it can be used for other assets as well. You donate the property to the charitable institution of your choice, but retain a life interest, which allows you to continue inhabiting or otherwise enjoying the donated property. In turn, you remain responsible for paying property taxes, maintaining proper insurance, and ensuring upkeep. When you die, the "remainder interest" in the property passes directly to the charity. This technique is also sometimes called a "Life Estate Agreement."

Remainder interests offer several advantages. The charitable organization already holds title to the property, so the transfer bypasses the probate process upon your death. This saves the charity time, and in some cases money. Additionally, the property is shielded from any claims creditors might make against your estate. If you wish, you can accelerate the end of your interest in the property during your lifetime as well – for example, if your family no longer uses a vacation property or if you one day need to move out of your residence into a facility that offers medical supervision. This flexibility allows you to retain or give up the property during your lifetime depending on circumstances that are hard to foresee. You can provide the life interest to someone besides yourself, though you should note that (unless the person is your spouse) doing so many trigger federal gift tax liability.

This sort of gift can also offer an additional tax benefit if the property you donate is a personal residence (including a second home) or a farm. Donating certain properties that meet the IRS' definition of conservation or historical value may also create an additional income tax deduction. Generally, your charitable deduction will be equal to the remainder interest, not the entire value of the property at the time of the gift.

Donors with debt-free property may consider combining a charitable gift annuity with a remainder interest, which creates an income stream in addition to retaining lifetime rights to use the donated property. This technique works best for older donors, and usually requires help from a financial adviser or other professional.

## Endowments

An endowment is a form of donation, usually in the form of investment funds or other property that is intended for a specific, stated purpose. Endowments are often discussed in conjunction with educational, religious or arts institutions, but most nonprofit organizations have the ability to handle an endowment. Endowments are often used to fund academic scholarships or to underwrite a performing arts season.

Most endowments are designed to keep the principal of the initial gift intact for a long period, often indefinitely, while using the investment income to support the designated cause. In some cases, the organization is permitted to withdraw a certain percentage of the endowment's total assets annually, which could include withdrawals of principal depending on investment returns.

If you wish to support an existing endowment, most organizations have mechanisms in place to support donations of cash or securities. If you wish to set up a new endowment, many organizations will work with you in order to draft an endowment agreement for your gift. Some nonprofits go as far as providing donors or their families with annual reports about the state of the endowment, so they can keep up to date on the endowment's performance and how the withdrawals are put to use. Like a private foundation, an endowment can offer a more durable philanthropic legacy than a one-time gift or bequest. Unlike a foundation, the administration of the endowment usually falls to the organization in question. While this gives the donor less control, it also means less responsibility for maintaining and administering the ongoing gift.

---

## Eric's Advice

### Can my family foundation employ my children?

Your family foundation can hire your children. However, there are strict IRS rules that prohibit certain "disqualified persons," which usually would include your children, from engaging in self-dealing with the foundation. Compensation for services rendered by your child must be reasonable and necessary to carry out the foundation's exempt purposes. Let's say you hired your son to be the foundation's bookkeeper. You would want an independent party to determine his compensation, and you might look to salary benchmarking studies for guidance.

-EM

---

### Charitable Gift Annuities

Charitable gift annuities, or CGAs, are a giving method that certain nonprofits oversee in order to encourage donations. Many colleges and universities offer them. The donor and the nonprofit organization sign a contract whereby the donor transfers cash or property to the nonprofit in exchange for an immediate partial tax deduction and a lifetime stream of annual income. At the donor's death, the entire remaining gift goes to the nonprofit.

The annuity is calculated so that the charity expects to realize a net gain on the annuitant's death. Generally, about 50 percent of the original gift is expected to go to the charity by the end of the CGA. Though each nonprofit can set its own annuity rate, many use rates calculated by the American Council on Gift Annuities. These rates are typically lower than those offered by commercial annuities because of the contracts' charitable component; however, the immediate tax deduction included in a contract often lessens this gap. In a low interest rate environment, the difference between a commercial annuity rate and a charitable annuity rate is smaller still.

CGAs offer other advantages over commercial annuities. They minimize your investment risk and management expenses and, should anything cut your own life short unexpectedly, the windfall will go to an organization you find worthy rather than to a commercial insurance company.

Much like a CRT, a CGA allows a giver to realize an immediate tax benefit while retaining an annual income stream from the donated asset. However, the institution administers the annuity, making a CGA simpler (and less costly) from the donor's point of view. It is therefore worthwhile for gifts smaller than those that would make sense for a CRT. CGAs are also quite flexible. The donor can control what sorts of assets are donated, can designate an annuitant (or annuitants) other than him- or herself, and can decide how frequently payments are made. And, while the payments can only span the annuitant's lifetime, annuity payments can end earlier if the annuitant no longer needs the income stream.

Tax reporting is also simpler with a CGA than for a CRT. Each payment from a CGA will include a portion taxed as ordinary income and, if you donated appreciated assets, a portion taxed as capital gain. Annually, the nonprofit will issue a 1099-R form for use in your personal tax return. After the investment is fully recovered, the annuity payment is entirely treated as ordinary income. A CGA can also control or minimize capital gains tax, much as a CRT would. As long as you or your spouse is the annuitant, the transfer generally doesn't count against gift or estate tax exceptions (though you will generally need to file a gift tax return). If you name a skip person – a descendant more than one generation removed from you – as the annuitant, be aware you may trigger generation-skipping transfer tax rules.

Not every nonprofit institution offers CGAs. Religious groups and private colleges often offer them, as they are likely to have supporters who are willing to make a long-term, irrevocable gift. Most institutions that offer CGAs have minimum gift sizes and rules about certain assets they will and will not accept. And unlike a CRT, a CGA can only benefit one institution.

CGAs are not without risk. Such a gift is irrevocable, so if you give to a small or financially unsound institution, it is possible it may not meet its annuity obligations. In cases where the organization defaults, you cannot retrieve your original gift. Instead, you become one of the organization's many creditors, and you are unlikely to be at the front of the line. Some states prohibit CGAs altogether, so you should also be aware of the rules of your home state, and the institution's state if it is different.

## Combining Charitable and Non-Charitable Objectives

There are many financial planning objectives that can naturally partner with philanthropy. We have touched upon some of them in describing means of charitable giving.

One of the main benefits of charitable giving can be the charitable deduction on your income taxes. As noted earlier in this chapter, outright gifts to charities, as defined by Internal Revenue Code section 501(c)(3), can be deducted up to 50 percent of AGI for cash and 30 percent of AGI for appreciated securities. Gifts to private foundations may be deducted up to 30 percent AGI (cash) and 20 percent (appreciated assets). Amounts over these limits may be carried forward for five years.

The largest tax consideration in giving is timing. Compare your current year taxable income to your past earnings and what you expect to earn in the future. If the current year's income is unusually large, it might be a good time to consider making a charitable gift. Strive to match high income years with large deductions. Besides outright gifts, you can also secure tax deductions through donor-advised funds, CRTs, gifts to private foundations, and endowments. You can also partially deduct gifts to a CGA.

If you want to secure a steady cash flow from your gift, consider a CRT or a CGA, both of which can direct income back to you. If you want to quickly diversify a concentrated stock position without triggering large capital gains tax liability, you can contribute a concentrated stock position to a split-interest trust (either a CRT or a CLT, depending on your other needs).

You can also use charitable giving as a shortcut if you need to diversify your investment holdings. For example, if you contribute a concentrated stock position to a split-interest trust, the trust can immediately sell without worrying about a large up-front capital gains tax. Instead, you will pay the tax as it is distributed to you (in a CRT) or potentially not at all if the capital gains end up going entirely to the charity. This can either spread out or reduce your ultimate capital gains tax for the asset.

Those who want to combine philanthropy and recognition or a legacy will likely be best served by an endowment or a private foundation. A private foundation will also allow them to involve other family members in their charitable work if desired. This can either be a means to provide others with higher visibility and prestige, or as a way to cement shared family values in younger generations.

There are many ways to support worthy causes. Some are highly complex and some are relatively straightforward, but ultimately they all come down to using your wealth to accomplish your goals. As in all areas of financial planning, prudent decisions can help you accomplish something important more quickly or on a larger scale than would otherwise be possible. Philanthropy is a part of many sound financial plans, and planned, methodical giving can help you do the most good to yourself and the causes that matter to you.

# 19

# A SECOND ACT: STARTING A NEW VENTURE
## Paul Jacobs, CFP®, EA
## Eric Meermann, CFP®, CVA, EA

Though the popular conception of a successful retirement is the ability to spend time in leisure, whether enjoying family or relaxing on the beach, the reality is that you have a great many options when considering what to do with your time and resources once you leave your primary career. After your children are grown and you have provided for your own financial needs, there are many dreams you can use a well-planned retirement to pursue.

One option is not to really "retire" at all, but instead turn your hand to working at something you love. Starting your own business isn't always a simple endeavor, but it can be an intensely rewarding enterprise. You might draw on skills you learned during your career, but parlay them into an independent business where you can be your own boss. You might turn a hobby into a business, capitalizing on talents that you hadn't formerly monetized. Or, if you have an entrepreneurial bent, you might have an idea for a new product or service that you never previously had the chance to bring to reality.

Whatever the drive behind your new business, this chapter will give you an overview of things to consider as you get started. Knowing the ground rules is one of the most important ways to ensure your business is successful, no matter what you want that success to look like.

## Setting Up a Business

As far as the IRS is concerned, an activity is a business if it is carried on with a reasonable expectation of earning a profit. Of course, the agency uses a more complicated system for determining whether that is the case on an individual basis, but it is a useful guideline. If you make a pie every now and then, even if you sell one occasionally at a bake sale, you probably don't have a pie-making business by default. However, if you make a website to advertise your pies, invest in an industrial oven so you can bake more of them, and have a set price scale for pies of different sizes, you have clearly moved in the direction of a proper business.

It is important to decide at the outset what you want out of your new business. Is it a profitable hobby, which you would like to pay for itself or maybe earn a little extra? Is your business going to be your main source of income, replacing a former job? Or do you envision your business as the start of a lasting enterprise that will increase your wealth and outlast your involvement? No one choice is better than another, but your goals will shape how you set up the business and what expectations you set for its future.

No matter what sort of business you envision, you will need working capital and a business plan to get started. Working capital is the difference between your (or your enterprise's) current assets and current liabilities. Current assets here mean liquid assets – either cash or assets that can easily be converted into cash. Current liabilities are obligations due within one year. Because working capital is the difference between these two amounts, it can be either positive or negative at any given time. But it will need to be positive over the long run so your business can succeed.

You will also need a comprehensive and articulate business plan. The plan is not only necessary to organize your thoughts, but to demonstrate the strength and practicality of your idea to potential investors or lenders. As such, you want to be sure your business plan is as polished as a résumé, free of errors or awkwardness. You may want to consult an accountant or legal expert in creating your plan, though if you do, it is important to make sure the professionals you approach are accredited and have experience in the field pertinent to your business. Your business plan should also convey your professionalism and expertise, so investors who don't know you personally have reason to believe you will succeed.

How to format your business plan will depend upon the type of business you start. However, there are some elements that all good business plans should share. Start with a cover sheet, as you would a résumé. Then lead with your executive summary. This should be the heart of your business plan. It is your opportunity to explain what your business is about, as well as to demonstrate market analysis you have performed, present evidence you can succeed in your market, focus on your personal background and experience, and discuss your plan for the business' ultimate future. Though you lead with this document, many experts suggest it be the last thing you write, once you have the rest of the plan completed, as you will then be in the best position to present yourself well.

After your cover letter and executive summary, it's a good idea to include a table of contents, dealing with the rest of the body of your business plan and supporting documents. You should include a detailed description of your business, including a concrete timeline for at least the first year of operation, and your intentions over a longer time horizon as well. The plan may also include some or all of the following documents:

- Marketing plans

- Analysis of the competition

- Proposed operating procedures

- Plans for staffing and personnel

- Data on business insurance

- Loan applications

- Capital equipment/supply lists

- A balance sheet, if you have assets and obligations to list

- Breakeven analysis

- Assumptions upon which projections were based

- Personal financial statements

- Copy of proposed lease or purchase agreement for building space

- Copy of licenses or other legal documents

- Copy of your résumé (and résumés of any other principals)

- Copy of letters of intent from suppliers

The business plan will not only help you succeed by making sure you think through the timeline and details of your business launch, but will also be essential in demonstrating your seriousness and potential for success to investors and lenders. Raising capital and crafting a solid business plan go hand in hand.

Once you have a business plan, what are some of the ways you can raise capital for your new business? The two main categories most businesses use are equity financing and debt financing.

## Equity Financing

Equity financing is an exchange in which someone contributes capital and receives a share of ownership in the business in return. It's an appealing way to raise capital, because it lets you as the business owner focus on making your products or services profitable, rather than worrying about immediately paying interest or principal to lenders. However, it can mean a loss of autonomy over your new business.

There are a variety of sources to consider for equity financing. If you have the personal assets available to support starting your enterprise, doing so will ensure your autonomy; however, you will also bear the financial risk alone. Speaking to your financial adviser can help you decide what portion of your business capital is appropriate to fund yourself.

A prevalent source of equity funding is angel investors or venture capitalists. As a general rule, angel investors tend to be wealthy individuals investing their personal funds as a contribution to society or because they believe in the company or product. Therefore, they may not expect as high a return as a venture capitalist, and they are less likely to require or want control of operations or to conduct lengthy due diligence. Venture capitalists tend to expect a high return on investment, and may demand a voice in the management of the business. They usually have more capital to invest and carry out a more detailed process for vetting potential investments than do angel investors. While relying on angel investors or venture capitalists to invest in your business may mean giving these investors a say in your business' future, it is also a sensible option for those who are not in a position to fund their business themselves or who prefer not to go into debt at the outset.

## Debt Financing

Debt financing basically means taking a loan, often from a bank. These loans can be secured or unsecured, and there are different types to fit the needs of different business owners.

Bank loans are generally classified by the size of the proposed business. Common types that might apply include start-up business loans, small-scale business loans, and new business loans. As with other types of bank loans, you can often apply either online or in person. Many banks also offer online loan calculators that allow you to estimate monthly payments or how much funding your new business will need.

Government-backed loans are also available to new business owners in many circumstances. The Small Business Administration (SBA) acts as a guarantor for a network of local lenders, who then extend commercial loans structured to meet SBA requirements. Because the SBA reduces risk for the lending institutions, they are often willing to offer SBA loans on better or more flexible terms. On the other hand, you must meet the agency's minimum criteria and furnish details including the proposed business profile, the amount of the desired loan, and personal financial statements, among other information, in order to qualify for such loans.

A secured loan involves putting up collateral, such as real estate, as a deposit to secure the loan. Unsecured loans do not require collateral, but generally will not be as large as a secured loan might be. Both sorts of loans will rely on your credit rating; while it's good financial sense to know your credit rating generally, it is essential before considering whether debt financing is the right way to raise capital for your business.

Family members and personal friends can also lend money to your business. In some cases, this scenario can be ideal; people who know you personally already have a sense of your trustworthiness and may find your project exciting. Because you may not need to pitch your business plan as thoroughly, these loans can often provide quicker funding than going elsewhere, and family members may be inclined to offer you a relatively low interest rate (though it is important they not charge too little, or the IRS may view the loan or the foregone interest as a gift).

However, it's important to be cautious. You don't want people to lend money out of a sense of guilt or obligation. Also, family members may feel they should have a direct say in business decisions or operations by default after they lend any start-up capital. You don't want to sacrifice your personal relationships, and you certainly don't want to make poor business decisions to appease a family member or friend. Material in Chapter 2 of this book on talking to adult children and family members about finances may be helpful, should you decide to pursue this source of funding.

**Quick Tip:**
Consider all options when it comes to taking out a business loan.

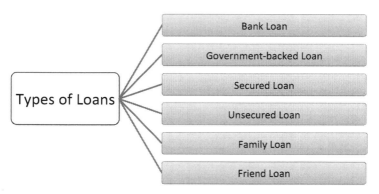

Whatever sort of funding you pursue, you should research your options. There is no one-size-fits-all choice.

It is also essential to estimate what your start-up expenses will be before you approach either equity investors or lending institutions. Starting a business can entail a rather steep commitment at the outset. If you plan to rent an office, you will need to secure the space and pay for utilities; if you work from home, you may still need to purchase equipment and supplies in order to do business smoothly and professionally. You will need to factor in marketing and research and development costs for your product or service. You will need to pay for technological expenses, including set-up costs in many cases. And, if you plan to hire employees within your first year, you will need funds for payroll and benefits too.

**Fixed and Variable Expenses**

Startup expenses can be divided into two types: fixed and variable. Banks and investors will want you to have an idea of each, as well as the total start-up cost that results from the combination of the two. Fixed expenses, as the name implies, are things that won't fluctuate month to month: rent, insurance, utilities. Variable expenses may include items such as shipping costs or sales commissions. Variable expenses are by their nature harder to predict than fixed expenses, but it is important not to neglect them in your estimate for necessary start-up capital.

Insufficient funding is one of the primary reasons that many new businesses fail. The product or service can meet a real need or find a willing audience, but if the business owner has badly underestimated the costs of running the business, it never has time to get off the ground. In an effort to save a floundering new venture, business owners will often sharply limit their expenses, rather than seeking out new sources of capital, which in turn limits the business' viability and potential for growth. Be realistic about how much your business will cost to run, especially in its beginning stages, but also be willing to raise more capital early on if necessary.

As you continue to craft your business plan and raise your working capital, you will need to decide how to organize your business. There are many organizational structures to choose from. We are going to focus on the limited liability company (LLC), which is often the best choice for a small business given its flexibility and protection from liability, but we will also briefly touch on a few other common organizational structures as well.

## Organizational Structures

*Limited Liability Company*

An LLC is a hybrid structure, combining features of a corporation and a partnership. LLC owners are called "members." Depending on your state, members can be just you (a sole owner), or two or more individuals, corporations, other LLCs or some combination of these. Unlike a corporation, the LLC is not usually taxed as a separate entity. Instead, all the LLC's profits and losses are "passed through" to each of the LLC's members. The members then report the profits and losses on their personal tax returns.

Each state has slight variations on the rules for forming LLCs, but all include some general principles. You will need to choose a business name, unique in your state, which indicates the business is an LLC (e.g. including the words "Limited Liability Company" or ending "LLC"). The process of forming an LLC automatically registers your business name; you won't have to do that separately.

You will also need to file "articles of organization," a simple document to legitimize your LLC. It will contain information such as your business name and address, and the names of the LLC's members. In most states, this will be filed with the secretary of state, but you should check local procedures. Not all states require operating agreements, but they are a good idea for multi-member LLCs even when not required, because they spell out the LLC's rules, allowing you to avoid disagreements later on. Of course, you should also make sure to obtain a business license and the permits relevant to your state, locality, and industry. A few states require you to announce your new LLC in a newspaper.

If your business does not have a brick-and-mortar location, or if you plan to serve clients in more than one state (through Internet sales, for example), it may make sense to form your LLC in a state that offers favorable tax laws or attractive corporate infrastructures. Delaware is such a state, and one that is quite popular for business incorporation, due to its favorable laws and business-friendly tax rules. Nevada and Wyoming are also popular choices. Consider your options thoroughly before making a final decision about where your business entity should establish its domicile.

Setting up your business as an LLC offers several advantages. As the name implies, the structure protects you and any other members from personal liability for your company's business decisions or actions. This means if someone sues your company, your personal assets can't be reached in most cases. An LLC also offers smaller start-up costs and fewer recordkeeping requirements than some other business structures.

The LLC option does come with some disadvantages as well. In certain states when a member leaves an LLC, the business is automatically dissolved. However, in many cases you can include provisions in your operating agreement that will avoid this outcome, if you wish. As an LLC member, you may also owe self-employment tax on your income, reflecting both the employer and employee share of Medicare and Social Security costs. Still, these downsides are relatively minor, and for many small business startups they are not enough to prevent an LLC from being the most appealing business structure solution.

*Sole Proprietorship*

While we recommend an LLC for most small businesses getting started, it is not the only way to structure your enterprise. A sole proprietorship is a common, simple organization that is more or less what it sounds like: Your business is unincorporated, owned and run by you, with no legal distinction between business and owner. You are entitled to all its profits and responsible for all its debts and liabilities. It does not require any formal action beyond obtaining the necessary licenses and permits to operate. This form of organization is common among freelance writers and designers, for example. Sole proprietorships are uncomplicated and inexpensive to start, but offer no liability protection. Owners of sole proprietorships also often find it hard to secure outside funding due to perceptions of risk from investors or lenders.

*Partnership*

Should you wish to go into business with at least one other person, you can also set up your business as a partnership, in which each partner contributes to all aspects of the business and, in turn, shares in the profits and losses. Although most states do not require formal partnership agreements, it's important to have one, specifying the type of partnership, how profits will be divided, how disputes will be resolved, and how to dissolve the partnership, among other considerations. The three most prevalent partnership arrangements are general partnerships (in which profits and liability are divided equally among partners), limited partnerships (in which certain partners have limited liability and a limited role in management decisions), and joint ventures (general partnerships limited to a period of time or a particular project). Like sole proprietorships, partnerships are generally easy and inexpensive to form, but can leave the general partners exposed to personal liability.

*Corporation*

A corporation (often referred to as a C corporation to distinguish it from an S corporation) is in many ways the opposite end of the spectrum. While in a sole proprietorship there is no legal separation between the business owner and the business, a corporation is an independent legal entity owned by shareholders. The corporation, not the shareholders, is held liable for the business' debts and actions. Corporations tend to have costly administrative fees and complex tax requirements, and are usually more useful for larger, established companies with multiple employees. Especially for a small business owner or stakeholder, one of the largest downsides of a corporation is that profits are subject to double taxation: Earnings are first subject to corporate income tax and are then taxed again as personal income when they are paid out as dividends to shareholders.

An S corporation is a special type of corporation in which profits and losses pass through to the shareholders' personal tax returns, avoiding the double taxation most corporations face. An S corporation can offer attractive tax savings, but can be costly to maintain. In addition, there are limitations on who can be a shareholder of an S corporation. For example, an S Corporation is limited to 100 or fewer shareholders, and partnerships and certain trusts cannot own stock in an S Corporation. If one of these "prohibited entities" accidentally comes into possession of shares (by gift or bequest for example), this can lead the S corporation's status to be declared null and void by the IRS, and it will revert to a C Corporation. (There are, however, procedures to correct inadvertent terminations of S corporation status.)

## Recordkeeping

Whatever business structure you choose, it is essential to establish regular and thorough recordkeeping procedures from day one. It is much easier to set up a good recordkeeping system from the outset than to play catch-up once your business is underway. Keeping your records complete and well-organized will help you with a variety of important tasks: evaluating the performance of your business and identifying areas that can be improved; preparing your financial statements for creditors and investors; and keeping track of income and deductible expenses to be reported on your tax returns.

There are many other recordkeeping considerations, such as whether to use print or electronic records and how to set up your journals or ledgers, which are beyond the scope of this chapter. Depending on your background, it may make sense to consult an accountant when setting up a recordkeeping system in order to make sure the system works for you and addresses all your legal obligations.

## Business Taxes and Tax Planning

Starting a business will inevitably introduce new taxes and tax issues to consider. Not being taken by surprise is essential in properly meeting your obligations and building them into your business plan.

*Sales Tax*

Sales tax is an obvious place to start for any business. The first thing to do is check state regulations – depending on where your business operates, items you sell or inputs that you purchase for internal consumption or resale may not be subject to sales tax. Additionally, if you sell goods online to a customer located in a different state, you may not be required to collect sales tax either, though this principle is currently under legal dispute and the rules may change in the future. Except for these scenarios, however, and assuming you live in a state with general sales tax, you will need to make sure you are charging the right rate and paying the government at the correct times. You may also need a sales tax permit.

*Income Tax*

As a business owner, you will also need to consider income taxes. Income is usually taxable unless the law specifically exempts it. When you received a W-2 form from your employer, your reportable income was clear-cut, but when you are the employer, it is up to you to make certain you list all taxable income properly. Depending on how you chose to set up your business, the impact may mainly fall on your personal income taxes or on the business itself.

If you already have a personal financial adviser, you will want to involve the adviser in your tax planning decisions as soon as possible. If your business is especially complicated, it may be a good idea to consult a tax professional at the outset.

Depending on the way you set up your business, you may be subject to estimated income tax, which is discussed briefly in connection with retirement in Chapter 11. Broadly, estimated income tax covers any income not subject to withholding and is due quarterly. More information about how to calculate estimated income tax and who must pay it is available from the IRS. It is important to thoroughly understand whether you must pay estimated tax and when you must make payments in order to avoid penalties.

*Payroll and Employment Taxes*

If you hire employees, you will need to consider payroll and employment taxes. You must generally withhold federal income tax from your employees' wages; you also withhold half of the employee's Social Security and Medicare taxes and pay the remaining half yourself. As an employer, you are also responsible for federal unemployment (FUTA) tax. You must keep track of and report withholdings for tax purposes and, at year end, you must complete W-2 forms for your employee(s).

If you are self-employed, you should also be aware of self-employment tax, which is a Social Security and Medicare tax similar to those withheld from employees who earn wages. While employees see only half of their Social Security and Medicare taxes withheld from their paychecks, the self-employed have to pay the full amount out of their income.

Other requirements, often imposed at the state or local level, can include obtaining disability or workers compensation coverage for your employees, paying state unemployment taxes, and complying with minimum wage and mandatory time-off rules that can vary from standards imposed at the federal level. It is easy to overlook some of these requirements, and penalties for failing to comply with them can be substantial.

*Managing Business Taxes*

This may seem like a lot to cope with. Although the United States does require compliance with many taxes and regulations, it is still one of the easiest places in the world for new business owners to get started. As of this writing, the World Bank ranked the United States fourth internationally for ease of doing business. Its high per capita gross domestic product reflects a country that, even with its recent economic struggles, still offers the capital to commit to new ventures and a culture that encourages the entrepreneurial spirit. Despite all the taxes and regulations to manage, basing your business in America remains a smart business decision.

So, then, how to manage these taxes and regulations? The best way to keep on top of your obligations as a business owner is through good planning. First, and perhaps most important, is to take the time to do thorough research – or to hire a reputable adviser to do it for you. There are a lot of factors at play, and it's easy for a non-professional to miss something crucial, especially when starting out. Also be sure you are classifying your business correctly, and that you have taken all the necessary steps to set up whatever structure you chose.

Especially for small business owners, it's important to capitalize on all the deductions available to you to keep your tax burden under control. Be aware of opportunities such as the home office deduction, accelerated depreciation for asset purchases, and travel expense deductions, and use them whenever appropriate.

---

## Eric's Advice

---

**What is a common mistake new business owners make regarding their tax planning?**

Self-employed individuals may not realize that they must pay income taxes throughout the year, not just when they file their tax returns. When you run your own business, you are responsible for making estimated tax payments that are due on April 15, June 15, September 15 and January 15 (of the next year). These estimated payments can be based on your current earnings or, in many cases, your prior year's taxes.

-EM

---

### Next Steps

Once your business begins to thrive, you may find yourself shorthanded as you cope with growing demand for your goods or services. At some point, you may wish to hire one or more employees. Before you place a "help wanted" ad, however, you must take steps to make sure you are a legal and responsible employer.

First, you will need to obtain an Employer Identification Number (EIN) from the IRS. You can apply for this online or by contacting the IRS directly. Your EIN is necessary to report withholding taxes and for submitting other employer documents to the IRS. You won't be able to hire without one.

Additionally, you should be sure you have copies of all the forms your new employee or employees will need to complete, such as Form W-4 for tax withholding. One form all employers will need is Form I-9, which verifies an employee's eligibility to work in the United States. Your new employee will also need to provide supporting documentation within three days of hire. While I-9 forms do not need to be submitted to the government, you must retain them for three years or for one year after the employee's termination, whichever is later.

You may also need to obtain workers' compensation insurance, either through your state's workers' compensation insurance program or through a commercial carrier. Once you have employees, you will also need to display certain posters and notices in the workplace informing your workers of their rights and your responsibilities. Which precise posters you need to display will vary by state.

You should also be sure you are set up to offer the employee any benefits that you must provide by law, which may vary depending on your business' location. Optional benefits, such as health insurance coverage or a retirement plan, are a good way to attract and retain talented workers, but it is up to you to decide if they are worth the cost to your business. Benefits can have tax and legal implications, so research your options thoroughly.

Depending on the sort of help you need, you may want to consider hiring an independent contractor instead of an employee. Independent contractors are able to control how they go about their work, and set their own business hours. Because they are self-employed, you are not required to withhold Social Security, Medicare, or income taxes from their pay. Many small business owners find hiring a contractor an appealing option for these reasons.

However, it is important that you be aware of the Fair Labor Standards Act, which outlines the legal definition of an employee. While there is no single test to determine whether an individual is an employee or a contractor, the distinction generally depends on the amount of control the employer exercises over the work being done. It is also important to consider the permanency of the relationship, whether the contractor has other clients, and the independence of the contractor's operation. Misclassification can be costly, so it's important to be aware of the differences between employee and contractor and treat individuals who work for you accordingly.

Once your business is on its feet, another important consideration is estate and succession planning. Depending on whether you consider your business a hobby, a job, or an enterprise, you may have one of several outcomes in mind for whether and how your business will one day continue without you.

Whether you plan to transition your business to your heirs or someone within the company when you step down, or if you plan to sell it outright when you depart, effective succession can require years of planning, so it's best to start on it as soon as possible. Ideally, it's something to consider shortly after you have set up your business.

The first step is to decide what outcome would be best for you. If you think it is likely that your business will close after you are no longer a part of it, your business is considered "owner-dependent." In this case, you will want to generate the most income possible each year, and then take the profit as current income (or retirement savings) rather than reinvesting in the business to any great degree. You have no need to develop a management team or successor. There is nothing wrong with this model, but it should be a conscious choice, rather than an accident due to lack of planning.

If you want to transfer your business, matters get a little more complicated. It's important that your succession plan, like your business plan, be formal and that it exist in writing. It may make sense to consult an attorney when you create a succession plan, and you will certainly need to discuss your plan with all those involved in its execution, so your wishes don't come as a surprise to them.

Your first step will be to choose a successor. Depending on your business' size and scope, this could be someone within the company or it could be a family member. (In the case of a family business, your successor might be both.) If your successor is a family member, your succession plan should be especially sensitive to estate or gift tax issues that may arise.

---

# Paul's Advice

---

### Should you give children joint control of your business?

If your children all contribute labor and skill to the business, and if they work well together, joint control may be a good option. But joint control can invite trouble if some are interested in the business while others are not. It may be better to make interested children earn their place through labor or by buying out siblings' share. And it is sometimes wise to consider putting non-family employees in charge, or to sell the business outright.

-PJ

---

For either sort of successor, it's important to create a training plan, as well as a timeline leading up to your departure. Though there is a certain amount of uncertainty involved in any sort of transition, having a "best case scenario" still leaves you a template from which you or your heirs can improvise if necessary. It's also important to mentally prepare yourself to let go of your business when the time comes. Your own peace of mind will increase dramatically if you are sure your successor is prepared to step seamlessly into your former role.

Should you have more entrepreneurial ambitions, perhaps you hope to eventually grow your company to a point where it can be sold. An outright sale has the advantages of speed and a quick receipt of payment. If you need to raise cash for a separate reason, or if you want to rapidly divest a business you are having trouble sustaining, an outright sale may be the way to go. Be sure to consider your personal tax implications and the effect the sale may have on your existing estate plans. You will also need to find an interested buyer who can afford to pay outright, which may limit either your asking price or your pool of potential buyers.

If your need for liquid assets isn't pressing, you can also sell your business gradually. By transferring ownership slowly over time, you can ensure a smooth transition and afford opportunities to buyers who might find a gradual payment plan more manageable than a lump sum. If you'd like to sell the business but still retain some exposure to its future growth, you can structure the sale as an "earn out," where some, or all, of the purchase price depends on a pre-agreed formula.

However you sell your business, you should draw up a formal sales agreement, even (or perhaps especially) if you are selling to a friend or family member. You should be as specific as possible in defining what you are selling, any specific fees involved in the transaction, what sort of access to business information is included, etc.

You can easily find guidance and sample sales agreements online, though as always, you should make sure the sources you use are reputable. Matters of valuation, or what the business is worth, are a very important aspect to selling a business. For the simplest businesses, the price paid could be agreed upon in advance in a buy-sell agreement. However, an independent third-party expert in valuation should be called in for valuing businesses of greater complexity.

## Business Startup Checklist

To review, here's a basic overview of the steps you should either take or consider as you form your business.

1. Decide the aim of your business: hobby, job or enterprise.

2. Write a detailed business plan.

3. Select a name and a legal structure (such as an LLC).

4. Earmark or raise capital.

5. Apply for an Employer Identification Number.

6. Open a company-specific bank account.

7. Lease space or prepare your home work area.

8. Obtain all proper licenses and permits (federal, state, local).

9. Set up a detailed recordkeeping system and account tracking.

10. Research and plan for applicable taxes.

11. Obtain business insurance.

12. Begin considering an exit strategy or succession plan.

And, of course, you should develop a quality product or service, start cultivating a brand, and market your business to grow its customer base. Remember that the point of all this work is so you can spend your time on an endeavor that you find useful, important and enjoyable. There are many resources available on the subject of how to make your small business succeed, but many business owners forget to pay attention to the details discussed in this chapter. If you follow the steps outlined here, you can rest assured that your business has been structured properly for the future. While it may all seem a bit overwhelming, exciting new businesses are created every day, and with some hard work and good fortune, your business could be the next big thing. Good luck!

# Index

*Index created by Schroeder Indexing, Inc.*

# About the Authors

Photo by Jonathan Zornow

**Larry M. Elkin, CPA, CFP®**, has provided personal financial and tax counseling to a sophisticated client base since 1986. After six years with Arthur Andersen, he founded his own firm, which would eventually become the Palisades Hudson organization, in 1992. The firm moved to its Scarsdale, New York, headquarters in 2002, and has since expanded to Fort Lauderdale, Florida; Atlanta, Georgia; and Portland, Oregon. Its clients reside in more than 30 states, as well as in several foreign countries. The organization's investment advisory business currently manages more than $1.25 billion.

Larry is the author of *Financial Self-Defense for Unmarried Couples* (Currency Doubleday, 1995), the first comprehensive financial planning guide for unmarried couples. He also is the editor and publisher of *Sentinel*, a quarterly newsletter on personal financial planning, and the lead author of the firm's daily blog. Larry received his B.A. in journalism from the University of Montana and his M.B.A. in accounting from New York University. He is a director of the Mental Health Association of Westchester and a past president of the Estate Planning Council of New York City, Inc., which gave him its first Lifetime Achievement Award in 2009.

**Anthony D. Criscuolo, CFP®, EA**, has extensive experience in the firm's tax, investment management, estate planning, and accounting practices. As a client service manager, Anthony provides a wide range of services to clients and also serves a member of the firm's investment committee. Anthony began his career with Palisades Hudson as an intern and became a full-time staff member in 2008. A native Floridian, Anthony is based in the Fort Lauderdale office.

Anthony graduated *summa cum laude* from the University of Florida's Warrington College of Business Administration with a degree in finance and minors in leadership and entrepreneurship. While earning his degree, Anthony was a member of the Warrington Finance Scholars and was elected to the Golden Key International Honor Society. Anthony has authored numerous articles for *Sentinel*, the firm's quarterly newsletter, and has also been quoted in a variety of national, regional and online publications.

**Shomari D. Hearn, CFP®, EA**, is the senior client service executive in charge of Palisades Hudson's Florida practice. As vice president, he is responsible for firm-wide technical quality, advanced research and professional staff development. Shomari also provides a wide range of services to clients across the United States and abroad and is a member of the firm's investment committee.

Shomari is a member of the Estate Planning Council of Greater Miami and the Financial Planning Association of Broward County. He is also active in the Greater Fort Lauderdale Chamber of Commerce. Shomari is a regular contributor to *Sentinel*, the firm's quarterly newsletter on personal finance, and has been quoted by financial columnists for publications including The Wall Street Journal, CNN Money and Forbes.

A New York City native, Shomari is a 1997 graduate of Duke University, where he obtained a B.A. in economics and a certificate in markets and management study.

Photo by Jonathan Zornow

**Paul Jacobs, CFP®, EA**, as chief investment officer and chairman of the firm's investment committee, directs a team of portfolio managers and associates focused on finding the most efficient and cost-effective ways to implement client portfolio strategies. He oversees more than $1.25 billion in client assets, including all aspects of investment strategy, portfolio management and due diligence.

Paul formerly served as the firm's chief compliance officer and has extensive experience in the firm's investment management and tax compliance practices. In 2008, he moved to Atlanta to establish the firm's Georgia office. He is a member of the Financial Planning Association of Georgia.

Paul has written numerous articles for *Sentinel*, the firm's newsletter, and multiple posts for the firm's blog. He has been quoted by publications including The Wall Street Journal, Reuters and NBC News. Paul graduated from New York University's Stern School of Business with degrees in finance and accounting.

---

Photo by Ashley A. Dandridge

**Melinda Kibler, CFP®**, rejoined Palisades Hudson in 2013 as a client service associate and investment analyst in the Fort Lauderdale office and became a client service manager in November 2014. Following an internship with the firm, Melinda was also part of the Palisades Hudson team full-time between 2009 and 2010. She works across multiple disciplines, including investments, taxes, accounting and estate planning.

Graduating *cum laude* from the University of Rochester, Melinda earned Bachelor of Arts degrees in economics and statistics, as well as a Certificate in Management focused in accounting and finance. A native of Wappingers Falls, New York, Melinda has embraced her home in South Florida, serving as a member of the Junior League of Greater Fort Lauderdale. She has authored or co-authored many articles for the firm's *Sentinel* newsletter. She has also been quoted as an expert by various national and regional news outlets.

Photo by Jonathan Zornow

**Eric Meermann, CFP®, CVA, EA**, joined Palisades Hudson after graduating from New York University's Stern School of Business with a degree in finance and international business. He has been a client service manager with the firm since 2004. Eric is based in the Scarsdale, New York, office, where he supervises the staff of client service professionals.

Eric has had extensive experience in the firm's investment management, retirement planning, estate planning and tax compliance practices, and is the lead manager for the firm's business valuation practice. He is also a member of the firm's investment committee. He holds the Certified Valuation Analyst designation from the National Association of Certified Valuators and Analysts, of which he is a member.

Among the many publications in which Eric has been quoted are Forbes, The New York Times and Businessweek. He has written many articles on diverse topics for *Sentinel*, the firm's quarterly newsletter.

---

Photo by Jonathan Zornow

**ReKeithen Miller, CFP®, EA**, a native of Tallahassee, Florida, started his career at Palisades Hudson in the Fort Lauderdale office and has been based in the firm's Atlanta office since 2008. He currently serves as a member of the firm's investment committee. As a client service manager, ReKeithen is fully involved in the broad range of services Palisades Hudson offers. He has been directly engaged in cross-border tax planning issues for international clients, estate tax preparation and planning, business acquisitions planning, financial recordkeeping and financial management, among other client services.

ReKeithen is a member of the Financial Planning Association of Georgia and is regularly quoted as an expert by national publications including Barron's, Kiplinger and Fox Business. ReKeithen has written articles on a variety of topics for *Sentinel*, the firm's newsletter. He holds a B.S. in finance with a minor in entrepreneurship from the University of Florida.

Photo by Jonathan Zornow

**Rebecca Pavese, CPA**, is the client service manager responsible for supervising the delivery of income tax planning and return preparation services to the firm's clients nationwide. She is based in the Atlanta office, where she supervises the staff of client service professionals.

Rebecca joined Palisades Hudson after graduating from the University of Pittsburgh with a B.S. in business administration. While an associate at the firm, she earned her master's degree in accounting from Pace University. Rebecca has worked extensively in the firm's tax, financial accounting, and estate planning and administration practices. She also supervises Palisades Hudson's accounting and administration services for estates and trusts.

Rebecca is the author of several articles for *Sentinel*, the firm's quarterly newsletter. She has been quoted as an expert in a variety of national publications, including The New York Times, The Wall Street Journal and Bloomberg.

---

Photo by Ashley A. Dandridge

**Laurie Samay** joined the firm's Scarsdale office full time in 2012, after earning her B.S. in business administration, majoring in finance and French, from Washington University in St. Louis. She began her Palisades Hudson career as a summer administrative intern, focusing on the company's social media presence and internal training practices; she completed a client service internship with the firm in the summer of 2011. Laurie is currently involved in all areas of the business, including accounting, tax and investment. She has written several articles for the firm's *Sentinel* newsletter.

Laurie is a member of the Beta Gamma Sigma Honor Society, which honors academic achievement in the study of business. While in college, she was a brother of the international coed business fraternity of Delta Sigma Pi, and received that organization's Scholarship Key. She is a native of Hastings on Hudson, New York.

Photo by Jonathan Zornow

**Benjamin C. Sullivan, CFP®, EA**, since joining Palisades Hudson in early 2007, has been extensively involved throughout the firm's asset management, personal financial planning, tax and valuation practices. He became a client service manager in 2010. He serves on Palisades Hudson's investment committee and is a member of the New York chapter of the Financial Planning Association. He is based in the Scarsdale office.

Ben is regularly quoted regarding personal financial planning in national media publications, including The Wall Street Journal, Money Magazine and U.S. News & World Report, among others. He has written many articles for *Sentinel*, the firm's quarterly newsletter on personal finance.

A native of East Hanover, New Jersey, Ben graduated *magna cum laude* from Tulane University's Freeman School of Business with a degree in finance and legal studies in business.

---

Photo by Jonathan Zornow

**Thomas E. Walsh**, a *cum laude* graduate with a B.S. in finance from the University of Florida, joined the firm's Atlanta office in 2011. He is involved with all areas of Palisades Hudson's financial planning, investment and tax practices.

Thomas is a native of Ormond Beach, Florida. While attending UF, he helped to organize "Wake Up!," a club dedicated to informing and educating students about current events, specifically the economic crisis and future implications of budget deficits. He was also a member of the Business Administration College Council (BACC), the Entrepreneurship Club and the Delta Epsilon Iota Academic Honor Society. Before joining Palisades Hudson, Thomas traveled to Europe in order to broaden his cultural understanding and polish his Spanish language skills.

Thomas has authored several articles for the firm's *Sentinel* newsletter, including one about financial planning and management for musicians on tour.

Photo by Jonathan Zornow

**David Walters, CPA, CFP®**, joined Palisades Hudson as an associate in the Scarsdale office after receiving his Bachelor of Science in finance and accounting from New York University's Stern School of Business. He became a client service manager in 2006, and moved to Fort Lauderdale in 2007. A Wisconsin native, David established the firm's West Coast presence in 2012, when he relocated to Portland, Oregon. He also serves as a member of the firm's investment committee.

David has extensive experience in the firm's tax, investment planning, estate planning and accounting practices. While at the firm, David has obtained his credentials as a Certified Public Accountant and CERTIFIED FINANCIAL PLANNER™. He is the author of several articles for *Sentinel*, the firm's newsletter on personal finance, and has been quoted in numerous national publications, including The Wall Street Journal, Money and Forbes.

# About the Company

T wo principles have defined our firm since it was founded in 1992:

1. Effective financial advice must consider all the issues confronting affluent individuals. Investment, tax, accounting, estate planning, insurance, business management, retirement and philanthropic considerations — among others — must be addressed together, not in isolation. We accept the challenge to furnish knowledgeable guidance and excellent service in whatever areas our clients require.

2. Our loyalty lies only with our clients. We accept no compensation from anyone else. All charges to every client are clearly disclosed and agreed upon in advance.

Today we serve clients in more than 30 states, and as far away as Brazil, from our offices in Scarsdale, New York, Fort Lauderdale, Florida, Atlanta, Georgia, and Portland, Oregon. Our investment advisory affiliate has more than $1.25 billion in assets under management. Our services to clients range from providing tax returns and household financial management to operating sophisticated real estate and energy investment companies.

There is much more information about our firm, our staff and our work, including many of the articles we write or in which we are quoted by major publications, available on our website at www.palisadeshudson.com.